"DEAR MASTER"

*Letters of a
Slave Family*

"DEAR MASTER"

Letters of a Slave Family

EDITED BY

RANDALL M. MILLER

CORNELL UNIVERSITY PRESS

Ithaca and London

First published 1978 by Cornell University Press.
Published in the United Kingdom by
Cornell University Press Ltd.,
2–4 Brook Street, London W1Y 1AA.
Third printing 1978

International Standard Book Number 0-8014-1134-3
Library of Congress Catalog Card Number 77-90907
Printed in the United States of America
Librarians: Library of Congress cataloging information
appears on the last page of this book.

FOR MY LINDA

God gives the desolate
a home to dwell in;
he leads out the prisoners
to prosperity;
but the rebellious dwell
in a parched land.
—Psalms 68:6

Contents

Illustrations

Maps

Preface

This book relates the story of an American slave family, the Skipwiths, a family separated by time, place, and circumstance from their Virginia home. Some members of the family were freed to emigrate to Liberia, a frontier society in Africa; others were settled on an absentee-owned plantation in Alabama, then the frontier of the cotton South. In time, different circumstances led to different interests, values, and personalities among the family members. But the family survived, for a common folk tradition and a deep commitment to family unity bound the Skipwiths together. Ironically, the slave owner who separated them also joined them: he established a correspondence with two generations of Skipwiths, and through him the family bridged the two continents of their residence. This correspondence—probably the largest and fullest epistolary record left by an American slave family—traces the history of the planter, the freedmen, and the slaves. It is the substance of this book.

Students of black slavery in America have long lamented the lack of adequate sources. True, we have learned much of the South's peculiar institution from planters' personal papers and business records, from government documents such as manuscript census schedules and court records, from travelers' accounts of the South and contemporary periodicals, but such sources have serious limitations. While valuable for understanding the white community's attitudes toward slaves and slavery and for discerning the mechanics of slavery and race relations, they present a distorted picture of bondage. They all refract slavery and the Afro-American experience through a white lens. The American slave remains elusive. This situation is especially vexing when we seek answers to questions of slave values, slave behavior, slave relationships with the master class and with one another, the dynamics of the slave quarters, the nature of slave religion and family life, and slave self-perception and personality development.

To learn of black perceptions, of what it meant to be chattel and to be free, scholars must consult the surviving testimony of the slaves and the freedmen. Few historians have done so. The prevailing opinion among historians writing on slavery has been that direct evidence from the slaves themselves is hopelessly inadequate. Kenneth Stampp, a leading authority on slavery, recently reminded us that well over 90 percent of the slaves were illiterate and even the small literate minority rarely spoke or wrote with candor. Stampp, like many others, discounts the value and breadth of the former slaves' testimony to slavery's travail. For him the "ubiquitous white man, as master, editor, traveler, politician, and amanuensis," intrudes at every level to stand between historian and slave. He concludes that however inventive the historian might be, "he will always have trouble breaking through the barrier, and he will always be handicapped by the paucity of firsthand testimony from the slaves themselves." Perhaps.

Abundant literary material from the slaves themselves, in varying degrees of quality and usefulness, has been available for a long time. This evidence consists of several hundred slave narratives (autobiographies) written in the nineteenth century by emancipated or fugitive slaves as well as the rich oral tradition of Afro-Americans recorded by folklorists, particularly the Fisk University and WPA Federal Writers' Project collections from the 1930s.

Still, there are problems. We must treat the narratives with caution, as we do all historical evidence. The products of rebels and resisters rather than accommodators, the narratives constitute a sample of the work of only a limited number of the total slave population. The narrators were largely from the upper South, were male with few exceptions, and were highly skilled, town-oriented slaves rather than rural, plantation-oriented slaves. In addition, the narrators often dictated or recorded their stories many years after successful escapes or manumissions so that experiences of freedom partially blurred memories of servitude. Because many of the fugitives and freedmen were illiterate, white editors and amanuenses helped them to prepare their autobiographies. One result was that the narratives were sometimes distorted to fit the needs of antislavery polemicists. Although immensely valuable for unraveling the interior world of the slaves, the narratives suffer from the corrosive effects of white intrusion and of time.

Similar problems diminish the worth of the interviews with former slaves conducted by folklorists in the 1930s. Remembrances of antebellum life were taken down so long after slavery that postbellum experiences colored the accounts. Recalling a life in childhood, when bondage was less onerous (or, for many, even less visible), many former slaves evinced few signs of bitterness. To be sure, some mentioned brutal whippings and humiliations, or a spare diet of fatback and cornmeal mush sometimes served in a common trough, or a vermin-infested cabin. But many spoke kindly of their former masters and remained silent on their intimate lives in the quarters. Mary Colbert of Georgia, a former slave who learned to read and write during Reconstruction, summed up the problem nicely for a WPA interviewer: "I have often considered writing the history of my life and finally decided to undertake it, but I found that it was more of a job than I had expected it to be, and then too, I would have to tell too much, so I thought best to leave it alone." Rather than tell too much, many other slaves and freedmen left no written testimony of their lives. They became part of that great mass of the inarticulate—the men and women who leave no records and so seemingly no history.

The unwillingness of many former slaves to speak candidly in the 1930s was largely due to the inhospitable interviewing environment. Blacks were usually excluded from the Federal Writers' Project interviewing lists, and white interviewers had not been trained to establish the kind of rapport with blacks that was necessary to evoke confidence and produce candor. The South of the 1930s was the South of Jim Crow, Scottsboro, and lynch law, of debt peonage, grinding poverty, and physical want exacerbated by a depression, and of careful rules of social etiquette and racial deference. Many informants, chosen for their expected docility, still lived on or near farms of their former masters and depended on the masters' descendants for charity and succor. The white interviewers may have been the former masters' descendants who commanded a deference incompatible with the integrity of the ex-slaves' responses. Some interviewers, hoping to preserve a plantation idyll or an ancestor's reputation for kindness, consciously suppressed unfavorable accounts or refashioned responses. Thus, the recollections of former slaves recorded in the 1930s, while providing the largest body of firsthand slave testimony available, must also be used with caution.

Some slaves left a more traditional record of bondage and slave values in the form of letters written to their masters, families, friends, or organizations, especially antislavery societies. These documents do not have the limitations of the narratives and interviews with former slaves. Third parties do not intrude to corrupt the language and structure of the letters. The letters also have the advantage of immediacy of time and, more important, of showing change over time. Most slave letters are isolated items, but the Skipwith family letters span two generations. They are personal documents uncorroded by time and are timeless in their revelations. Their worth rests in their casual, almost accidental nature. They are not polemics or arranged interviews. They are, rather, the reflections of a people's day-to-day concerns.

If literature is a distillation of a people's history, the Skipwith slave letters are seemingly of limited utility in enabling us fully to comprehend the nuances of slave life and culture. Letters were not a common form of expression among enslaved Afro-Americans, or among freedmen for that matter. Most slaves were illiterate people who relied upon the spoken word to convey the full compass of their emotions and thoughts. The written word cannot fully catch the flavor of the call and response, double entendre, gesture, and rhythms of oral communication. But the Skipwith letters offer rare, if sometimes tantalizingly brief, glimpses into the lives of particular slaves and freedmen over two generations. Insofar as individual lives inform and reflect the lives of many, the Skipwiths remind us of the diversity of slave types and experiences in the South, and out of it. And they echo and refine the central themes of the slave South—family, religion, and the continuity of life.

Editorial Method

In order to preserve the integrity and flavor of the letters and to capture any distinct Afro-American dialect, the letters are printed as found in the originals, with the few minor exceptions described below. End-mark dashes have been rendered as periods when this seemed to be the writer's intention. When no end mark exists but the sentence is complete, the sentences are separated by extra space. Otherwise, punctuation and spacing follow the practice in the original. Capitalization conforms to the writer's style. When it is impossible to decipher the erratic habits of the writers regarding capitals, the letter in question is rendered in the lower case. The placement of the dateline, salutation, farewell, and signature has been regularized. All editorial emendations and additions are placed inside square brackets. Thus, if the original manuscript is torn or illegible, this fact is so indicated: [torn] or [illegible].

All the letters are from the Cocke Papers. A source note follows each document, indicating the exact location of the manuscript in the Cocke Papers at the Alderman Library of the University of Virginia, Charlottesville. Explanatory notes, numbered consecutively by document, briefly identify individuals and significant events mentioned in the text of the document. In order to keep scholarly apparatus as unobtrusive as possible, and, more important, to highlight the central characters in the book, the Skipwith family, I have provided only the barest descriptions of secondary personalities and minor occurrences mentioned in the letters. Unless otherwise indicated, all quotations are from materials in the Cocke Papers. Background sources are described in the Bibliographical Essay.

All of the Skipwith family correspondence known to exist has been collected and printed in this book. None of the Cocke letters to the Skipwith family has survived.

Acknowledgments

Editing historical documents and writing history are simultaneously communal and solitary enterprises. In the course of gathering data about a subject, the editor/historian interacts with many individuals, as my own experience has revealed. They direct him, or her, to sources, they correct his misconceptions and errors, they improve his prose, they provide differing perspectives and arguments with which to judge his material, and, if they are kind, they encourage him and remind him of the importance of his subject. They become active agents in the editing and writing process. The success that the final product enjoys is owing partly, but significantly, to their participation and cooperation. In the end, however, the editor/historian is left alone with the subject and becomes the final judge of the evidence. He imposes the final order on the material and attempts to draw meaning from it. In so doing, he makes the work "his" work more than "their" work. He is responsible for the accuracy and the common sense of the final product. His name on the title page signifies his recognition of that responsibility. But it should not diminish the role of those others who lighted the way.

And so it is with this book, for it is the product of many hands. In the five years it took me to prepare the manuscript, I learned many different things from many different people, and I thank them for it. Because I did not always heed their advice about editing and writing this book, I can hardly hold them responsible for any of its shortcomings. Because I did listen to them in many instances, I happily acknowledge their assistance in giving this book whatever importance it may come to have.

George H. Reese and Dorothy Twohig nurtured my interest in Cocke and the Skipwiths when I was an intern at the Institute for the Editing of Historical Documents at the University of Virginia. They taught me much about the editorial method and the importance of accuracy, and without realizing that Cocke and the Skipwiths would become my preoccupation thereafter they encouraged me in my work. For three summers Edmund Berkeley, Jr., Gregory Johnson, and the staff of the Manuscripts Division of the Alderman Library, University of Virginia, provided a congenial working environment for me. They patiently assisted me while I sifted through the thousands of items in the Cocke Papers and related collections. They were unfailingly efficient, friendly, and knowledgeable, and so lightened my research tasks and added to my understanding of Cocke, the Skipwiths, and their world.

The staffs at the following institutions also offered me kind and useful assistance: Alabama Department of Archives and History, University of Alabama at Tuscaloosa, Auburn University, Balch Institute in Philadelphia, Duke University (manuscripts division), Haverford College, Historical Society of Pennsylvania, Library Company of Philadelphia, Library of Congress (manuscripts division), Mississippi Department of Archives and History, National Archives, New York Public Library, University of North Carolina at Chapel Hill (Southern Historical Collection), University of Pennsylvania (rare book room), Presbyterian Historical Society, Tulane University (manuscripts division), Virginia Historical Society, Virginia State Library, College of William and Mary, and Williams College. Finally, the staff at the Drexel Library of Saint Joseph's College, particularly Richard Behles, assisted me in gaining materials through the interlibrary loan service.

During the course of my research and writing many fellow scholars offered suggestions on content and style and shared their own information with me. Svend E. Holsoe left his own important work on Liberia to locate Liberian sources for me, to correct my drafts and notes on the Skipwiths' Liberian experience, and to make innumerable other valuable contributions to the Liberian section. James M. Gifford read an earlier version of the Liberian chapter and made useful suggestions for sources. Michael L. Nicholls, Tom W. Shick, and Bell I. Wiley led me to Liberia-related materials. At a crucial stage in my annotation, John W. Blassingame kindly offered several observations on slave testimony and the editing of slave materials. Charles B. Dew, William K. Scarborough, and William Van Deburg criticized a paper I delivered on slave drivers, and their comments helped me to rethink my position on privileged bondsmen. Stanley Engerman made several corrections and improvements. Finally, John M. Mulder read the entire manuscript and made countless improvements in the style and direction of my writing.

Saint Joseph's College provided institutional and financial assistance to the project. Thomas P. Melady encouraged me in my work and ensured that the school's part in the project went smoothly. Maria Monzo assisted me in cataloguing the Skipwith letters. Paul Cimbala performed many errands and assisted me in the preliminary bibliographical work.

This project received support from several institutions. The American Council of Learned Societies provided a grant that allowed me to complete my research on the Skipwith experience in Alabama. Joseph R. and Norma Starobin opened their home and the Robert S. Starobin Memorial Library to me in 1975 so that I could complete my draft of the introductory chapters. The National Historical Publications and Records Commission endorsed my editorial project.

Portions of the Preface appeared originally in my article "When Lions Write History: Slave Testimony and the History of American Slavery," *Research Studies*, 44 (March 1976), and are published with the kind permission of the editor. Parts of the chapter on the émigrés were published in my article "Home as Found: Ex-Slaves in Liberia," *Liberian Studies Journal*, 6 (1975), and are published with the permission of the editors. Several passages contained in this book appear in my article on black slave drivers written for *American Heritage* magazine and are reprinted with its permission.

The letters are published with the kind permission of the University of Virginia Library and of John Page Elliott and Joseph F. Johnston, the heirs to the literary rights of the Cocke Papers and unselfish friends of scholarship.

The dedication of this book is to my wife, Linda Patterson Miller, and conveys only in part the debt I owe to her for her unflagging support and encouragement. She accompanied me on my research trips, typed notes, looked up sources, and, more important, kept asking questions. She lived this book with me in many ways. For that, and for much more than can ever be expressed verbally, I give this book to her.

RANDALL M. MILLER

Philadelphia, Pennsylvania

The Cocke and Skipwith Families

John Hartwell Cocke Family (one generation only)
John Hartwell Cocke (1780–1866)
  m. Anne Blaws Barraud (1784–1816)
      John Hartwell (1804–1846)
      Louisiana Barraud (1806–1829) m. Dr. John Faulcon
      Philip St. George (1809–1861) m. Sally Elizabeth Courtney
        Bowdoin
      Anne Blaws (1811–1862) m. Nathaniel Francis Cabell
      Cary Charles (1814–1888) m. Lucy Williamson Oliver
      Sallie Faulcon (1816–1879) m. Dr. Arthur Lee Brent
  m. Louisa Maxwell Holmes (d. 1843)
      no children

John Hartwell Cocke's Siblings
  Sally (b. 1775) m. Nicholas Faulcon
  Anne Hartwell (b. 1776) m. Merit M. Robinson
  Elizabeth (b. 1778) m. Arthur Sinclair
  Mary Kennon (b. 1783) m. John Faulcon
  Robert Kennon (1785–1789)
  Martha Ruffin (b. 1788, died in infancy)
  Rebecca Kennon (b. 1791, died in infancy)

The Cocke Plantations
In 1801, when John Hartwell Cocke reached his majority, he became the master of the Cocke family estates on the James River in Surry and Fluvanna counties, Virginia. About 2,500 acres of his land were in Surry County at the old homesteads of Mt. Pleasant and Swann's Point, plantations that were adjacent to one another. When he first married, Cocke occupied Swann's Point; his sisters lived at Mt. Pleasant. Cocke sold most of his Surry County interests to his sisters when he moved to Fluvanna County. Sally (Cocke) Faulcon, Cocke's sister, worked Mt. Pleasant for many years. Cocke's son, Philip St.

George Cocke, later moved back to Surry County and lived at a plantation known as Four Mile Tree. Philip tried to restore the exhausted family lands in Surry County, but after repeated failures he disposed of Four Mile Tree and moved to Belmead, a James River plantation in Powhatan County, Virginia, which he turned into a showplace. Philip later established cotton plantations in Mississippi.

When Cocke moved to Fluvanna County, in 1808, he divided the family property, known as Bremo, into three plantations, each approximately one thousand acres in size: Upper Bremo, Lower Bremo, and Bremo Recess. Both Upper Bremo and Lower Bremo fronted the James River; Bremo Recess was situated northeast of Lower Bremo, away from the water.

Bremo Recess was originally run by John Hartwell Cocke, Jr., but his epileptic condition prevented him from managing the estate successfully. After he died, in 1846, Cocke and his son Cary Charles Cocke managed Recess. Later that year, Cocke gave Recess to his daughter Sally as a life right possession. When she married Dr. Arthur Brent, she moved to Recess and assumed control.

Cocke lived at his Upper Bremo plantation until 1855. Cary Charles Cocke resided at Lower Bremo and shared the management of the Bremo estates with his father. It was at Upper Bremo that Cocke constructed the magnificent buildings that earned him so much praise from contemporaries and students of architectural history. In 1855, Cocke exchanged Upper Bremo for Lower Bremo.

Cocke's cotton plantations, Hopewell and New Hope, in Greene County, Alabama, are described in the text.

Skipwith Family

Children of Lucy Nicholas, who cohabited with Jesse Skipwith
    Peyton Skipwith (d. 1849)
      m. Lydia Randall (1804?–1834)
        Diana (1822–1844?) m. Moore James (b. 1820?)
        Matilda (b. 1824)
          m. Samuel Lomax (1823?–1850)
            infant (died)
            Eliza Adala
            Lydia Ann
            child (died)

        m. James Richardson (d. 1860)
           child (name unknown)
      Napoleon (1825–1839)
      Felicia (1828–1834)
      Martha (b. 1830?)
      Nash (1831–1851)
  m. Margaret Skinner (b. 1820?)
George Skipwith (b. 1810)
  m. ?
      Howell (b. 1830) m. Polly Brown
           four children
  m. Mary
      Martha (b. 1837) m. Albert Morse
           two children
      William
      Richard
      Thomas
      James (d. 1860) m. Patsey
           two children (names unknown)
      Isaetta (d. 1863)
      Peyton (died as a boy)
      Lucy
        m. ?
          Betsey (b. 1844)
          Maria (b. 1847?)
          Dinah (d. 1850)
        m. Armistead Hewitt
          one child (died young)
      Mary (d. 1862)
      George (d. 1857)
      daughter (name unknown)
      daughter (name unknown)
Jesse
Erasmus
Gerry
Lavinia

Introduction

To the casual student of black slavery in America, it might seem wrongheaded and mean to begin a black family chronicle with a paean of praise to a white slave owner. But then, of course, John Hartwell Cocke of Bremo was no ordinary planter. He was, as Clement Eaton once observed, a "free lance of the Old South," gallantly and sometimes testily thumbing his nose at every shibboleth of Southernism—tobacco planting, strong drink, and the rightness of slavery. Still, he was a slaveholding planter, and so to many critics he deserves no place in a book by and about slaves.

In truth, he deserves every place in it. There was no wholly separate Afro-American nation in the slave South, as there could be no wholly separate white Southern-American nation, however distinct their respective origins and self-perceptions. The lives of black and white—slave and master—were inexorably bound up with one another in that peculiar symbiosis that was the antebellum South. By proximity and necessity they worked together, they sometimes prayed together, they sometimes played together, and they even slept together. Violently, yet even lovingly, their lives intersected in countless complex ways. In varying degrees of intensity this theme echoes through all of the literary remains of black people—in their narratives, in their folk tradition. And it forms the adhesive mix, although not the only one, for the Skipwith slave family letters that comprise this book.

The Planter

Born in 1780 into one of Virginia's great landed families, John Hartwell Cocke enjoyed all of the advantages of his gentry class, yet cherished none of its vices. At his Fluvanna County, Virginia, estates, clustered on the James River midway between Richmond and Charlottesville, Cocke allowed himself one ex-

Portrait of John Hartwell Cocke, 1820s, by Edward Troye. (White House Collection)

travagance. There he built "Bremo," a pisé Greek Revival mansion which has evoked encomia from generations of architectural historians. But the true interests of this tall, raw-boned man of quiet dignity are more sharply etched in the sturdy slave cabins, the "Temperance Well," and the brick plantation schoolhouse and chapel that stand today as monuments to Cocke's humane values, good order, and sense of noblesse oblige.

Forsaking political preferment, General Cocke chose the life of the planter. He called for enlightened husbandry of every kind to restore the economic vigor of the South. By writing and example he demonstrated the profits accruing to the farmer who diversified his crops and replenished his soils. Throughout his life Cocke promoted careful livestock breeding, marling and the application of animal manures, crop rotation, horizontal terracing and ditching, deep plowing, reforestation, and pomology.

Cocke's principal contribution to Southern agricultural reform was his lifelong campaign against tobacco cultivation, a crop that exhausted the soil and absorbed labor. In his influential pamphlet, *Tobacco, the Bane of Virginia Husbandry* (1860), he scourged tobacco planters as harmful to the South. Their preoccupation with tobacco cultivation forced them to import meat and corn for their tables and hay for their livestock. This shackled them and their region to the North, the source of their provisions. Cocke also found tobacco morally repugnant. By his account, tobacco consumption led to a host of maladies including dwarfishness and insanity. Tobacco had no place in a Christian society. Such extreme arguments, which also characterized Cocke's lifelong war against alcoholic beverages, subjected his ideas to ridicule, but Cocke remained fixed in his beliefs, apparently confident that God and Nature were on his side.

Cocke's claim to our attention, however, rests on something more than his scientific agriculture and his antitobacco crusade. Cocke was of a school of conservative reformers, North and South, who after the War of 1812 formed benevolent societies to give purpose, continuity, and permanence to the reforming tremors of the age's religious revivals, and so responsibly to hasten the millennium. The increasingly powerful

Miniature of John Hartwell Cocke, 1830s. (From Virginia State Library, Richmond, Virginia)

denominational churches encouraged social reform and imparted to all reform a religious cast. Conservative reformers hoped that Christian benevolence and guidance would secure the republican social order against the excesses of democracy by promoting the middle-class virtues of self-reliance, thrift, industry, and sobriety. Through meliorative agencies such as the American Bible Society, the American Tract Society, the

American Temperance Union, to name several, Cocke and these good people hoped to eradicate intemperance, poverty, ignorance, sloth, and a welter of related evils. In this way they would remake America into one homogeneous Protestant nation. To that end, the presence of a swelling tide of black slaves posed an urgent, central problem.

With his generation, and those after for that matter, Cocke could not imagine two races living harmoniously together. One inevitably enslaved or devoured the other. Cocke thus shuddered, as did his ideological mentor and friend Thomas Jefferson, in the knowledge that justice would triumph in the end. He knew that Providence would visit His wrath upon the unrepentant people. Nat Turner's rebellion in 1831 offered grim evidence of that awful, impending truth. Cocke's letters, especially in 1831 and 1832, revealed his fears and outlined his solution: to save Virginia, indeed America, men must remove the curse of slavery. They must also remove the blacks.

And that was just the rub. No removal, no freedom. There would be little of either, however, for Southerners unfailingly hitched the millstone of exportation of the blacks to all abolition schemes. Most eighteenth-century and early nineteenth-century Southern liberals, including Cocke, Jefferson, and James Madison, advocated the colonization of American blacks as a solution to the race problem in America and indirectly as a way of promoting gradual emancipation.

Colonizationists rooted their programs in the conviction that America must be a white man's country, but something more than racism alone informed their appeals for mass deportation of blacks. Supporters of colonization in Virginia, the seedbed of what little gradual emancipation sentiment existed in the South, wanted to eradicate slavery because it discouraged local industry and manual labor among whites. To free whites from lethargy and tyranny, the South must free slaves. In addition to liberating whites, the emancipation and deportation of slaves to Africa would open up the dark continent to American religious and commercial influence. Once the African natives were "civilized," they would demand American trade goods and missionary support. The colonizationists were not blind to the irony of charging American blacks with the great mission to uplift and outfit their racial brethren in Africa while being de-

Bremo, Cocke's home in Fluvanna County, Virginia. Exterior view, southwest. (A 1930s photograph reproduced from the Historic American Buildings Survey collection, Library of Congress)

nied the capacity to prosper in America; rather, they argued that prejudice prevented the American blacks from fulfilling their ambitions in America. Only in Africa could the former slaves give full compass to their talents and serve God's larger purpose. Finally, as Cocke wrote in 1831, only colonization would encourage even the most gradual emancipation in the South. Few planters would divest themselves of their valuable property unless they received some form of compensation. More importantly, nonslaveholding whites would not act on their latent antislavery sentiments unless they were confident that black emigration would proceed simultaneously with black emancipation.

Colonization, then, was an amalgam of humanitarianism, racism, commercialism, missionary purpose, and even diluted abolitionism. However impractical it appears in retrospect, it

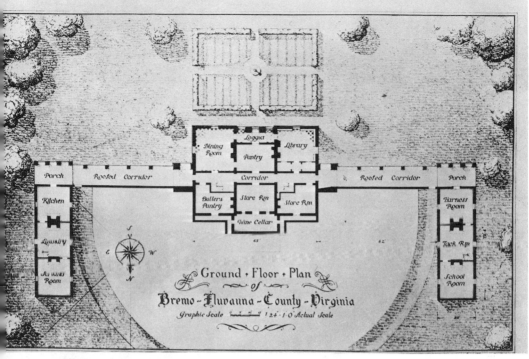

Bremo, ground floor plan. (A 1930s photograph reproduced from the Historic American Buildings Survey collection, Library of Congress)

was not a wild visionary scheme. Short of war, there was no other means of ending slavery in the South. Whites manifested an open hatred of blacks everywhere in America. Segregation, restrictions on movement and on political and social activity, and countless other humiliations reminded free blacks of their lowly status in the North as well as in the South. Blacks were unwelcome in America, unless enslaved, and there was little prospect that white racial prejudices would soften. Most importantly, there were examples of successful voluntary mass emigrations in the nineteenth century which fueled the hopes of the most patient colonizationists like Cocke. Migration was the central fact of American history. During the first half of the nineteenth century hundreds of thousands of Europeans ventured to America and tens of thousands of Americans uprooted themselves to move westward. Movement to escape economic

Daguerreotype of John Hartwell Cocke, 1850s, by W. A. Retzer of Charlottesville, Virginia. (From Bremo Recess deposit, Cocke Papers, University of Virginia, used by permission of Mrs. Raymond Orf)

Slave cottage at Bremo. (A 1930s photograph reproduced from the Historic American Buildings Survey collection, Library of Congress)

and social restraints was built into the American ideology of self-help, and so it could be charitably extended to blacks. Recognized as people who suffered because of prejudice, blacks were offered the chance to improve their position by emigrating to the virgin land of Africa. Such logic ran throughout colonizationist literature and was both explicit and implicit in Cocke's own thoughts on the subject.

The practical difficulties encountered in early attempts to transport and colonize liberated slaves in Africa dashed any hopes for a meaningful, general emancipation. Some men, like Cocke, dreamed on. They founded the American Colonization Society in 1817 to lobby for governmental aid for colonization and to educate the public on the need for colonization. The society purchased a beachhead in West Africa and attempted to settle manumitted slaves and free blacks there, but the society lacked the financial resources to carry out the project successfully. Worse, it lost the support of many Northern white and black reform leaders who charged that colonization was a proslavery plot to strengthen the South's peculiar institution by removing free blacks from the country. Wanting direct government assistance, the society transported fewer than seven thousand freed slaves to its tiny colony of Liberia in West Africa. Little matter, for by the 1830s time had run out on the John Hartwell Cockes of the South. An increasingly militant Northern antislavery movement combined with the haunting specter of slave revolt to cool Southern interest in the most gradual abolition proposals, or discussions of them. Proslavery apologists bullied the South into a quiet acceptance of their arguments as they pushed the nation toward civil war. Even colonizationists fell suspect in the South for their implicit assumption that slavery was somehow not right. Indeed, Cocke suffered a frightful beating in 1835 for persisting in his moderate antislavery witness.

General Cocke survived ostracism and the rough handling and referred to such practices as object lessons on the morally debilitating influence of slavery on Southern manners. Surely slavery cursed the land, wrote Cocke in his letters to Southern friends and Northern reformers. It bred indolence, sexual laxity, and brutality in the master and denied intellectual fulfillment and scriptural counsel to the slave. Just as surely, slavery remained the most effective means to restrain the passions of the darker race until they could be safely returned to Africa. But slavery was wrong, Cocke concluded, and to escape God's wrath, the good master must treat his slaves humanely while he prepared them for freedom and resettlement in Africa.

In his blasts against chattel slavery, Cocke fused the natural rights principles of the eighteenth century with the scriptural invocations of the nineteenth. The one he acquired while a student under Bishop James Madison at the College of William and Mary, and the other he received from his own conversion and the good example of his two wives. After the death of his first wife in 1816, Cocke rededicated his life to humanitarian causes, and in choosing Louisa (Maxwell) Holmes as his second wife he found an austere Presbyterian equal to him in

Christian ardor and charity. They took their religion straight and interpreted the Scriptures literally. Early each morning they rose to read the Bible together, as well as other Christian works such as *The Imitation of Christ* by Thomas à Kempis. Daily, they also reviewed their sins. They labored tirelessly to become worthy Christian examples for others. Confirmed Sabbatarians and temperance advocates, Louisa (Maxwell) Cocke and John Hartwell Cocke renounced the worldly life. Cocke often chided his friends and even his children for their weaknesses. Few people satisfied his high demands for self-denial. Both of Cocke's wives vigorously supported his various philanthropic enterprises and endorsed his desire to liberate his slaves and colonize them in Africa.

Except perhaps for temperance reform and scientific farming, no other human interest so dominated Cocke's attention as did colonization. And no other interest yielded such meager rewards. By 1859 he would concede the impracticability of his dreams, but until the failure of his various manumission experiments was apparent, Cocke stood publicly on the side of gradual emancipation and colonization. As late as 1857, he was reading Hinton Rowan Helper's *Impending Crisis*, a devastating critique of slavery as an economic system and a call for nonslaveholders to overthrow planter dominance. He was also recommending this banned book to his friends. The implacable resistance of the South to any discussion of abolition, his personal failures, and the opposition of his children, and finally the embittering experience of civil war and the loss of a son all combined to erode Cocke's liberalism. Still, by translating his antislavery words into action Cocke showed a courage and a vision that were all too rare among the other scions of the master class in the South.

Simply put, Cocke's manumission plan for his own slaves relied upon a merger of material stimulants of cash and kind with a policy of moral uplift to convert each slave into an individual worthy of trust and therefore of liberty. Cocke pledged a percentage of plantation profits toward repaying his investment in his slaves, and he encouraged his large force of slave artisans especially to work overtime to earn money for self-purchase. Through religious training and regular preaching he endeavored to infuse in his slaves the virtues of thrift, temperance, loyalty, and self-reliance. Cocke did not fail to remind detractors that such a policy redounded to the planter's advantage as well as to the slave's. The slaves gained the blessings of Christianity and purged themselves of vicious habits. Ultimately, they obtained their freedom. The planter, in turn, received a steady application of hard labor from the sober, devout slave who toiled longer and with less disruption than the querulous, besotted slave who knew only the driver's lash.

Cocke refused to release any slaves incapable of assuming the full burden of freedom and colonization in Africa. Better that they remain under the care of humane masters, he later opined, than that unskilled, un-Christian slaves should be turned loose on civilization to embarrass colonization and their race. Generous for his day, Cocke ascribed the slaves' alleged ignorance to their unhappy condition, not to their color. Throughout his letters Cocke revealed his manumission dreams as an entrenched faith in the mutability of man through scriptural revelation and useful employment, a belief that weathered many disappointments in his colonization schemes. The linchpin of his plan, then, was successful religious and moral instruction.

At Bremo, Cocke and his Christian wife Louisa began a daily program of religious indoctrination and reading among the slaves, a program which also included tutoring in letters. Cocke initially staffed his plantation chapel and his infant and Sabbath schools with Northern teachers and clergymen, but he quickly ran afoul both of public opinion and of a Virginia law prohibiting slave education. Thereafter, Cocke directed family devotions, and Mrs. Cocke guided the slave children through the rudiments of reading and writing. Plantation work requirements inevitably interfered with adult education, but the slave children daily gathered around the stern mistress to recite their lessons. Impatient of progress, Mrs. Cocke was quick to record in her diary any illumination among her "house scholars." In 1834, one precocious girl especially impressed her as being "much above the ordinary cast of them." Little Lucy, the daughter of the slave driver George Skipwith, "of her own accord" one evening entertained Mrs. Cocke with several hymns and "many questions." This performance gave Mrs. Cocke "pleasing proof" that at least one slave had "profitted much by her instruction in the Infant Sch." Thus encouraged, she continued her ministrations, and her husband waxed stronger in his emancipation convictions.

In 1833, Cocke freed Peyton Skipwith and his family and sent them to Liberia. In choosing Peyton, Cocke wrote in 1832, he found a servant who was "prepared for the change, advantageously to himself & useful to the Colony." Earlier Cocke had trained Peyton as a stonemason, and in time he invested great confidence in Peyton's ability and industry. In a July 27, 1825, letter to J. C. Cabell (Cabell Papers, University of Virginia), Cocke described Peyton as "an intelligent & skillful man for his station." What impressed Cocke more, however, was Peyton's commitment to temperance and his Christian devotion. In his certificate of emancipation for Peyton (October, 1833), Cocke elaborated on Peyton's qualifications. Peyton had given Cocke thirty-three years "of faithful service." He possessed a "culti vated mind" and "first rate" skills as a craftsman, but "above all" he had a "Christian walk & conversation." Cocke was not then able to find another slave so eminently qualified for freedom.

Cocke did not gloss over the formidable difficulties confronting the slaves and their would-be emancipators. Virginia law imposed a snarl of obstacles to discourage manumissions and required any newly freed slave to leave the state within a year of liberation or face re-enslavement. Other states had passed similar repressive laws, often in the wake of Nat Turner's insurrection. Furthermore, as Cocke wrote in a September, 1831, letter detailing his arguments, the mass of field hands were so ignorant that they could not even count to twenty. Only the romantic or the callous could delude themselves that such people were fit for freedom. A consummate gradualist, Cocke insisted that educating the slaves for emancipation, and the public mind to accept the idea, would take so long "as to preclude the men of any one generation from the honor of its accomplishment."

Over the next twenty-five years Cocke's manumission plans took their final form. To prepare his slaves for emancipation on a wider scale than possible at Bremo, Cocke purchased a plantation, "Hopewell," in Alabama's Black Belt. Conservative reformer that he was, he combined philanthropy with profit. Cocke selected the most likely candidates for improvement and sent them and their families to work the Greene County, Alabama, cotton plantation under the direction of an overseer and slave driver, Peyton Skipwith's brother George. The earnings from cotton sales, less the costs of maintenance, would buy freedom for the deserving. While in Alabama, the slaves would learn useful industrial and agricultural skills and further their studies in letters and religion. By managing their own affairs with minimal white supervision at this "school for freedom" as Cocke called it, the slaves would learn the arts of self-government. If their pecuniary and moral progress moved apace, they could expect to earn their freedom and passage to Liberia in five to seven years.

While Cocke awaited the results of his Alabama experiment, he surveyed the fortunes of the Peyton Skipwith family in Liberia, on which the future prospects for emancipation seemed to him heavily to depend. The experiences of the Skipwith émigrés in Liberia comprise the first section of this book, while the Alabama experiment provides the background for the letters of George and Lucy Skipwith printed in part two.

PART I

LETTERS FROM LIBERIA
1834–1861

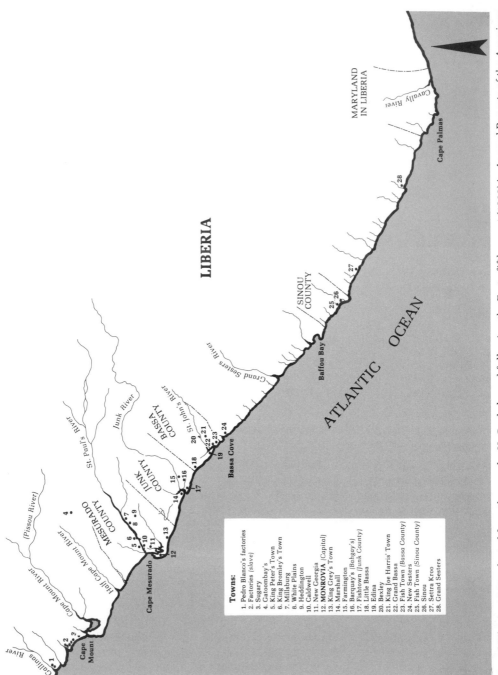

Towns:

1. Pedro Blanco's factories
2. Factories (slave)
3. Sugary
4. Gatoombay's
5. King Peter's Town
6. King Bromley's Town
7. Millsburg
8. White Plains
9. Heddington
10. Caldwell
11. New Georgia
12. **MONROVIA** (Capital)
13. King Grey's Town
14. Marshall
15. Farmington
16. Barquay's (Bohgoy's)
17. Fishtown (Junk County)
18. Little Bassa
19. Edina
20. Bexley
21. King Joe Harris' Town
22. Grand Bassa
23. Fish Town (Bassa County)
24. New Sesters
25. Fish Town (Sinou County)
26. Sinou
27. Settra Kroo
28. Grand Sesters

Map of Liberia, 1845, adapted from the map by H. Coyle bound following the Forty-fifth report (1862) in Annual Reports of the American Colonization Society. Spelling of towns and rivers follows the Coyle map.

The Emigrés

The gentle Peyton Skipwith, son of the Bremo plantation black ma and nurse Lucy Nicholas, became the first beneficiary of Cocke's colonization program. In 1833, Cocke released the thirty-three-year-old Peyton with his wife Lydia and their six children to search out a new life in Africa. After several months' hesitation Peyton agreed to go. A temperance man and, like so many slaves, a Christian steeped in an evangelical faith that sustained him through enslavement, Peyton seemed to Cocke a fit vessel to carry American genius and the Gospel to Africa.

Aware of the appallingly high mortality from fevers and pestilences among settlers, a fact which discouraged Liberian immigration throughout the nineteenth century, Cocke instructed the American Colonization Society agent in Norfolk to postpone the family's departure until the end of the West African rainy season. Peyton was never a man to squander opportunity, and he soon found work in Norfolk while waiting to embark. He also polished his reading skills and accelerated the schooling of his oldest daughters, Diana and Matilda.

In the company of approximately two score other black immigrants and several missionaries, including Cocke's friend and the colony's physician, George Todsen, the Skipwith family sailed out of Norfolk aboard the *Jupiter* on November 5, 1833. Although prolonged by calm, the fifty-five-day passage was pleasant until a violent thunder storm ominously greeted the sighting of Grand Cape Mount. The *Jupiter* cast anchor in Monrovia Bay on the last day of the year. With the first glimmer of the new year the hopefuls disembarked to begin their African adventure.

First impressions of Liberia hardly flattered any expectations of plenty. Despite modest progress in commerce and political expansion since its establishment in 1822, the colony pre-

Ashmun Street, Monrovia, in the late nineteenth century. (Reproduced from the collection of the Library of Congress)

sented a rough-hewn appearance. In Monrovia, the capital and largest settlement with a population of approximately 2,000 persons in 1833, a veneer of polite society and prosperity obtained in the several handsome government buildings under construction, but most private dwellings were little better than crude wooden shacks, giving the town an aura of impermanence. Stone warehouses and wharves dominated the architecture and underscored the town's distinctly commercial cast. It was a brawling seaport and frontier town with a large population of floaters and speculators. It was also a town of promise. Since Peyton was familiar with Richmond and Norfolk, it is unlikely that he was awestruck by the bustle and cacophony of town life. But he could hardly have been cheered. The aesthetic disparity in the buildings mirrored the gross inequalities of wealth and political power in Liberia, with most of both monopolized by the free black population who came with money and skills. This situation initially angered Peyton and later impoverished his daughter Matilda.

In time, thanks partly to Peyton's masonry, Monrovia took on a more finished quality, which elicited accolades from travelers. The city had a commanding view of the sea on two sides and the jungle at its back. Settlers looked to the sea for sustenance, fishing and trading with Americans and Europeans in material goods and ideas. Since the soils around Monrovia were inferior and the lush, verdant jungle close to the coast unyielding, settlement moved up the St. Paul River or more generally laterally down the littoral. The settlers gathered in small communities according to geographic origin in America. Effective occupation of the interior proved difficult and dangerous, for hostile natives and deep ravines imperiled any inland trip. Consequently, the Skipwith family, like the vast majority of colonists, settled in or near Monrovia.

Once in Monrovia, Peyton commenced a correspondence with his family in America and with his former master —a correspondence that, continued by his children, spanned almost thirty years. Few of the missives sent to black relatives in America are extant, and none of their or Cocke's letters to the Skipwiths survive. The manuscript letters of Peyton, daughters Diana and Matilda, son Nash, and nephew James to members of the Cocke family total over fifty and constitute probably the fullest family epistolary record emanating from former slave colonists in Liberia. All of the Skipwith Liberian letters known to exist are published below.

Significantly, none of the irreverence toward former masters that crowds the fugitive slave narratives distinguishes the Skipwith family letters. Through two generations of writing, Cocke remained "dear master," "dear Gen'l," "Honr'd Sir," and "friend." Matilda endearingly addressed one note to "dear Philip" since she remembered Philip St. George Cocke, the general's son, more as a playmate than as a scion of the master class. Among the Skipwith women correspondents, affection was manifested through the exchange of gifts and confidences. The often plaintive Diana delighted in receiving handkerchiefs and other finery from her former mistress and family and sent native fruits, mats, and handicrafts in return. On one occasion she dispatched a set of whips with alligator skin handles to Cocke. The women correspondents also discussed marriage interests and gossiped, although these exchanges were always guarded in tone.

The fact that the Skipwiths bothered to maintain a link with their former master implies something of trust and affection. To be sure, each party derived special benefits from the contact, with the advantage clearly resting with the white. Cocke, ever hungry for reliable intelligence on Africa and colonization, secured competent and detailed testimony about the colony, especially its political and economic history. He also continued what must have been a psychologically rewarding paternal oversight over his former slaves through timely charity and admonitions to thrift and sober habits. Perhaps Cocke felt that letters from Liberia, if read aloud to slaves at home, might work to assuage the refractory and to prod the indifferent to diligence by reminding them of the master's past benevolence.

The Skipwiths, however, were not free agents in the exchange. Friends and family held in America and a dependence upon Cocke's philanthropy to tide them over lean years, of which there were many in Liberia, tempered any visible signs of hostility or disapproval. Discreet enough not to appear grasping, the Skipwiths, like those who came after them, filled their correspondence with cries of distress and calls for provisions—a hogshead of tobacco for the interior trade, tools of every kind, seed, and sundries—and so kept their relations with Cocke in good repair.

Like the letters of immigrants to the United States in the nineteenth century, the Skipwith letters are often businesslike and prosaic. This reflects the formal, distant relationship with the Cockes which the Skipwiths assumed after long absence from America and gaps in the correspondence, but it also illustrates how survival dominated the everyday lives of these pioneers. More than this, it reveals the materialistic urges of the settlers who often framed their image of liberty in terms of progress and prosperity, as did many white Americans of their day. The Skipwiths, like other settlers, looked upon Liberia both as a mission field and as a fertile ground to build their fortunes. Peyton Skipwith, at least, understood that true independence came only with economic security. The Skipwiths were initially dependent upon the American Colonization Society which provided all settlers with food and home-building supplies for the first six months they were in Liberia. When the rationing ended, the Skipwiths turned to Cocke for assistance.

It was a temporary expedient, they hoped, but one that bound them to Cocke. As the emotional bonds joining Skipwiths and Cockes slackened over time and as a new generation of correspondents grew up with only dim childhood memories of one another, material interests increasingly defined the relationship between the two families. Nash was a stranger to the Cockes, and Matilda too was far removed from their world. Among the second generation of Skipwith correspondents, only James knew America well and recognized any deep personal debt to Cocke. His letters rekindled the warmth of the early family correspondence.

Perhaps, then, the Skipwiths are deceiving us in their statements of affection for the Cockes and in their seemingly chatty manner in some of the early letters. Since the bulk of their letters from Liberia went to whites, we can never know how much, if at all, the émigrés lifted their masks. Even letters to fellow blacks passed into white hands and so, perhaps, contained no genuine self-revealing commentary. But however illusory and fragmentary, these letters from Liberia furnish some of the most illuminating evidence available on slave attitudes, values, and skills that survived emancipation, and of the early social history of Liberia.

From the beginning, misfortune dogged the path of Cocke's missionaries of Americanism. Within a year after their arrival, the dreaded "African fever" carried off Lydia and daughter Felicia, and dysentery, near blindness from the African sun, and a hernia laid Peyton low. Given up for dead by the colony physician, Peyton secretly received West African medicine-man nostrums and scored a remarkable recovery. Other maladies were more lasting. The primitive economy and the oppressive climate of Liberia offered only irregular, seasonal employment to a stonemason, and while combating the "wild" Gola, Peyton sustained a leg wound that incapacitated him for over a year. The sweep of death and ill fortune left Peyton emotionally prostrate. He thought often and wistfully of his old Virginia home, and daughter Diana yearned to return there.

Happily, conditions improved. Peyton regained his health and found steady work. Affluent Monrovians built detached houses of two stories that were composed of a stone basement and a wood-frame body with a portico on both the front and the

Monrovia, Liberia, 1850s. (*House Executive Document #1*, 1st Session, 33rd Congress; reproduced from the collection of the Library of Congress)

rear. Whenever possible, they constructed their homes entirely of stone because the scarcity of whitewash or paint, the humidity, and the ravages of termites gave frame buildings a dilapidated appearance and a short life. As the colony matured economically and socially, the preference for stone in all public and in many private buildings afforded the stonemasons numerous opportunities to find work during the milder months. Home builders of all kinds commanded high wages throughout the nineteenth century in Liberia. Often, however, payment was in trade goods rather than money, and these goods had to be exchanged, sometimes at a stiff discount, for staples. Peyton complained of this practice, but he eventually prospered in spite of it.

Peyton's business grew rapidly as the local economy expanded. To meet an increasing demand for his work, he took in several boys as apprentices, including John Faulcon, a manumitted slave Cocke bound over to him. The Skipwith household grew with Peyton's trade, since Faulcon and the other apprentices, who numbered as many as six at one time, shared the Skipwith table and shelter. According to Faulcon, Peyton was a model of propriety and a powerful advocate of sobriety and enterprise. This was in marked contrast to George Skipwith, Peyton's brother, who was the driver and community leader at Cocke's Alabama plantation. Freedom thus allowed the one brother, who was by temperament and training quieter and more resolute than his younger counterpart, to exercise true leadership and to develop a sense of purpose and self-worth.

By 1837, Peyton declared himself to be satisfied with his new home and to "desire no other." He claimed his government land allotments and purchased town lots in Monrovia. As Matilda later ruefully recalled to a visitor, the family lived "comfortably and had a fine house" until her father's death in 1849, at which time the estate "got into court & was completely swallowed up by lawyers." Peyton remarried, mixed with other temperance men among the settlers, rejoiced in a Sabbath school to instruct his children, and drew strength from Baptist ministrations. His three surviving children all enjoyed fair prospects, and his adopted country fared well economically. Opportunity for upward mobility beckoned. The Protestant mission boards in America were expanding their ministries in Liberia, opening new schools, and increasing contact between America and Liberia. Son Nash followed his father into the mason's trade, and, joyfully for Peyton, Diana and Matilda were reborn in Christ. Finally, Peyton counted himself a man of local eminence, for he was elected to a minor rank in the militia. This was an honor reserved to rich and well-born whites in his native Virginia. The Skipwiths' Liberia was a frontier society and therefore a participative society in which the settlers were expected to assume responsible self-government. Peyton's service in the militia and as a juror gave him a personal involvement and emotional investment in his young community which helped to transfer his loyalties from Virginia to Liberia. Ten years in Africa were enough to transform him into a Liberian in habit and mind, a man proud of black achievement and eager to trumpet the blessings of freedom and Liberia.

Joseph Jenkins Roberts, first president of the Republic of Liberia. (From *Frank Leslie's Illustrated Newspaper*, December 26, 1868, p. 235)

Liberia worked a similar metamorphosis on James Skipwith, Peyton's nephew by his brother George. After removing from Philip St. George Cocke's Belmead plantation in Virginia, James labored eight years in Alabama as a waiter, a steward, and a river-boat pilot in order to purchase his freedom. Unhappily, he lacked sufficient funds to satisfy the claims of his wife's owner, Cocke's son Dr. Cary Charles Cocke. Despite Cocke's repeated insistence that Cary Charles release James's wife and children, the doctor, who did not share his father's views on slavery, adamantly refused to bend. James sailed for Liberia in 1858 without his family. Despondent, he almost quit Africa. Travel and lengthy discussions with black community leaders, particularly Joseph J. Roberts, a native-born Virginian who became president of the new republic, and who had been a friend of Peyton Skipwith since they traveled together on the *Jupiter* in 1833, led James to concede that his first impressions of Liberia were unjustified; rather, James came to believe that Liberia afforded the sole refuge from prejudice for his race. He reported that "with alittle help we can live heir as well as we can in America." Reflecting upon the success of President Roberts and other black architects of Liberian independence—which was granted by a financially exhausted sponsoring society in 1847—James praised the black republic as worthy to stand with any nation in the civilized world. He chose well the metaphor of "building the wall of Jerusalem" in describing the Liberian experience. In this, he appropriated a theme common to the slave narratives, that of God's anointed recovering their lost patrimony. This African manifest destiny, for James at least, translated into black pride. Like Peyton, his participation in Liberian civic life and his investments in land and business increasingly bound him to Liberia. Liberia's success reflected his own and stood as a symbol of his own self-worth.

But whose Africa was it? What image of Africa did these privileged bondsmen, still close to their former master's interest, entertain? As one recent student of Liberian settlement rightly contends, bonds of culture proved more durable than bonds of race in settling the colony. The settlers claimed nothing in common heritage with the peoples of West Africa. Rather than cast off American manners and institutions, save slavery, the settlers sought to transplant an American society to Africa. The Skipwiths, like the rest, remained Americans, and unfortunately for the success of assimilation thereafter, their perceptions of West Africa and her inhabitants were framed in the antebellum South. In order to secure a station denied to them in America, for they countenanced a society based on privilege, they exaggerated real and subtle differences that distinguished them from the Bassa, Gola, Kru, Dei, and Vai tribes occupying the grain-coast region of Liberian settlement. Perhaps fearing that in the wilderness of Africa they too would become like savages, and heathen, they retained American tastes in food, dress, manners, and housing. These became fortresses of civilization amid the savages and the jungle. As Gus Liebenow and W. W. Schmokel have shown, the West Africans acknowledged the cultural distance by styling Monrovia "the America place" and the settlers "white men."

The unhappy and bloody early history of colonist-native relations confirmed the separation. Land transactions and bargains struck between the colony and the native chiefs from the first palaver in 1822 through the mid-nineteenth century precipitated frequent misunderstandings, exacerbated by faulty surveys and conveyances, rival claims, defaults on payments, alien concepts of land appropriation, and a voracious appetite for land on the part of the colony—a history which elicited few objections from the Skipwiths. The colony's encroachment on the native trade monopoly further strained relations. To bolster sagging incomes, settlers engaged in a petit trade with European and American traders in palm oil, cassava, camwood, cane sugar, ginger, rice, and other African products, the exchange of which cut into native middleman profits. The colony relied upon trade with local tribes for essential food supplies and for export commodities. Both as a colony and a republic the Liberian government took a direct hand in promoting and securing such trade and consequently embroiled Liberia in local tribal politics. The colony also disrupted the native economy by waging vigorous campaigns against the slave trade. Slave trading did not diminish with the arrival of the Americans. It actually increased during the 1830s when Pedro Blanco, for a time, expanded his slave-trading operations at New Sesters. As Peyton Skipwith relates, it took concerted action by the colony and the British navy to drive the slavers away, but the problem nagged Liberian relations with the natives throughout the 1830s and 1840s. On numerous occasions the natives met these challenges by waging war; indeed, through most of its early history, as graphically detailed in Peyton's full, and sanguinary, accounts of Liberian military prowess, the colony was immersed in armed struggle with one or more of the local potentates.

The very process of defending the exposed settlements along the coast reinforced the settlers' separateness and feelings of superiority over the West Africans. Locking arms with the politically dominant free blacks in Liberia, the former slaves became integrated as the second tier of a distinct Americo-Liberian community, while they became further estranged from the local West African populace. Sadly reminiscent of the Europeans' confrontations with American Indians, Liberian leaders ascribed the natives' alleged inferiority to their heathenism and their wilderness habitat and justified military subjugation in the interests of advancing a superior civilization and forestalling inevitable treachery from the savage host. The relish with which Peyton discussed slaying Africans speaks volumes on his disdain for these people and their culture. Only James Skipwith doubted the wisdom of the protracted conflicts with the natives. He cited reasons of economy.

Prejudice against Africa extended to diet and manners. Except for rice and fresh fruit, the Skipwiths initially declined to eat West African foods. They preferred to purchase imported American wheat flour, corn, and pork when these items were available at modest prices. The former slaves were also shocked by the seminudity and the crudity of manners displayed by the natives who were, as Matilda put it in describing Ibo and Congo tribesmen recaptured from slavers and settled in Liberia, "the most savage, blud thirsty people I ever saw or ever wishes to see." Peyton insisted that despite prodigious efforts to "civilize and uplift" the natives through scriptural enlightenment, they remained ignorant and vicious. Indeed, he once questioned the possibility of any ancestral link between the former slaves and the West Africans.

Unsure of their own place in the nascent Americo Liberian community, many former slaves labored hard to differentiate themselves fully from the West Africans. They early threw up communal breastworks against African culture that were impenetrable in the short run at least. In their relations with the natives the former slaves discouraged the most casual liaison between native and colonist children, something that the free-born settlers, more confident of their status, did not do. The former slaves practiced endogamy, restricting access often to former slaves from similar geographic, religious, and occupational backgrounds, thus shoring up communal ties. The cultural boundaries between free-born colonists and the former slaves, however, overlapped and blurred. Permeable rather than rigid, these boundaries posed no barrier to ambitious, successful former slaves who might watch their children pass into the dominant free-born society via marriage. This did not happen with the Skipwiths, who married former slaves, but who significantly also chose marriage partners from the elite or privileged bondsmen class.

Social distinctions among slaves and free blacks in the antebellum South also confused the social picture of Liberia. In urban centers in America lighter skinned, affluent free blacks formed exclusive social and fraternal organizations that insulated them from contact with slaves and darker, poorer free blacks. In Southern port cities the presence of a caste system among the blacks had put distance and distrust between various segments of the black population. This legacy passed to Liberia where poorer, darker former slaves lacked the wealth, skills, education, color, or connections in America to claim social and political equality with free black émigrés. In this sense the former privileged slaves like the Skipwiths stood in the middle as moderators or conduits between the two groups. The early history of the colony reveals an economic and social fluidity that allowed for considerable movement in and out of the various levels of black émigré society, but the desire to establish social standing forced the poorer settlers and the former privileged bondsmen to define their place vis-à-vis dark heathen natives accordingly. As white influence in Liberia declined in the 1830s and the settlers became more confident of their own abilities and leaders, color and caste barriers between settlers from America broke down. This was necessitated by the need to preserve an American cultural hegemony. There were not enough light-skinned, rich, free black émigrés to preserve the caste through intermarriage. By mixing with the natives and with the former privileged bondsmen and women, they produced darker offspring. In addition, there were many free black émigrés from the upper South who were dark. The Skipwiths maintained friendships with several such families. Consequently, the color differentiation was never powerful enough to serve as a means of fixing status in the new country. Material success would prove to be a better yardstick, perpetuated of course by access to political power. By his friendship with Roberts, the leading political figure in Liberia in the 1830s through the 1860s, with the politically and socially influential Teage family, and with church and temperance leaders—not to mention his own rising economic fortunes—Peyton Skipwith enjoyed a stature unknown to him in America. Although not of the ruling class, he was close to it and supported its interests.

Once in Liberia many colonists turned to trade, much to the dismay of the American Colonization Society, which favored agricultural development. The Skipwith letters reveal the degree to which members of the family subsisted on the petit trade. Nobody thrived in it. In fact, Matilda's second husband, a former house servant characterized by John Barraud in 1857 as "a lazy worthless fellow working only enough to keep from starving, even when work can be obtained," dragged that sorely

Monrovia, 1860s. (From *Frank Leslie's Illustrated Newspaper*, December 26, 1868, p. 236)

tried woman into penury by his devotion to barter that far surpassed any abilities he had in it.

Belatedly, the Skipwiths considered agricultural pursuits. Perhaps they had earlier connected farming with slavery, or, more probably, they lacked the resources and skills necessary for that difficult, risky undertaking in Liberia. Until colonists learned native farming techniques and the colony subdued or pacified the interior tribes, agriculture was a perilous occupation. The dense forest growth yielded grudgingly to the ax. Much of the arable land on the flat coastal plain was engrossed by early arrivals in the colony. Heavy West African rains washed out crops, strange and terrifying crop pests ravaged the fields and drove farmers to perplexity, and American crops and farming practices were inappropriate to conditions in West Africa. But with a liberal government land policy luring them inland, it was hard to resist inducements to commence farming. Moreover, the wealthy American planters, who operated absentee rice, coffee, and sugar-cane plantations that were cultivated by African recaptives, hired native workers, and native apprentices, were earning handsome profits once West African farming methods were applied. The period of the 1840s through

1860 was one of general prosperity for the republic. The staple crop plantations around Monrovia produced abundantly and supplanted the garden-style agriculture of the colonial period. Peyton Skipwith, who had attacked the monopolist tendencies he saw among planters in 1834, was contemplating farming twelve years later. Immediately before his death in 1860, James Skipwith described several nascent farming villages and was preparing to occupy his own upcountry holdings.

Contrary to the proslavery denigrations of the Afro-American as congenitally indolent or to the abolitionist insistence that chattel slavery infected the slave with a permanent, if purposeful, sluggishness and distaste for work, the Skipwith letters reflect a healthy attitude toward work on the part of these former privileged bondsmen. For the Cocke slaves it had been less the lash and the boot than the promise of improved shelter and enriched diet, sweets and calico for the women and, before Cocke started his antitobacco crusade, a plug of tobacco for the men, released time, barbecues, or other crude wages which had inspired them to industry and enterprise while in bondage. The artisan in bondage did not necessarily challenge a work ethic that gave surety of rewarding earnest, honest labor and virtue with material comforts, upward mobility of a sort, and even emancipation, for within the carefully prescribed bounds of plantation regimen, slaves of talent and ambition realized marked advances in status and remuneration. To trade the unwieldy "Negro hoe" for the mason's trowel was no small recompense for someone of a creative bent. Slave artisans enjoyed a large measure of self-direction, controlling their own work pace and, if fortunate, hiring their own time. Furthermore, the demands of Cocke's neatly ruled ledgers and modern farm management had dictated tutoring the slave artisans and foremen in the forbidden arts of ciphering, reading, and writing. To read their letters, the Skipwith émigrés were not wholly ungrateful for these few advantages. After all, Cocke's training had given them freedom.

More than a puritan work ethos, cultural impedimenta, or their slow absorption into the Americo-Liberian community, the most salient attitudes expressed in the Skipwith letters are the émigrés' powerful attachment to family and religion. The letters are laced with gossip and queries on family matters.

Closely intertwined with familial affection was a tenacious commitment to temperance and, more importantly, an evangelical Christian thrust that ran deep.

A timelessness and an otherworldly flavor permeated their advice on good behavior and Christian witness and revealed a debt to the survival of inchoate West African religious values imbedded in their own Southern evangelicalism. It was a debt perhaps greater than the Skipwiths would care to admit. Their blurring of time boundaries of past, present, and future—a means of bearing up under afflictions by projecting one's own suffering backward and forward in time—owed its origins to West African culture. Too, their veneration of elders was of a magnitude and kind to be decidedly non-European. Their faith did not simply promise immediate, temporal deliverance— certainly an impossible goal in the South. No religion could long prosper on such a false premise. Rather, their faith imparted to them a calm, a solace, and a comfort in the divine assurance of restored fellowship in the end. For the Skipwiths, condition and color were not the final arbiters of salvation. All of the "folk," white and black, who honored the covenant of grace would reach jubilee, and about this they were exultant.

In this context, Peyton's emotional restraint following his father's death and his more apparent grief over the loss of his "cussan Charles" take on greater meaning. Redemption was already accomplished with the father, whose place at the family table was thus assured for all time. But with Charles's conversion in doubt, Peyton despaired of a full family reunion in eternity.

Religion also broke the monotony of the settlers' lives, particularly affecting the insular world of the women. The letters of the Skipwiths relate the progress toward salvation of loved ones and neighbors, and tell of the great sectarian controversies that racked Liberia during its formative period. Religion dominated the lives of the Skipwiths, as it did for so many settlers. The churches provided community life, educational facilities, intellectual sustenance, and an important link with the past. The churches also provided opportunities for assuming leadership positions, although the continued control of church policy and property by American mission boards retarded this development during Liberia's early history and aggravated many of the settlers who wanted to take their religious life into their own hands. As Peyton Skipwith's accounts show, the missionaries carried their sectarian loyalties to Liberia and sucked some settlers into the vortex of sectarian disputes. This retarded true nation-building by setting settler against settler, but the Liberians overcame this obstacle after political independence.

But religious disputes did not shatter family unity. Nothing could do that, for the love ligaments binding family were strong. In many instances, family ties had been fostered during slavery by humane masters who sought connubial orthodoxy and stable social units on the farms. More importantly, strong family ties among slaves grew up because the slaves bitterly contested any disruption of their family life. As many scholars have recently argued, the patrifocal, monogamous family unit survived slavery as the ideal and the real for many Afro-Americans in the South, and the former slaves jealously guarded this arrangement in Liberia. In the American South the enslaved father might earn the respect of his children by virtue of his role as chief correction officer in the cabin, by hunting, fishing, gardening, or pilfering to stock the family larder, and by working extra tasks for money, which meant gifts, home amenities, and expanded freedom for all. Separate slave cabins further helped to insulate individual family units. Such had been the case on the Cocke plantations.

The clear male focus of the slave family immediately appeared in Liberia, as it did in the Reconstruction South. The wives retired to home and hearth, the proper province of the Victorian "lady," to practice domesticity, piety, and submissiveness. The letters of the Skipwith women, like those of other women settlers, are strikingly similar to letters written by contemporary Southern white women in this regard. The world of all women in the nineteenth century rarely extended beyond the domestic circle. Women married young, bred often, remained confined to the home, and settled quickly into the life of the commonplace. Life was narrow and provincial and family-centered for most women in Liberia as it was in America for their white mistresses. Health greatly concerned the women: their letters generally began with a review of the family's health and the health of the community. Family gossip and news of religious affairs often filled up the rest of the letters. The preoccupation with domestic themes in the letters of the Skipwith women points to the principal roles women settlers assumed in Liberia, as it also marks the degree of absorption of Victorian values among these former privileged slaves.

Only when economic adversity intervened, which occurred with tragic frequency for the twice-widowed Matilda, did the Victorian lady leave the home for outside employment. Significantly, women settlers eschewed field labor whenever possible and sought, with mixed success, home-related jobs such as washing and ironing. According to John Barraud, a white visitor to Monrovia in 1857, Matilda, who was burdened with three small children and a "no-count" husband, chased traders and sailors to take in their wash and so augment the deflated family income. Although deprived of her former comfortable accommodations, she did not complain of her shabby surroundings. Her husband's lot was hers, and if she expected more, she never presumed to vent such hopes to white visitors or correspondents.

Expressions of love for family run like a litany throughout the Skipwith letters. Family fragmentation caused by migration greatly disturbed the settlers. James agonized over his separation from wife and children, and the Skipwith women wrote of a sense of "great loss" and "grief" or of being "buried in sorrow" because relations had passed away. But the family identity among the Skipwiths reached beyond the nuclear hub to embrace one vast cousinage of the Cocke slaves. Migration uprooted slaves from kinship and companionship networks of the extended family. Despite long-distance separation, the Skipwith émigrés sought out the psychological warmth of the old relations, and in Liberia they perpetuated extended family identity by bringing Cocke freedmen into their households. Letters to Cocke and his daughter Sally besieged them with requests to remember the former slaves to brothers and sisters, grandparents, nieces and nephews, cousins, aunts and uncles, what-have-you. Peyton maintained a steady pressure on Cocke to inform him of his brother George's progress and to honor his pledge to free George and reunite the family in Liberia. Out of loneliness or a desire to recapture youthful memories, the Skipwith girls eagerly solicited news from homefolk. Another former slave writer in Liberia reported that Matilda, whose road he called "quite hilly," "jumped with joy" after Cocke broke a long silence with a note, and she once admitted her wish "to visit again the scenes of childhood." Diana's heart, as ever, "blead" for her relatives and friends left in Virginia. Arrivals from the United States needed only to locate kin, however distant, to have homes opened to them. Thus Matilda invited in cousin James and eased his transition to Liberia, as the family had earlier received the Faulcon, Sturdivant, and Creacy immigrants from Cocke's plantations.

Pride in family was demonstrated in other ways. The Skipwiths took care in choosing marriage partners, since no one wanted to embarrass the family by wedding someone below the family's station. Diana refused to marry an African. Matilda alone made a bad match in marrying her second husband, but his failure was one of personality rather than any lack of class status. Peyton felt a keen sense of loss after the death of his first wife, but he did not rush into marriage again. He waited until he met a well-mannered Methodist woman fit to raise his children. To family members in Virginia, he also preached vigilance and temperance lest any shame the family by licentious and vicious habits.

The settlers in Liberia struggled hard to ensure a promising future for themselves and their progeny. Parents sacrificed much to send children to school and lobbied for educational reform in Liberia. When formal instruction was deficient or unavailable, they made do with home tutoring. Nash, for example, conscientiously added requests for histories and a dictionary to his list of necessaries from America. In many respects, the Skipwiths' engrossing faith in education anticipated the experience of the freed slaves in the postbellum South when young and old alike crowded into makeshift schools to unravel the mysteries of the written word. James had this hunger for education. Although twenty-three years old, he enrolled at a Baptist high school soon after arriving in Liberia. To prospective colonists and friends among the Cocke bondsmen, he also kept up a barrage of counsel to seize every opportunity for learning, which he considered the surest vehicle to self-reliance and influence. In this, he echoed the thoughts of his uncle Peyton. Education thus combined with religious faith and a strong sense of family to shape the Skipwiths' personalities and their adjustment to new modes of thought and living as free men and women in Liberia.

The letters from Liberia underscore the resiliency of American values and institutions, an amalgam of West African and European values really, during the period of settlement in Liberia. The Skipwiths ordered their world in Africa in terms of the old world in America that they had helped to create and sustain. As long as their prior cultural assumptions proved tenable in this raw, frontier environment, they clung to familiar, comfortable American social arrangements and institutions. But the Skipwith family letters also document another story. They reveal the slow erosion of the old values, the blurring of cultural boundaries, the very process by which these transplanted Virginians became Liberians. Reverberating through their letters is an emerging, swelling pride in their young, fragile republic, a nation wrought with their own black hands.

The letters of Peyton and James especially show that they wanted not only to be free but also to escape race prejudice. In America, privileged bondsmen, like the free blacks, keenly felt the sting of prejudice in their dealings with hirers and tradesmen away from the plantation. This common suffering bound them closer to the free blacks from the South. For both, Liberia appeared to be an inviting land where they could give full scope to their skills and aspirations. Despite the shock of the rugged frontier conditions and want which they found in Liberia, the Skipwiths overcame their initial disappointments and found satisfaction in their new land.

As a people who had survived the rigors of chattel slavery, their adaptability was of a tough and sturdy kind. African fevers that claimed family and friends, an enervating sun, hostile native tribes, and an often capricious Nature disheartened them, and, indeed, drove several other of Cocke's former slaves from Liberia to seek employment aboard American trading vessels or to find new homes in the West Indies. The Skipwith family, however, dug in for the duration. They were determined to achieve in Liberia what had been denied them at the old home in America—namely place and freedom.

Letters from Peyton Skipwith

Monrovia   Liberia   Febuary the tenth 1834

Dear Sir

I embrace this oppertunity to inform you that we are all in
moderate health at this time hoping that these few lines may
find you and yours enjoying good health   after fifty Six days
on the ocean we all landed Safe on new years day and hav all
had the fever and I hav lost Felicia[1] but I thank god that our loss
is hur gain   as Job Sais the lord gave and he taketh   I thank
god that he has mad it possible that we may meet to part no
more   I thank god that we are all on the mend   I can not tell
you much about Liberia   I hav not been from monrovia yet

as it respects my Self and wife we are dissatisfide in this
place   their is Some that hav come to this place that hav got
rich and anumber that are Sufering   those that are well off do
hav the nativs as Slavs and poor people that come from america
hav no chance to make aliving for the nativs do all the work

as it respects farming their is no Chance for it unless we
would get the nativs to work for us and then you must be wit
them and at the Same time when we ought to put in our grain it
rains So hard that we dare not be out unless exposing our
health   their is no chance for farming in monrovia for it is a
Solid body of Stones but they Say at Caulwell is achance but
Still I find that but few fower it   as it respects Stone masons
thay can get a good price three   dollars and ahalf aperch   A
pearch is for foot high and four foot wide but the Sun is So hot
that people from america can not Stand it in the dry Season and
in the wet it rains to much   their has Some come from america
that hav learnt the nativs and they hav hierd them to put up a
too Story house eighteen by twenty for twenty galens of rum

as it respect Coffe it Sells at 50 Cents per pound   I hav Seen
the coffe tree and all So Coffe on them   their is but afew treas
in their gardens and as it respects that wich grow wild the

nativs and monkeys take it   the nativs do brings theirs to town   loaf Shugar Sells at twenty eight dollars per hundred brown Shugars at twenty five dollars per hundred pork twenty five dollars per hundred   we have alittle fresh beef and it Sells at twelve Cents per pound   as it respects the fruit in this Country it is to tedious to mention at this time but new comers dare not eate much of it   I hav not Seen enough of the Country to tell you much more at this time but will tell you more when I See more of the place   I want you if you please to write to me by the first oppertunity and let me no on what terms I can come back for I intend coming back as Soon as I can   I must Come to aclose   Give my respects to all the famely and all So to all inquiering friends   my wife all So and children Sends their respects to you all   direct your letters to monrovia

Peyton Skipwith

Source: #5680, Cocke Papers
1. Felicia, aged six, died from a combination of the African fever and a fall "from a very elevated bed" onto a nail that drove into her leg. See George P. Todsen to John Hartwell Cocke (JHC), March 6, 1834, Cocke deposit, Cocke Papers.

Monrovia   March 6th 1835

Dear Sir

I embrace this oppertunity to write you these few lines to inform you that I am not well with a blindness of nights so that I cannot see.[1]   all the information that I can get from the doctors is that [I] must stop laying stone   I have lost my wife[2] she died on July 2d 1834   the rest of my family are tolerable well   Sir This is the third letter that I have wrote to you and have received no answer   I would be thankfell if you would write by the first chance and I do not know of any better chance than to write by Mr. Jos J Roberts[3]   I wonce had a notion of coming home and still have a notion but I want to go up to Sirrilione as I am advised by the doctors to quit laying sone for it is injurious to my health & if I get my health by going there I will say there   If not will return back to America   give my respects to your family also to the people   let my Mother know that you have received a letter from me   I dont want you to say any thing to [her] about my being blind but let her know that I will return. Dianah send her love to Miss Sally[4] and all of the family and is very desirous of returning back again   she wants you to write her word also by the first oppertunity   let her know how Miss Nancy Cavil and her family[5]   I have put myself to a great deal of truble of searching the servent of Mr Cavil and also that of Mr Haris[6] but I cant find eather of them nothing more but

I remain yours truly
Peyton Skipwith

Source: #5680, Cocke Papers

1. According to the colony's physician, Dr. George P. Todsen, Peyton suffered from nyctalopia, or night blindness.

2. Lydia (Randall) Skipwith (b. 1804?) died of overexposure and the African fever. For further details on the circumstances of her death see George P. Todsen to JHC, May 27, 1835, Cocke Deposit, Cocke Papers.

3. Joseph Jenkins Roberts (1809–1876), free-born mulatto from Virginia, prospered in Liberia as a merchant and a politician. In 1842 he became the first black governor of the colony, and after independence was proclaimed in 1847 he was elected the first president of the Republic of Liberia. He held office until 1854, and he served again as president from 1872 to 1876. Roberts accompanied the Skipwiths to Liberia on the *Jupiter,* and on at least one occasion he wrote a letter to Cocke concerning the colony's progress.

4. Sally Faulcon Cocke (1816–1879), Cocke's daughter who befriended Diana Skipwith (b. 1822?) and Matilda Skipwith (b. 1824?). She later married Dr. Arthur Lee Brent and lived at Cocke's "Bremo Recess" plantation.

5. Probably refers to Anne Blaws (Cocke) Cabell (1811–1862), one of Cocke's daughters. In 1831 she married the agricultural reformer and publicist, Nathaniel Francis Cabell of Nelson County, Virginia.

6. Unable to identify.

Monrovia   Liberia   April 27th 1836

Dear Sir

Yours by Bro. James Byrd[1] came safe to hand. He arrived here after a passage of about thirty six days. When I wrote you by Mr. B. Wilson,[2] I truly were in a distress situation. My health at that time was not good, and I expected to become blind as my eyes faild me daily, and the Doctor had advised me to stop work and travel for my health.

The idea of being in a new country with a large family of helpless children, who could depend only on me for support, & I being so indisposd as to be of no use to them nor myself having no means and the prospect of their suffering made me feel distressed and greatly so but thanks be to God my health and sight is recovered and that day of awful gloom is gone and I feel satisfied with my present home and desire no other   I write by almost every opportunity but cannot tell how it come to pass that only two of my letters have [been] received   For sometime passed we have not had a regular School as we have at present. I have two of my children now in school and the others I instruct at home

I cannot express the comfort it gives me of hearing of your health of the family and my friends and relations in general and would be [torn] I had time to write your at greater [torn] but this is now in haste as the [torn] Vessel is expected to sail in a few hours   I am still single myself and so are my daughters. I received the tracts on temperence   am still an advocate for the cause and rejoice to say that as to the use of ardent spirits there never was a more temperate community. it remains now to be put down as as an article of trade and the point is gained   the amt of ten Dollars you requested Mr. McPhail[3] to forward, never reached me. If you find it convenient to send us such articles as provisions they will be of more use to us than any thing else for there are times that we are obliged to suffer for such things as must be expected in a new country where we are not yet prepared to raise for ourselves enough for supprt

give my love to all the family both white and colored and all my friends in general   I shall end[eavor] to give evry [torn] the next time I write

Respectfully Yours
in the bonds of Christian affection
Peyton Skipwith

Source: #5680, Cocke Papers

1. James Byrd (d. 1856), free black from Virginia who arrived in Liberia in April, 1836, on the *Luna.*

2. Rev. Beverly R. Wilson (d. 1865), free black from Virginia who came to Liberia with the Skipwith family on the *Jupiter.* He directed the Methodist mission at the Cape Palmas settlement, established a manual labor school at Millsburg, and participated in politics frequently.

3. John McPhail, a Scottish-born Presbyterian elder who handled affairs for the American Colonization Society in Norfolk, Virginia. He chartered and fitted out expeditions to Liberia, and organized the Skipwith family departure.

Monrovia, January 30th 1838

Honored Sir:

I embrace this opportunity of writing you these few lines to inform you that my health is very bad at present. I have a wound that has lasted me for more than five months, and it is not well yet. I have not been able to do any work for nearly that length of time. The wound is not well, though I believe it is on the mend. My two small boys have wounds, for such are the diseases of a tropical climate: the three girls are in good health;[1] and as these leaves us in as good health as could be expected, we hope that they may find you and your family enjoying of very good health.

Your letter dated the 12th of Nov. 1837, was received a few days since, by the arrival of the ship Emperor and read with much pleasure. Sir, here permit me in a very few words to lay before you, some of the difficulties that I have had to encounter with since my arrival in Africa; as it respects my trade, I can get as much work as I can well attend to when I am in possession of my health, and have the use of my feet. Rock work is worth from Two Dollars and fifty cents, to Three Dollar per perch; and day work is worth per day $1,50: but the payment which workmen get here for their work is of the most inferior sort, and at the dearest rate; viz: cloth, Tobacco, powder, pipes, &c. all of which are paid to workmen at the highest market price, so that we are unable to trade them off at the least advantage. I have put a stone wall for a school house, 30 feet by 20, for the Ladies Society in Richmond,[2] one story and a half high, for $275 per perch,[3] but I have not the money for it yet. I under stand that Rev. J. J. Matthias, Governor to Bassa Cove,[4] is empowered to settle the claim, as he has the money in hand, which I presume he will pay shortly, according to what Leut. Gov. A. S. Williams[5] says; being employed by him to put up the wall. By the ship Emperor forty days passage from Norfolk Virginia, I received the hoghead of Tobacco, which you sent me, for which you made a demand of $55; but I do not think it prudent in me to send the money by this Brig as she is bound for New York. But the ship Emperor will sail after trading a little on the coast, then I will send you the money. I am very much oblige to you for the Tobacco, indeed, but is rather short, notwithstanding it arrived here in good time. The shortness of the tobacco may prevent the quick sale of it, as we use it principally for native trade, though I may be able to sell it in the rains, which is fast approaching. I would be glad if you would appoint an Agent in New York, and write me his name, the street on which he lives, the number &c. so that I may have some person to send your money to. John[6] is living with me, he arrived here safe and in good health, he has not got the fever yet, he is much pleased with his new home, and bids fair for usefulness in this place; though all new-comers seem well pleased with the place. John is going to school every day to the Methodist Mission School—you says that you wish me to let you know what things I stand in need off, which I will do in another letter. noth more at present but

Remain yours &c Truly
Peyton Skipwith

Source: #5680, Cocke Papers

1. Nash (b. 1831) and Napoleon (1825–1839); Diana, Matilda, and Martha (b. 1830?).

2. Ladies Society of Richmond, originally the Female Colonization Society of Richmond and Manchester, Virginia, sought to establish a school for orphan and destitute children in Monrovia. The school languished for want of books and financial support.

3. Certainly he meant $2.75 per perch.

4. Rev. John J. Matthias (d. 1861) served a brief and undistinguished tenure as governor of Bassa Cove settlement from 1837 to 1838.

5. Rev. Anthony D. Williams (1799–1860) assumed effective control of the Bassa Cove settlement in the absence of Ezekial Skinner, the appointed agent, and he later served as vice-president of Liberia (1850–1854).

6. John ("Jack") Faulcon (b. 1822) was emancipated by Cocke and apprenticed to Peyton in 1838. In 1841 several of Faulcon's family, who received their freedom in the will of Cocke's sister, Mrs. Sally (Cocke) Faulcon of Mt. Pleasant in Surry County, Virginia, joined him in Liberia. Cocke freed Faulcon's mother and a brother and sister in 1851. Several Faulcon family letters from Liberia are preserved in the Cocke Papers.

May 9 1838   Monrovia
John H Cocks

Dear Master

I rite you theas fue lines to imform you that I am very unwell but the rest of the family are well and I hope that theas fue lines wil find you the Saim

I rite you by the Brig Susan Elithebeth but I dont know
whither they come to hand or not   as it respect the Tobaco you
Send me I have not Sold it and I wil give you my reasen why
if I sel it at publick Auction it wil fetch verry little and thire
have bin So much Fiting with the Natives that they dont Come
to town   thire-fore I thought best to wait A whil as I knew that
you was not in amediant want of it at pressent   I am in hopes
in a Short time this war among the natives wil be done; the
head man Jinkens have bin at war with the Golar Tribe Come
down to our agence & desiar him to Stop the war and Show him
plan what to fall upon that the war might be Stop and the plan
that he fall upon was Sinply this that he wil not fite the Golar
tribe and if the golar wil cetch his people he want to know if
our governor wil portect him   a commity of 3 men was Chosen
to goe and See what termes would the golar Stop upon but the
Commity has not return yet[1]

I will now go ond to tel you of a Sertain Death took place by
M[r] D Logan a Gentleman from the city of Richmon[2] he was
a man of wealth and had a great deal of influance a mung the
heathens but he got whimsical and thought proper to leave the
Cape and to go to and Seak a cuntry Seat a bout 9 miles from the
Cape   he went on doing bisiness with the natives trading and
So forth   after he had bin thire about 5 mounts they came
down a large tribe of heathens with Bullocks Camewood & ivry
and amoung them thire was some that was in debt to him and
they had a Bullock which he went up and seas and give it to a
nother gentleman whome he had as a companion   as Soon as
he don that the natives Sirround him and Say that he Should
[not] have it & they attemp to tak it & he cill one of the men
Mr Logan was brot down to Stand a trial   he was brote in gilty
by the grand Jurry and the pettiJury Clear him   Mr Logan was
then advise not to go to his cuntry Seat a gain but he say that he
would for he and Mr harris[3] was not afraid & he return back to
his farm and was not thire 3 weaks before thire came another
tribe down to him with Camewood and ivory for him to by &
whiles he was waing the wood one of them draw of with his
Cutlis and Struck him down to the ground & cilled him   Mr
Harris Saw that he up with a hatchet & maid the attemp to cill
this fellow but he mist it and the others saw this throw thire
Spear at him and he being up to thire Capers Caught it and run

Peyton Skipwith's letter to John Hartwell Cocke, Monrovia, May 9, 1838. (From the Cocke Papers, University of Virginia Library, Manuscript Division) away with it and then they Shot him cilled and they took every thing that they wanted out of the house and then put Logan in it and Set it afire

a nother Sircom Stance thire was a Mr Grean[4] a Emerican ho keep factry at little Bassa his money growed Short and he went in the cuntry and took two natives boys and he told thire fathers that he was going to learn them to Speak inglish he brote them to his factory and the ver night one of them run a way & he rose up in morning and took the one that [was] lef and carried him to the Slave factory and Sold him he Sold him for 2 Two Dubble lowns and one peace of cloth cost about 5 Dollars; in a short time the news reach Edina which is about 20 miles from little Bassa and they send and had him arest by the natives they brought him to edina for a trial he resist against the natives and would not be taking by them but they wounded him verry much he was tried before the jestos peace and they found that they had no power to try a Sienson of Monrovia and he was Sent up Monrovia to have a trial and he Stud two trial and at last the petti Jury clear him; I dont know what wil become of the Colony

the richest of the men seam to be failing for they hav mogage thire propity to the firroners & I exspect before long thire wil be a great desstress with them Captain Tailor[5] is hear now an inglish man and he has given his agent power to Sue for his rits

one thing what pleas me they have not got no money and they are oblige to go to farming you may know that this is the fact for thire is two vessel in harber; hats that use to be 5 dollars is orford for 150 cents Brass that use to be $1 is offerd for fifty cents clothes and varias things is orford as cheap durt and thire is not money in the colony to bye I had the pleasur of Seing Mr Mils[6] last Sabbath evening he hold praers in my house this is the second time I have sean him since he hav bin out hear he is now about to leave for amerrica and by him I rite you I wil be verry glad if you wil Send me a cag of Shingles nails and some Riting paper I wish you to appoint an agent in new york or some person whome you can place confident in John is got through the fever verry well So far he is now going to School you desire me to rite to whither my children was going to the Richmon Ladies Sosiety School or not they never was A School thire for it so much out of the way it is

unconvinent for them to go but as Soon the new School house
is don I wil Send them   give my respect to all of your family
and to Miss Nancy Moldon[7]   pleas to give my love Mr and
Mistress C T Cabble[8]   give my love to all inquireing friends
I have nothing more to Say at present but I Stil Remain yours
Peyton Skipwith

Source: #5680, Cocke Papers

1. Fan Fila Yenge, whom the settlers called Chief Jenkins, broke away from
the Gola confederation centered at Gon in 1833 when the leader of that interior
political grouping died. According to the *African Repository*, XIV (1838), 66,
252, 253, Jenkins sought to extend Gola influence over the coastal region occupied by the Dei tribe. He frequently attacked the Dei towns. He also waged
war against the Condo confederation, an ethnically diverse political state with
its capital at Bopolo, or Bopulu. In 1838 Jenkins and his Gola followers attacked
the last Dei town of consequence, killing 200 Dei inhabitants. Jenkins' depreda
tions spilled over to hurt the colonists, and the destruction of Dei power disrupted the balance of power among the coastal tribes. Combined with the
celebrated Logan murder (see note 2 below), Jenkins' warmongering offered the
Liberian government an excuse to extend its authority into the interior by
subduing Jenkins and restoring order.

2. David Logan, a farmer and trader in the Dei country, was murdered by
Mandingo tribesmen in revenge for Logan's slaying of a Mandingo. The Liberian government, which was attempting to exercise a supervisory and mediat-
ing power over the native tribes, blamed the crime on the Dei tribe and forced
the Dei chiefs to grant the colony a land cession as compensation for the loss of
a colonist.

3. The account in the *African Repository*, XIV (1838), 251, describes Harris
as an American who, along with a Gola and a Bassa, was carried off by the
Mandingo warriors.

4. Green Hoskin, a citizen of Monrovia, was charged with selling slaves. The
inhabitants of Edina settlement pressed the charges against him but lacked
jurisdiction. Despite intense lobbying by Bassa Cove and Edina settlers, he was
acquitted for lack of evidence at his trial in Monrovia. See *African Repository,*
XIV (1838), 165–166.

5. Unable to identify.

6. Perhaps he refers to Nicholas Mills, the manager of the Virginia Colonization Society during the 1820s.

7. Nancy Moreland (1778–1842) was born at the Cocke estate at Swann's
Point and remained with the Cocke family as the Nanny to John Hartwell
Cocke's children after the death of Cocke's first wife in 1816.

8. Unable to identify.

May 10 1838   Monrovia Liberia   Lucy nichels

Dear Mother[1]

I rite you theas fue lines to imform you that I am verry unwell
but the rest of the family is quit wel and I hope that these fue

lines wil find you in good health; I am in hopes that you will
not greav after Father[2] because I beleav if he keep the faith he is
gone to beter world then this   all that you wil have to do
mother is to prepare to meat death for the Lord giveth and the
Lord takeeth and blessed is the nam of the Lord   I have not
greave after my father for I beleave that he is gone to a better
world than this   I was more Shock when I heard the death of
Cussan Charls[3] because you did not rite me whither he maid his
peace with god or not   tell my brother Erasmus[4] deal fair with
his self for I know that if the love of god ever was applied to his
troubleed contion he know it; you wish to see me but cant be
more desires to see me than i am to see you all   I Calculate to
come and see your all this year but this wound have throw me
so far back I dont know when I shal be able to come and thin
Mother I hope wil give you Consolation if you never see me no
more in this world I am triing to meat you in a better world than
this whare we Shal part no more   tell Brother George that I
hope his faith has not fail   ask him is he a Solder do he mean
to fite in the indureing of the war. If you dos you go on for I am
bound to meat you

tell uncle ned[5] that I am verry glad that he is got his family
and that he is liveing well but I am verry much Surprise that he
have not rote me a letter Since I have bin hear   ask brother
gerry[6] do he mean to dy a Sinner or what is calculation   tel
him to write me for I feel consurned bout Situation   tell
Lavinia[7] that I Shant say much to her because she told me when
I com from home that nothing Should Seperate her from the
love of god   tel me by your nex letter if all the membres of the
temperance Sosiety[8] that I leave is hold out faith ful   I wil tel
you uppon the oner of a man that I have ceeping pleg for I have
not baught one gil of Spirrit since I leave emerria nor use it in
no way

give my love Father Primas and his wife[9] and the rest of his
family   tell Charls[10] most that I wish to se him verry much

it is so teagest for me to call all of people naim but give my
love to Cissiah[11] and her children to Sam Kello[12] and to all of
my inquireing friends fer and near   the children all send thire
love to every body   matilda Send her love to ned and aunt
Luvina and to the rest of the family   I get the ribbens and
hankerchief and one pare of Socks   I have not sene mr minor[13]

yet but if my health wil admit I expect to go to capepalamas for to work [nax dries?] and thire I Shal Se him if he dont leave for Emerrica before that time   I have nothing more to say

Peyton Skipwith

Source: #5680, Cocke Papers

1. Lucy Nicholas (1782–1852), Peyton's mother and the wife of Jesse, was the favorite nurse and house servant of the Cocke family, who fattened her with extra food in life and mourned her in death. Like her husband Jesse and her son Peyton, she became a devout Baptist and an ardent foe of alcohol. She was the mother of Peyton, George, Jesse, Erasmus, Gerry, and Lavinia. Although she married Jesse Skipwith, she did not use his last name. Some of her children also went by the surname Nicholas.

2. Jesse Skipwith, then the coachman and shoemaker at Upper Bremo. As a young man, he worked as the hostler at Upper Bremo. In 1821, Cocke persuaded him to become the foreman at Upper Bremo and to run the plantation without a white overseer. Cocke was very pleased with Jesse's work, but Jesse apparently was not happy with his new responsibilities. By February, 1822, he had returned to caring for the horses and the mules. See JHC to John Hartwell Cocke, Jr., November 12, 1821, Johnston deposit, Cocke Papers.

3. "Old" Charles (b. 1777?), the carter at Bremo Recess.

4. Erasmus Nicholas was Peyton's brother, whom he later joined in Liberia. He worked at Mt. Pleasant, the plantation of Sally (Cocke) Faulcon in Surry County, Virginia. He was a friend of temperance.

5. Ned Edwards (d. 1862) was Cocke's manservant. In 1834, at Ned's pleading, Cocke purchased Ned's wife Felicia and their two children, Berthier and Lucy, in order to bring the family together. Ned was a Baptist and a temperance advocate.

6. Gerry and his predicament remain elusive.

7. Lavinia, Peyton's sister, was a house servant and Sabbath schoolteacher who married a stonemason named Anthony Creacy, the son of "Old" Ben and Judy. Lavinia later moved to Bremo Recess to serve Cocke's daughter Sally (Cocke) Brent.

8. The Fork Union (Va.) Temperance Society where Cocke's abstinence men gathered.

9. Primus Randall, the husband of the Bremo shepherdess Betsy, was the foreman at Upper Bremo and a temperance follower. He died in 1849. Primus and Betsy Randall were the parents of Lydia, Peyton's first wife.

10. Charles Morse (or Moss) was born in Virginia in 1803. In practicing his mason's trade he became close to Peyton, his cousin. He took a leading part in the Alabama experiment. For further information see the Letters from Alabama below.

11. Kessiah Morse, Charles's wife and the mother of seven children. She was the cook at Upper Bremo until the Morse family moved to Alabama, at which time she hired out her time as a cook in Greensboro.

12. Sam Kellor (b. 1796?), the head ploughman at Upper Bremo.

13. Rev. Lancelot B. Minor labored at the Mt. Vaughn mission at Cape Palmas for the Protestant Episcopal church from 1838 until his death in 1843. He was the son of Mrs. Mary Minor Blackford of Fredericksburg, Virginia, who liberated many slaves to settle in Liberia and fiercely opposed slavery by pen and action. For information on the Blackford antislavery witness and the Minor

slaves in Liberia see L. Minor Blackford, *Mine Eyes Have Seen the Glory, the Story of a Virginia Lady, Mary Berkeley Minor Blackford, 1802–1896* (Cambridge, 1954), especially pp. 23, 34, 62, 81–83, 85–87.

Monrovia Liberia   May 20th 1839

Dear Sir

haveing receving you letter dated Nov 10th 1838 stating about my wound I have it in my power to state to you that they are all well and once more spared to be getting on handsomely at my trade and am in tolerable good halth together with my children, I had the misfortune to loose my youngest son accasiond by a soar mouth   I certainly must say that you have bestowed a great kindness on me by giveing me the perceeds of the Hogshead Tobaco, my children are getting on very well and are going to school every Day and I have yet to maintain them all   John Faulcon have been Bound to me to learn my trade and appears to get on tolerable well at present and conduct himself very well[1]   I received the packages that you sent and was very glad of them also the children, Mr Minor has sent me word concerning the amt you placed in his hand but he it appears do not wish to send it to me he wishes to give it to me himself—in person—you stated in yours dated the 28th that you wish me to state to some particulars relative to the colony   for my part I am at a Loss what to say   there are so many things that I call trifling perhaps may be some advantage to you to know & hear that is the colony has made some effert to exonerate herself from hunger by a few of our ablest men turning there attentions to agriculture but before that we could have hardly thought that we could have existed for our dependence was mostly on the tribes of the country   Gov Buchanan[2] have arrivd in the ship Seluda and I hope that the Friends of the Society will either support her colony or let us alone   I beg to be excuse for thus addressing you so harsh as respects the Society But for three years we thought they had entirely forsaken us and left us to our own resources   we have continual wars amongst the natives arround about us so that trade is very dull and scarcly any thing doing. The fisherman at grand Bassa cove like to have taken that settlement and if they had not to have been such cowards it would likely been the case which war is not settled as yet.[3] I did hear that the Gov did make some effort to effect a peace when he was down there but am not able to know on what conditions but did hear that the head fisherman should say that he did not care how it was &c   the natives are very savage when they think they have the advantage.

I also wish to remind you that I see daily the Star Spangld Banner unfurled on the cost of africa as a protection for the slaver to keep the British man of wars from takeing them which we think as a handfull of people to that of the United States a disgrace to her Banner   we if we had vessels could defy them to take our cross & stripes and Hoist them to her mast head for the protection of the slave trade[4]   please to send me some stone Hammers & trowels by the Revd C Teage[5]

Yours in due Respect

Peyton Skipwith

Source: #5680, Cocke Papers

1. John Faulcon and Harrison Story, aged fourteen, were bound to Peyton Skipwith on November 12, 1838. Story, who was probably born in Liberia, remained with Skipwith for several years. For further information on the indentures see Commonwealth Court Monthly Sessions, 1838–1842, folder 20, Liberian Government Archives (LGA).

2. Thomas Buchanan (1808–1841) was a former governor of Bassa Cove settlement (1835–1837) who returned to assume the governor's office for Liberia in 1839. The popular Buchanan marked his brief administration by frequent attempts to reduce the slave-trading factories near the colony and by a heated political controversy with the Rev. John Seys (see also Peyton's letter of December 29, 1840, pp. 77–78 and n. 1).

3. King Joe Harris, a Bassa chief, terrorized settlers living on the coast. In 1835 his people surprised and razed a Quaker settlement at Port Cresson, and despite efforts to satisfy his demands, he continued to annoy the colony into the 1840s.

4. Sensitive of maritime rights, the United States refused to permit other nations the right to search vessels flying an American flag, a prohibition which extended even to suspected slavers. Likewise, the United States navy in African waters, the so-called African Squadron, foreswore interference with any ships under foreign colors. Encumbered as well with admonitions from Southern or pro-Southern administrators to go slow in pursuing violations and by a reluctance of American statesmen to negotiate a forceful international antislave trade pact, the navy all but abandoned any attempt to suppress the illegal African slave trade. As a result, slavers hoisted the American flag with impunity in order to escape searches by British officers. See Alan R. Booth, "The United States African Squadron, 1843–1861," in Jeffrey Butler, ed., *Boston University Papers on African History* (Boston, 1964), I, 83–84; and Warren S. Howard, *American Slavers and the Federal Law, 1837–1862* (Berkeley, 1963), *passim.*

5. Rev. Colin Teage (d. 1839) came to Liberia in 1821 as a missionary for the African Baptist Missionary Society of Richmond. He is best known for chairing the Constitutional Convention of 1838 in Liberia.

Monrovia   Nov 11th 1839

Dear Sir

I did write you by the way of the Ship Saluda when she was home Last voyage and exspected to receevd a letter from you and that the Revd Colin Teage should have Brought it to me but he did not reach his home but died in about fourteen days sail of Monrovia which was a great disappointment to me and friend and also not to receive any inteligence from you nor none of the family as I am always anxious to hear from you all and I thought that the Lord had favourd us by sending a regular packet to sail to and from said ports so as we might never want for an opportunity or have any excuse   It has been very sickly here and has occasiond some few deaths of our respectable citizens but I believe the rest of the settlers are enjoying tolerable good health at present with my family   the children are still going to school to days & Sunday school that has Lately been establish in the Baptist church of the Town of Monrovia

I think that our Laws Lately made by the agent & council are two binding upon the inhabitants, if they can get along with them in the end they may prove a great benifit[1]   I think that they have occasion the Inhabitants of Monrovia to see all ready by not suffering the spanish trader to come to the colony that they are in better circumstances, as relates to rice, abundance of rice has come in our Market and some of our little retail shops are over run but this would not have the case if the slaver dealer had to have been allowed to come in our town for he would have bought from them faster than they could have obtain it. I have sent you the Liberia Herald and Diannah the Luminary which will explain to you what Laws &c and what we about here   I no you all are desireous to see me but it is imposible to come home at this time. I am building a house and the rock and wood has to be carried by the hand of men so you must no that I can make but little progress in Building is my reason that I cannot come at this time but perhaps as soon if the Lord Blesses me with health and strenght to finish it then I will make some preperations if a live to visit you once more. John has been bound to me and keeps quite steady and Learn very fast and is glad that he undertook to learn the trade.

A Slaver dealer for sometime had a slave factory at Little Bassa and Gov. Buchanan after he came out orderd him away and said to him that he had no right to deal in Slaves in that teritory and that he must remove in so many days   it appears that he agreed to it and that he would not buy no more until he did remove the said factory but the gov. hearing that he did buy contrary to his agreement warn him again if he did not leave the place that he should destroy the establishment and all the property that it contained should be confiscated   he would not believe but still remaincd and we went down and broke up the factory and brought away all the effects say in goods and destroyd about fifty puncheons Rum which was turn Loose on the ground say the effects in goods &c to the amt of ten thousand Dollars   after we had taken the goods or a part we had to contend with the natives which fought us two days very hard but we got the victory and form a treaty before we left with one of the chiefs but not with the other and only got four slaves so we cannot say that we concluded a final peace without the other partys consent   we were gone fifteen day and only Lost one man in the Battle and he was a crooman   two or three of our men got wounded but not dangerously but we killed a great many of tribes on both of the parties say of Bargays & Princes as they were the prinpal head men.[2]

NB   you will be informed that we did not go from home to interfere with the natives atall and would not have done it if they had not began it themselves   You will give my best respects to all your family—and my Mother.

Nothing Moore at Present But
Remains Your affectionate
Friend & well wisher
Peyton Skipwith

Source: #5680, Cocke Papers

1. In order to meet the growing restiveness of the colonists who complained of the Society's arbitrary rule and niggardly outlays for public support, the debt-ridden American Colonization Society created the Commonwealth of Liberia which linked all of the independent settlements with Monrovia, save

the Maryland Colonization Society settlement at Cape Palmas. The Constitution of 1839, effecting the above change, granted greater autonomy to the colonial council, circumscribed the war-making and treaty powers of the parent organization, and established separate executive, legislative, and judicial branches of government on the American model. See Charles H. Huberich, *The Political and Legislative History of Liberia* (2 vols.; New York, 1947), I, 638–665.

2. In July, 1839, Buchanan dispatched an army of volunteers to chase the slave dealer from his factory. Aided by a British naval vessel, the Liberian force captured the barracoon and set the slaver to flight. Local natives, who were dependent upon the slave trade for income, attacked the Liberians. The two chieftains, Bahgay and Prince, eventually sued for peace and agreed to release slaves they held and to cede jurisdiction of Little Bassa to the colony. Prince failed to honor his promise. See *African Repository*, XV (1839), 277–282, XVI (1840), 35–36.

Monrovia   April 22 1840

Dear Sir

I receivd your letter and was very glad to hear from you and was very sorry that you did not see Mr Teage when he was in the states but he is no more   he never lived to reachd home   I also receivd the letter from Mother and was very glad to hear from her indeed   Dianna receivd her letter also from Miss Sally[1]   I am very glad that I can say that my health has been so good that I took my Rifle in hand to go to fight a savage King about three days travel through the forest slept one night in the bush and took his Town the next day about 6, o, Clock with my Capt Mortally wounded and other man, and two others with flesh wounds   there we encamped that night and on Sunday and Monday we set fire to the Town and took our line of March for home, and was two days in the wild bush, but a pretty country well waterd and timberd   I have as much work as I can well attend to at present with my apprentices and others you mention in your letter that you would like to no the prices of stone Masons pr day Carpenters &c.   the wages of stone Mason can get when work is to be had about $1.50 pr day Carpenter from 75 cts to $1.00 to $1.25

My daughters have a good time to improve themselves in education for they have nothing else to do much but to go school and I think they will improve   Dianna keeps up her night school as yet and also is a teacher in the sunday school of the Baptist Church   it would be well if we had some advantage in getting things cheap to this market for every thing that we get is at least from 100 to 200 per cent above cost which will forever keep the inhabitants poor   if the steam packets were sent and would sell there things cheap we would like to have them and to increase our population   it is something strange to think that those people of africa are calld our ancestors   in my present thinking if we have any ancestors they could not have been liked these hostile tribes in this part of africa for you may try and distell that principle and belief in them and do all you can for them and they still will be your enemy   It is a fact that agriculture has been carried on very rapidly but we must say a little on the retrogade   the gardens are tolerably well furnished with vegetable matter and pretty well supplies the market.

I saw Mr. Minor   he come out in the ship Saluda this time and settled with me in full.

apprentice Labour is worth from 50 to 75 cts pr day   we have Blacksmith one or two and they have as much work as they can do and more, I think a blacksmith that would follow his trade might make a Handsom living in this country   the Blacksmiths say they make from two to three dollars per day   I have no work cattle mules nor Horses but there are two or three Jacks on the cape and three Horses   cows are worth 18 to 20$ and ox the same again   I must say that the greatet war that ever was fought by man was fought at Headington a Missionary establishment about five miles from Millsburg   it was said that a savage host of this man that we took occassion to against sent about four Hundred men to attack this place about day Break   there was in that Town three americans and they took there stand in the House and whips the whole enemy   they killd on the feeld about 20 dead, and god he only knows how many was wounded and carread away   it has been said that a great number died but how many I do not no   with the lost of one Native man mortally wounded they then persued them and found the Generals body slighly intomed about twenty miles from the feeld of Battle   his head was taken from his body and now made an ornament in the Hands of the Governor Buchanan   the Battle lasted about one Hour fifteen minutes   how this was done they had and over quanty of musket loded and had nothing to do but take them up and poor the Bullets in there flesh and they would fall takeing fingers and tearing the flesh assunder[2]

Our selves we have made a company of rifle men and I hold an office in that company   the Churches is some somewhat in prosperous state and appear to thrive   I send you the Liberia Herald so you can acquaint yourself of the particulars about our goeing to Gatoombahs and what I fail writing you can correct yourself in that I try to write you every thing that I can think of.

there is a man in jail to be hung a crooman for killing an american boy the 2nd friday in May at ten o Clokk   this boy was shockenly murderd by this fellow   he broke his legs his arms and stabs him in several places and the next obsconded to Junk[3] about sixty miles and there he was detected and brought back to Monrovia an he had his trial in our seperior court at his first setting with two the ablest Judgest our town could afford Judge Benedet[4] & Gov Buchanan

Nothing More at Present
Yours
        Peyton Skipwith

Source: #5680, Cocke Papers
1. Sally (Cocke) Brent, Cocke's daughter.
2. From 1838 to 1840 the back-country settlements suffered the ravages of constant warfare among the rival tribes. No effective action was taken against the natives who occasionally raided Liberian towns until the time of Buchanan's administration. Following their victory over the Dei tribe, Gola warriors attacked the Millsburg settlement on the St. Paul River. The Bopolo, or Boporo, chieftain who headed the Gola confederacy was one Getumbe, or Gatumbah, the successor to Sao Baso, or "King Boatswain," who had established the Condo confederation of tribes living in the Bopolo hilly region. Getumbe resented Liberian interference in the slave trade and consequently pursued a policy of resistance and raids. The Millsburg incident prompted Buchanan to organize an expedition of two or three hundred militiamen to chastise the Gola invaders. Meanwhile, Getumbe allied with one Gotola, or Gotorah, a Loma chief in the service of the Condo who was believed to be a cannibal. With 700 men Gotola attacked the mission station at Heddington in 1840, but a small body of well-armed Liberians, commanded by Sion Harris, repulsed the attack and killed Gotola.

In a rare show of efficiency the Liberian militia then commenced the campaign against Getumbe's principal fort, drove him from it, and left him to wander in the wilderness. This victory overawed other interior tribes for a time and convinced them to sign peace treaties with Liberia. The country along the St. Paul River, the scene of so much bloodshed, remained underdeveloped for several years after the above events because settlers continued to fear native reprisals.

For details of this confusing chapter in early Liberian history see Sir Harry
Johnston, *Liberia* (2 vols.; London, 1906), I, 179–182; and Archibald Alexander,
A History of Colonization on the Western Coast of Africa (Philadelphia, 1846),
581–589.
   3. The Junk River.
   4. Samuel Benedict (1808–1854), longtime political foe of Joseph J. Roberts,
became the first chief justice of the Liberian supreme court. Nothing is known
of the incident described in Peyton's letter.

                                        Monrovia   Dec 29th 1840
Dear Sir
   The time has arrived again for me to write you by way of the
Bark Hobert hopeing that you are well and the family   I am
sorry to say that we have had a great confusion in our Colony by
the instigation of the Missionares of the Methodest Espiscopal
Church respecting a duty which they owed to our commonwealth   the collection waited on the superintendent of the
Mission for six Months at most or at least untill the Govr had
written to the Board of directors for an explanation of the Law
and the Board in there opinion considered that the duties was
lawfull to be paid when the superintendent considered that he
had no right to pay them for the Board had no more right to
make the Mission pay duties than the Mission had to make the
Board pay duties and that he would not pay it for five hundred
Dolls and that he wish the Collector to sue him which the
collector did after the Govr. could not prevail on him to pay
them   the suit was enterd against the superintendent in the
supreme court where the Gov resided a Jury impanneled on the
case and the trial commenced after many hissings &c from the
Mission Coleauges of the Govr peceddings but he discoverd it
and put and end to it   But through much confusion by the
citizens takeing sides with them the missioners after many witnesses were examined to prove that the Superintendent did
trade in so much as he paid goods for Labour and that other
citizens did purchase from him for money was out of the question he the superintendent considered that it was not trade and
he had no right to pay duties   the Jury retired and found no
Bill   the Govr dismissed the case.
   and on the whole the same like to have caused a serious time
in our Colony for myself I thought that we would have to take

arms one against the other to name them one of Seys party[1] & the other for the Govr   I believe it has nearly coold down but I believe it to be very rancoroeus in some of the leaders on the Mission side   perhaps you may get a paper or two and there you will see all the trial and what was particular on both side the Govr nutrial haveing got through the above in a broken way in trying to explain to you our situation you can judge for yourself and make the best of it you can. but shall I aquaint you that within the last month that the Large Establishment of Blanco[2] has been destroyed by one of his Majesties ships of war   it is said that they took one thousand slaves from that factory and destroyed and taken to the amount of one hundred thousand Dollars   Kennet[3] factory under the same firm has been given up by him to one of the cruisers with one Hundred slave and put himself under the protection of the English   he has been since that to the Town of Monrovia and was admitted to come on shore and he has proceeded to see the ruins of that splendid slave factory at Galenas that was belong that rich man Blanco. Sir I am more than happy to inform you that Both of my daughters have been I trust converted to God and has been Baptised and are now Members of the Baptist Church.

you stated in your last last letter that you intended to send some one out   I have not forgotten it   I have been makeing preparation for them and the sooner you send them the better.

Nothing More at Present But
Remain yours &c
Peyton Skipwith

Source: #5680, Cocke Papers

1. Rev. John Seys (1799–1872), born in the Danish West Indies, was superintendant of Methodist Episcopal missions in West Africa and later United States consul and resident minister in Monrovia. Through his newspaper, *African Luminary*, Seys criticized Buchanan for abuses of his veto power, his poor relations with the natives, his dismissal of the colony physician, and, especially, his attempt to tax the missions. Seys attempted to wrest control of the colony by vigorous campaigning, but his political maneuvers failed. Although unfriendly to Seys, the best account is Huberich, *History of Liberia*, I, 520–521, 670–674, 720–723.

2. Don Pedro Blanco, "the Spider of Gallinas," was a former Spanish sailor who operated lucrative slave barracoons, or depots, on the West African coast. He remained in operation in West Africa until the British navy cannonaded his Lomboko compound in 1841.

3. Theophilus Conneau, who was more generally known as Theodore Canot, ran a slave-trading factory at New Sesters (New Cestos) before retiring from the

ugly business about 1840. For a rare and revealing account of slave trading in West Africa see his *A Slaver's Log Book, or 20 Years' Residence in Africa* (Englewood Cliffs, 1976).

Monrovia   April 27th 1841

Honr,d Sir,

I have taken the present chance of conveyance by the Brig R. Groning now about to leave our port for the U.S. to acquaint my health and my family. I am happy to say that we are well, and that my children are improving as also my apprentice John who is learning his trade finely and I must say upon the whole is a very fine boy, and suits me very well, and I think will (if he continues thus) make a useful man.

The colony is not now as flourishing as it was not long since; trade is dull and country produce for subsistance scarce as the past season was very unfavourable to the growth of rice our main staff of life. The wars round about us is subsiding & the natives are about turning their attention to agricultural persuits as also many of Settlers, and a bright prospect of a good crop the ensuing season.[1]

You did not send those people of whom you spoke, should you make up your mind to send them I should be glad to see them, and do all I can for their advantage—if they are well provided for they will not suffer much.

Cattle sell here from 15 to 20 Dollars ea. Sheep from 2 to 3 dols. Goats 1.50 to 2.50. Hogs of different prices according to sizes fro 1 to 16 Dolls. Fowls Three dols. pr Doz. Duck 1 doll ea. &c   you will learn the state of the Colony much better than I can express as there will leave here about 20 pasengers from some of whom you will likely obtain information but if you take the papers you will learn all particulars about political affairs. Please give my love to my mother and relations and friends in general and receive the same for yourself and family from sir,

Your Obt. Hum. Servant
Peyton Skipwith

Source: #5680, Cocke Papers

1. The following lines were crossed out in the original letter: You did not send those animals which you spoke of in your former letter nor can I tell how

they would do here in this climate but as cattle and other animals except Horses have done well I think those perhaps may do well

Monrova   Liberia   Western Coast of Africa
Septr. 29th 1844

Dear Sir.

having reseived yours pr. American Ship Virginia, and was truly happy to hear from you indeed. Being as an oppertunity now affourds itself, I hasten to write you a short letter, which I sincerely hope will finde you and all in good state of Salubriety. I was very sory to hear that the letters I wote you by Govr. Roberts did not reach safe to you.

Sir You request to know how Peter[1] is getting along with our African Climate, he is quite well, and has a School in charge which I believe he is Compatant of teaching and I am in hopes he will be enable to make a living by it! he is not able to walk as yet & it appears as if he will never recover his strength in the legs again so long as he lives.

Dear Master, I am sorry to say that Erasmus[2] is displeased with the Country because he is of no trade, & therefore, he sees no way to make a living. I wanted him to come in and learn the mason's trade, but I could not prevale on him Enough to get his consent; it was so ordained by the Lord, that Mr Randolph,[3] the son of Mrs. Jane Randolph, came on shore here, from on board of the U.S. Brig Porpoise, and being acquainted with him gave him a recommendation, to the officers of the Ward-room: & he theire became a steward, and all the officers being much pleased with him advised him to go on to the states, with them, and he after consulting of me, Complied with theire request! the first Lieut. Mr.Wadkins from Gooseland County,[4] came on shore, and advised me to get his Passport, and said he would do all he could for him. Dear Master as to myself, I am as well satisfied as I can be in this little Community, & I must thank you sir, for the care you had over me while I was young, for when I was young & knew nothing you studied my interest. I am blessed with a trade, for you has sent me to this country where I can speak for myself like a man & show myself to be a man, so fair as my ability, allows me.

You are quite desireous to know the situation of our little Colony, which I think is in a prosperous situation: the farmers, is following their trade rapidly   they are very extensive in theire farms this Year, more so than I has seen them for some past Years, theire produce are as follows   Rice, Potatoes, Plantains, Corn, & Cassadoes. all the time I have been here I have seen no want for a mill, 'till this Year. I would be glad if you would send me on one, by the first affoarding oppertunity? Peace and harmony exists among us, with our savage natives. The U.S. Fleet; has done great good on the Coast of Africa they has in a measure dispursed the slave trade: & also, subdued the Natives, & brought them to know theire place, more so than they did before the arrival of said fleet. Since I has been here, the ministers of the "Gosple" were only allowed to preach the "Gosple" around about the Colony, but now they can go as fair as a hundred miles, in the interior; Though our ministers are out in the interior yet we has to keep an Eye single towards them; If you should see Mr. Randolph who has left for some time for the states, he can give you a true statement, about me, for every time he was in our Harbour, he would come on shore to see me. Please present my respects to all of my acquaintences both great and small, Particularly Master Phillip

I now beg to Come to a close by saying I Remain Truly Yours

Peyton Skipwith

Source: #5680, Cocke Papers

1. Peter Cannon (1803?–1847) was one of Mrs. Sally (Cocke) Faulcon's slaves emancipated by her will. Arriving on the *Maripose* in 1842, he settled in Monrovia with his brother Richard and the other Faulcon freedmen. For details on the terms of liberation and the character of the émigrés see the extract of Mrs. Faulcon's will, 1831, in "Copies of and Extracts from the Wills of Deceased friends of Colonization," American Colonization Society Papers (ACSP), microfilm reel 314 (Library of Congress); and JHC to William McLain, Sept. 27, 1841, "Domestic Letters Received," vol. 83:339, ACSP.

2. Erasmus Nicholas (b. 1814), who was able to write, accompanied his cousins James and Julia Nicholas to Liberia in 1842; all were part of the Faulcon contingent.

3. Beverley Randolph (b. 1823) of Clarke County, Virginia, was the son of William Fitzhugh Randolph and Jane (Harrison) Randolph. He was a midshipman on the brig *Porpoise* of the African Squadron.

4. Mayo Carrington Watkins (d. 1860) of Goochland County, Virginia, was a midshipman on the *Porpoise*, and reached the rank of lieutenant in 1847.

Monrovia   June 25th 1846

Dear Genl.

I write you a few hasty lines, by a vessel now about to leave this place for the states.

You earnestly request me to give you the particulars of our Colony. Since the Authorities has thought it proper to declare theire independence I Canot with Confidince say much about the present Situation of the Colony. It is not yet determined with the Colonist whither to receive the Constitution Sent on by the Board or not. The majority of this place is much in favour of independence, & those at Edina the Leeward Settlement are against it & that bitterly the Counsil has not Conveined to deliver the Constitution to the people as yet. It is thought that it will be done in July. It is my belief that the Majority of this place will gain the effections of those of Edina & Bassa Cove— and cause them to Join heart & hand with them; this is my expectations about the affair. We must be a people recognised by foreign Nations, or Else come under the Eye of some that will protect us when Called upon, you have I no doubt seen that there must be something of the kind done before we Can enforce our "Laws"; for it has been already said by the British that we hav no right to demand Anchorage Duties &c of them. If we are to remain in the state we are now in, it is deplorable Sir, I am in hopes that when the Constitution are presented that the Eyes of the blind will become opened.[1]

Though our love for the society is great we canot return her that gratitude of thanks that we due to her. Sir You wishes me to give you some information of the different productions. I myself do not farm it atall   I have my lot only planted down since here in Africa I have been, & it is all the farming I does. At the present time I feels an inclination to lay a side my trade and go in to Farming of it. we have had rather a sever season of it for bread kind. those who turned theire attention to farming some time past Caused us to weep almost at the Idea of paying theire Exorbitant prices for produce: we pay at this place for Potatoes 1.00$ Cents per. Bushel Corn 25 cents pr. dozen   Rice at this time brings 3$ per Bushel. Cassado at the present time is 50 cts. per Bushel and that in specie.

We are blessed with a good soil for raising Corn &c   we raises Corn from 12 to 13 inches in lingth and that good and full. Cotton can be abundantly raised here but no person seems to turn theire attention to it   Coffee grows wild in the woods and can be raised abundantly, if it was attended to. thire are only a few individuals who raises said article—and theirs is as promising as Ever I saw coff in the States. You wishes that I should say something about Miss Sally's people   I have and can do so a gain   Leander[2] is here and is well and all the people that came out with him is here   Excepting James Nicholas[3] he left this place for *Jamaca* & I have not been Enable to hear from him since. Richard[4] is now on board of one of the U.S. Ships of War Cruising on this Coast   Cousin Peter is at Mashall   he went theire to see if it would not be an addition to his health. I am very sorry that I did not turn my attention to farming when I first arrived to this Country, but It was Entirely out of my power, as I was alone in a manner & had no male kind to render me assistence. Now I am very well situated and has several apprentices with me Exclusive of some of the Barque Pons Cargo of Congoes[5]

You desired to know whither we Stood in kneed of Bibles. this we do not kneed so much as we do other Books. we have aplenty of bibles here, more than are used. If you deem it necessary you can send on some Valuable Books for my family Such as Historys &c &c   Please send me on some writing paper quills & wafers and you will be confuring quite a favour on me   As the Revd. A D Williams will be in the states you will be please to send me on some Flour & Pork and any other necessary article you may think will be of service to me

You promised me in your letter that you was going to send my Bro. George on to this place at the Expiration of three years & I would be happy indeed to see him and all the people that you have promised to send on. My love to all the family & inquiring friends. I beg to close by subcribing myself to be sincerly

Yours

Peyton Skipwith

NB Please remember my love to Master John Charles Phillip & Merret[6] also Mrs Nancy Cavel[7] & Family Miss Sally[8] also and Miss Coatny.[9] also tell them I am well

Source: #5680, Cocke Papers

1. In an attempt to control the profitable coastal trade, Liberia levied a six percent ad valorem duty on foreign traders, but British traders from neighboring Sierra Leone refused to acknowledge Liberian sovereignty or to pay the tax. The first major confrontation occurred when Capt. Dring, a British merchant, set up a trading station at Bassa Cove. Dring was armed with a letter from the British ministry refusing to recognize the claims of "private persons" (i.e., Liberians) to levy taxes or to interfere with British commerce. The Dring letter pointed up Liberia's anomalous diplomatic status and thus accelerated the drive for independence. In 1845 Liberian authorities seized a Sierra Leone ship moored in Bassa Cove. In an exchange of notes the British and American governments tried to clarify Liberia's status, but the United States revealed little interest in pushing the claims of a black government. The American Colonization Society, aware of its impotence, urged independence on the colony, which was declared in 1847. Since Great Britain entertained no imperial expansionist interest in Liberia at the time, she suffered the new republic to survive. See Johnston, *Liberia,* I, 192–195.

2. Leander Sturdivant (b. 1807?) became a farmer in Liberia and lived with his three children, Diana, Rosetta, and Leander. Cocke deemed the father "a young man of constant character" and the family "one of the best, color'd families, I ever knew." JHC to McLain, Sept. 27, 1841, vol. 83:339, ACSP. In 1843 Leander married Nancy Smith in Monrovia. See *Liberia Herald,* August 31, 1843.

3. James Nicholas (b. 1806?) left Liberia to farm in Sierra Leone in 1843 and ultimately went to Philadelphia, Pa.

4. Richard Cannon (b. 1807?), brother of Peter and cousin of Leander Sturdivant, attempted farming in Liberia before signing on an American naval vessel.

5. In 1845 the barque *Pons,* bound for Brazil with over 900 slaves, was captured off Kabenda by the U.S. African Squadron. The navy landed 756 survivors at Monrovia. The *Pons* recaptives generated much interest in Liberia as the settlers eagerly reached out to help these distressed individuals. Most of the *Pons* recaptives were Ibo and Congo tribesmen, and many were apprenticed as farmers in the New Georgia community, where they eventually prospered. Some colonists regretted the charity, for the refugees greatly taxed the country's meager resources; several Congo recaptives fled to the woods, where they fed themselves by making nocturnal raids on Liberian stock and crops. See *African Repository,* XXII (1846), 112, 137ff, 144ff, 154, XXIII (1847), 25, 77ff.

6. Cocke's sons: John Hartwell Cocke, Jr. (1804–1846); Dr. Cary Charles Cocke (1814–1888); and Philip St. George Cocke (1809–1861); and Cocke's brother-in-law Merit M. Robinson, husband of Anne Hartwell Cocke.

7. Probably Anne Blaws (Cocke) Cabell, Cocke's daughter.

8. Sally (Cocke) Brent, Cocke's daughter.

9. Sally Elizabeth Courtney (Bowdoin) Cocke (1815–1872) was the wife of Philip St. George Cocke.

Monrovia   June 27th 1846

Effectunate & Dear Mother

I embrace this favourable oppertunity of writing you a few

lines to inform you of my health which is very good at prsent and I hope this may finde you and all the same

Dear Mother   It has been for some considerable time since I have recd. a letter from you   I only heard from you through the Genls. letter to me bearing date 28 oct./45 to which I was very much pleased indeed to learn that you were in good health. In your last to me you expressed an anxiety for me to come over, but I am affraid that I shall never be enabled to cross the atlantic again though I would like much to see you once more in the flesh. Erasmus has not returned since he left here for the states & it appears as if I cannot receive eny intelligence from him. I would like much to hear something of him if he is in the States   You will be please to write me by Mr Williams and let me know whether you have heard any thing of him or no.

Should I never be blessed to cross the ocean again the Genl. has given me his faithful word that he wuld to send Bro. George on, whom I would be happy to see if it is the will of the Master.

Dear Mother   I find that the people are affraid to come to this country   I can assure you that any person can live here if they has a little money. all persons having any expectations to go to Monrovia Should endeavour to accumulate some money if they possibly can and that is no hard matter to accumulate in the States. In regard to this Fever that need not be much dreaded as we feel our Selves pretty much Skilled in regard to that part   every family more or less that has been here any time knows what to do in regard to the fever. Through and by the assistence of the Almighty we carried Miss Sally's People through without a death. Cousin Peter who was likely to have Did is yet a live and enjoying good health, I wishes to see some of the people from the very place I went from & that very much indeed. I think the people would go over if they were not affraid of the fever—that should not be an obsticle to any of them that knew me before I left the states. I have now been out theire nearly 13 years and Am ase well acquainted with the climate of the country   My efforts have been Crowned with Success from on high ever since theire I have been, & I canot thank him enough for his kind blessings that he has bestowed upon me since I left you all in the states

And I still feels as if the Lord will bless me in all my undertakings if I put my trust in him. Mother my confidence in the Lord is as bright now as it was when I first left—if any thing more so. when I went to Liberia I had no one that I was acquainted with. after a length of time a man came from Richmond in whom I was intimitly acquainted with & that revived my spirits. after a few Years the Lord brot it about so that Miss Sally sent on her People to Africa, which has been a consolation to me from that day to the present time. I still feeled buoyed up as Master has Promised to send on my Bro. Geo. & his family. I believ I shall have more help in this dark benighted land, to try and civilize the heathens and bring them to know life and life eternal. I now wish to close by subscribing myself to be your most Humble and obedient son

Peyton Skipwith

NB   Please say to Uncle Ned that I hope he still has Jesus in his Soul, and Heaven in his View   If so Uncle I shall meet you where we shall be blessed for ever through Endless days Please give my love to aunt Phalitia. tell sister Levina that I wants to see her very bad but if I should neve see her in this life I will to meet you we shall part no more. My love to all inquireing friends. tell them I am well & my confidence is still anchord in the Lord.

Source: Moore deposit, Cocke Papers

Letters from Diana Skipwith

August 24 1837

Dear Mis Sally[1]

I take this opitunity of riting yo theas fue lines to im form yo
that I and family are well and hope that theas fue lines may find
yo the saim   I am happy to im form yo that we are much beter
satisfy with the place than we was the last time we roten to yo
awl   we are much better now than we ever was; times has bin
verry hard for somthing to eat but now the natives ar [fishing?]
in rice and it is not so hard now

I think verry hard of yo not riting me aletter but howsoever I
suspose that yo had not tine   I go to school to Mr Leis
Jhonston and I think that heis one of the bes school masters in
the town[2] he is verry stud   my sister matilda go to Miss ivens[3]
the climet is geting much better than it was when we caim out
hear   my father has got A wound and he can not go upon it &
me and my sister keep house for my father   he has not got
marrid yet   there are 5 publick school   I hav mention in the
furst part of leter that me and my Brother Nash goes to Mrs
Luwis Johoston and my sister matilda and Napolun go to mis
ivens   Martha has got a wound one her foot goin on 6 munts
my father has bought him 2 lots   one of then had a house in
which he ar now living in both and groe stree   his lot what he
Drow he has im prove it and has got A deede and free stinple
we have got hogs   I have got one but we hav kill 3 and the
wild Beast has kild[3]   the things heare sell verry dear   evry
yard of cloth sell for twenty five cts pr yard   every pare of
stocken sell for 1[00] and dollar and half   the enfearist shoo in
the colony is 9 and three dollars a pare   yo cannot get even
somuch as one fould with out gaving twenty five 25 cents for it
so thire fore if yo are pleast to send us sone thing some tobaco
in pertilar for tobaco sell twenty five cents a pound   pleas to
send us out sone Flower or any thing that yo awl hav to spar

for we stand in neede of sonthin verry much   meat is a great
rerrity hear   yo aul mus know that we stand in need of theas
things for we awl like to starv this seasen and I hop that yo will
take us in considerration and send us sone thing   we have got
our gard planted in potatoes and cassaders   pleas to send us
out sone of awl kind of seeds for we can not any seeds to
plant   yo wil be pleas to send me out paper for I hav triing
two days and could not get any paper but this one sheet   tel
master and mistes that I think they treat me with comtenp
Gave myn best respect to them   I am glad to hear that master
injoy his health   I have no good noos to ri[te] yo at this time
pressent   we have to gave two dolars for half Bushel of rice
ther is sone of the Beauifully bullock bean that I ever saw and
sone of the largest   gave my best respect to my granmother
and ant luvina and to uncle geoge and tel then that dont think
as much of me as to rite me a litter pleas to rite me word if the
school is goin now and if Betsy[4] can rit good and tel her that
she would of send her love to me if noth else   I should like to
cone Back thire a gain and the expect of coming back again
gave my love to ant Lizy and to ant Cissiah and to uncle Ned
Gav my love to awl incuireing friends   this is some of my one
hand riting   do yo think I inprov or not   tel ned that the
children send thire love to him   Nomore But remain yours

Diana Skipwith

Source: #9513 "Bremo Recess" deposit, Cocke Papers

1. Sally (Cocke) Brent.

2. Mrs. Lewis Johnson ran an infant school in Monrovia under the patronage
of a women's colonization auxiliary in Philadelphia. The school prospered
throughout the 1830s. In September, 1836, William G. Crocker, a Baptist missionary, engaged Lewis R. Johnson, the son of Elijah Johnson, to teach in a
Baptist school in Monrovia for six months. The Johnsons were also affiliated
with a six-day school, a Sabbath school, a female academy, and an evening
school, all under Baptist auspices. The Skipwith children apparently attended
several of the schools. For more information on Johnson see R. B. Medbery,
Memoir of William G. Crocker (Boston, 1848), 143.

3. A Miss Evans operated a school for children in Monrovia. The school
suffered from a want of teaching materials and an inability of the parents to
clothe their children "sufficiently decent" to attend school. See *African Repository*, XIV (1838), 273.

4. Betsey Morse was a house servant at Upper Bremo.

Monrovia Liberia   May 7 1838

Dear miss Salla[1]

I rite you theas fue lines to imform you that I and family are well exsepting my father and he is verry unwell with his wound   the last of this month wil make 10 monts since he has hit a lick for hisself or any person els

the rest of the family is quit well   John H. Faulcon is going to school and the rest of the family all so   the fever was Quit faverable with him   I think that this Cuntry agrea with him

I was verry sorry to hear that my grand father was Ded But one thing Give me great consolation   I know that he is gone home to Rest and we have nothing to do but to pepare and meat him

I have nothing strange to tell you   times is verry dul hear in this coloney

I rote a fue lines to you by the Brig Susan Elithebeth   I send a small Bundle to you with some sowersap seads and some grean ginger for you to plant   I am going to send you some more seeds by Mr Mils   if you should get them you had better plant them in the hot house   sowersap is one of best fruit that we have in this cuntry   I am going to send you one of the seads which will be the larges sead and it is call the mangrove plum   it is somewhat like the plumb peach and verry nice in taste; I am verry glade to hear that the scholl is stil going on and that master has bild A church for the people   they had better be thire to be hear suffering Enlest they had some money to start with   you wil be pleas to tell the people that I would rite to them but I have not the paper   give my love to mistreess Ann Cabble[2] and tell her that I thought she would of rite to me before know   I have never reseave the money that you send to me yet but I hope that I wil get it in a time for I stand verry much in nead of it   I am verry much a blige to you for it   I wish that I could see your faice for I cannot take rest of nights Dreaming A bout you   sometimes I think I am thire and when I awoke I am hear in Liberea & how that dos greave me but I cannot healp my self   I am verry fraid I shal never see you faice a gain but if I never Do I hope I shal meat in the king-dom   give my best respect to Master and Master John and Master Chars and Miss nancy Moldan   I was verry Glad to hear that Master Philip was Marred   rite me ward whither you

is Marred or not   you wil be pleas to send me some paper &
some books   I have nothing Earging to say   I wil close by say
I remain yours

Yours
Diana Skipwith

Source: #9513-C "Bremo Recess Addition," Cocke Papers
1. Sally (Cocke) Brent.
2. Anne Blaws (Cocke) Cabell.

May the 8 1838   Monrovia

Dear Mistress Louisana[1]
    I reseave your Litter Dated oct 27 1837   I was hapy to hear
from you all   the family is well Excepting my father and he is
still down with his wound   if he is spard to see the last of this
month it will make 9 month since he has work any   John
Faulcon is quit well   he is still going to school   the fever
went quite Light   the money that Master send to my Father he
have not reseave it yet   he says as soon as he get it he wil let
him know   I know dout but what he wil say something to him
apond the subgect   you will tell grand mother that father
Talks of comeing back but his wound bother him but I think if
his wound ever get wel and if he canget money Enough he wil
come for he want to come back as bad as she want him to
come   we ware amase to hear that Grand Father was ded but
was hapy to hear that he was gonehome to rest
    we was hapy to hear that our uncle Erasmus is maid his peace
with god   all so I was hapy to hear that Master has bild A
church for the cullard people   I know that they injoy there-
selvs better than they would hear   they things that Grand
Mother send to us we get the hankerchievs and one pare of
socks but as to the frocks and socks we never get them   tell
betsy that I reseave the hankerchief   tel her for me if that was
her hand riting she can right wel enough to rite to me for I dos
want to get a letter from her verry bad   tell her that I was verry
much ablige to her for it   tell her school she wil mak a Mishi-
nary before long   I have nothing strang to tel you   I am going
to send some seads by Mr Mils to you and Miss Salla   the

largist sead that I wil send you must take good care of it   it is some of the inglesh fruit very nice   the nain of it is mangrove   plante it tall some what lik plant peach   give my love to all of the friends and tel them that I would of rote to some of them but paper was lacking   give my love to uncle nedd and his wife to ant Cissiah and tel them that I want to se them very bad   I have nothing more to say at Pressent but I still remain yours

Diana Skipwith

Source: #5213-B "Bremo" (Marshall deposit), Cocke Papers
1. Louisa (Maxwell) Holmes (d. 1843), Cocke's second wife.

Monrovia Liberia   May 20 1839

To Mrs Louisa Cock
My Dear madam
    though i not concious of having any thing to offer for the consolation of your mind yet i canot refrain from imbracing this oppitunity which pressent it self of sending you a line if it serve only to assure you that i reseave your letter in time   you request of me and my Father to come over to Emerrica but i do not exspect ever to come thire a gain not because i will not but because i cannot but i think that my Father will come over before long but it is quite conveninet for him to come by this oppitunity know that he have bin wonded so long but are now restore to his health a gain i could not arange his bisiness for to come just now   i Trust that i will see your face a gain but i am a fraid that i never will in this world   i am constrain to say like the monach to my Friends do they now and then send a wish or a thought after me. Oh tell me i yet have a friend though a friend i am never to see   it is my hart desiar to come but my Father say that he cannot trust the children to any body exsept me   you may judge by this whither i can come or not   i think that he will mention sonething concurning of his coming in master letters what time he will come   John Falcon is well and harty   he send much love to you   he is a good obident young man   he is now worken at his Traid   he wish you to give his love to his aunt Daphney[1] and all of his inquireing friends   we

reseave the Box that came from you all hands   we ware highly gratifide indead and we give thank to you for the things that you sont to us me in particular giv you thank for them   you will pleas to give my love to mrs Ann Cabell   he have got sone curiosities to send you all but for fear that you all will not get them i will ceep them untill my Father come and then i will send it but if he do not come i will send it by some other oppitunity   you said in your letter that you think some young Fellow have bin trying to make me think well of him but there is not a Native that i have see that i think that i could make myself hapy with   ware you to see them you would think that i am write in my oppinion all though they ar verry ingenious people   they make sone Beautiful Bags which i inted sending you all sone by my father   Remember me kindly to master and to mrs nancy moreland   my Father is not marrid yet and i do not think that he will get marreed a gain without he get one when he come over to emerrica   you will pleas to give my love to Aunt Liesa Cellar[2] and to aunt Casiah and to aunt mary[3] you will pleas to give my love to them all   you know that it would be Teagious for me to call all of thire naim but give my Respect to all of the people perticular to my uncle ned edward and his wife and children   Sister wish me to say to you that she know not how to return thanks to you all for the things that was sont to us and she wish you to give her love to all of the people perticular to master and miss nancy moreland and master John   she wish you to give her love to grandmother and to her aunt Luvinar and all so her thanks for the things that you have told me i have it to come true but now i must come to an close you will pleas to send your pertition to god that i may refrain my ways and turn to christ   i am your sincear and humble servant

Diana Skipwith

[Enclosure]
To betsey mors
Dear miss   it was with pleasur that i reseave your let and i inhopes that you will not make this the last time   i am quite well at the presst time and i inhopes that theas few lines will find you the same   it with pleasur that i now answer your letter   my Dear Betsey do you ever think that you will se me face to face a gain   i think not in this world but if we refrain

our wicked wais and turn to christ we will shorly se one nother
face to face but not in this world all though i would frealy come
yet i cannot   i reseave the things that you sont to me my Dear
miss and i give you thanks for them   you want to know
whither i am marrid or not but i am not and i dont know that i
ever shal all though win and tide can bring all things to work to
geter and god can when no man can hinder   you are far before
me the young man that you mention you was going to marrid to
but i do not know him   he is quite a stranger to me   where
was this mr Wilems[4] live   my Dear Betsey my hart in a maner
of speaking Blead when i think of you all and think that i never
shal se your all face a gain   your will give my love to one and
all of the people to my grandmother Betsy and father primis and
to all of my inquireing friends   i am your sinccar and Af-
fetionate servant

Diana Skipwith

Source: #5680, Cocke Papers
1. "Aunt" Daphne was the sister of Ann Sucky Faulcon, John Faulcon's
mother, and she was also the wife of Tom, the groom at Upper Bremo.
2. Lisa Kellor was the daughter of "Old" Cis and the sister of Spencer Kellor,
the blacksmith at Upper Bremo and later at Hopewell, Cocke's plantation in
Alabama. She married Jacob, the cartman at Upper Bremo.
3. "Aunt" Mary Skipwith, wife of George Skipwith and mother of James and
Lucy, all principals in the Skipwith correspondence. She was a milkmaid at
Upper Bremo before leaving for Alabama with her husband.
4. Unable to identify.

Monrovia L   March 7 1843

Master J H Cock Cenior
Sir   for the first time I now address you afew lines which
will inform you that we are all well at the present time hoping
you and your family are injoying the same blesing of god.
though I have exspress a great dissatisfaction with regard to
this place since I have bin out heare but now I can truly say that
I thank god & you too that I am heare   my mind are perfecly at
ease & I wish to make africa my home the longest day that I live
yet I do not pretend to say that I do not want to come back and
see you all. this is the place for collard people if they come out
with the exspectation of working for unles this is done thir is

no living out   in my last let to Miss S[1] I told her all about my self & sercomstance which I think you have heard therefore I think it needless to say any thing about it again. there was a temperance meeting got up heare this year of which my sister Matilda & my self have become a member July Nicholas[2] also by this sir you will see that we have not forgot the things that you use to instil in our Brest nor have we departed from nor I trust never will as long as we have our right sences   all of our family I mean those that was sot free by Mrs Falcon are well they have got out of the feever & not one of them is dead   we took them all and nurse them   they ware very poorly attende by the Publick   the prevision that ware given then weekly would not last them more than half of the week as to Bread kind   they ware ondly alowed three lb flour 2 lb met   had it not bin for us they must of had suffered

My Father is not home at the present   he have bin imployed by Doc Day[3] to do a Job of work down on the cors of this place therefor you will not get a letter from him this time

I have sont a box with a few articles for the friends & you will find two cuntry whips or natives whipes for your self and a nother Bag mad of skin that Mr James[4] send it to you but the whips I send you   they are not much but prehaps they will be a curiosity   one of them the handle is coverd in part with aligator skin   my sister is not marrid yet   the young man that will be the Barre of theas things if you will see him & talk to him he will tell you all about us   his name is Feny Smithy[5] will you if pleas sir be good enough as to send me out a little Tobaco & some provision   if you should send it pleas sir send some that is long   I mean Tobaco that is short will not trade hear   I know that you have bin very kind indead in sending us thing & I feel like I am intruding on good nature but rearly sir I am inhopes you will not think so   Sister & Couzen July sund thir kindest respect to you Mr James all so   I have sont you some news papers

your humble servt
Diana James

PS   pleas sir remember me to mrs Louisa & tell her that I have bin researving some mats for her & intended to send them by the first oppitunity but I find that I cannot send them   the Box is not long enough to hold them

Diana

Source: #5680, Cocke Papers

1. Sally (Cocke) Brent.

2. Julia Nicholas (1824?–1847), cousin of Peyton Skipwith, lived with the Skipwith family in Monrovia and worked as a seamstress.

3. Dr. James Lawrence Day (d. 1854), the colony physician until his retirement in 1843, at which time he entered the petit trade at Setta Kroo. Peyton was building a depot for him there.

4. Moore James (b. 1820?), Diana's husband, was free-born in North Carolina. He came to Liberia with his family in 1826, but by 1843 he had lost all of his family, save two brothers, Levi and Frederick. James was a seaman by trade when he married Diana. The newlyweds lived in the Skipwith household. Nothing is known of their history subsequent to 1843.

5. Unable to identify.

Letters from Nash Skipwith

Nov the 2 1849

Dear Sir

I take this oppotunity of wrighting you theas few lines to im form you of my helth which is at this time verry well and ihope that theas few lines may find you in the best of helth and all the family and this is the first time that I ever rote to you and ihope and trust it will not be the Last time   my reason for not wright-ing is becase I was so small when icome from thir and I did not know Enny one thir when I come from thire and I has to give you my best respects to all my Kindred and tell them all Pleas to try and send me something as iam in the want of it

Mrs. Genrel Cocks

Dear sir   if you can make it convenent as to send me a soote of Black Brod cloth as ihave Lost my Father and have now my silf to find and besides 3 Children and my father wife[1] and ihave to worke very hard and sometimes ihave but 1 dollar and sometimes non   and iam sorrow to say to my uncle Gorge this   I should heer that he would say his will ware [but as the Gone star flies of over his head?]

My father died in Ocr the 29 1849   will you pleas to send me a stoomstone for him   I no more to say at Present

Yours Respeteful

Nash P Skipwith

Source: Shields-Wilson deposit, Cocke Papers

1. Mrs. Margaret Skinner, a Methodist, married Peyton Skipwith on May 17, 1845, in the Baptist church of Rev. Abraham Cheeseman, a longtime friend of the Skipwiths. She was the widow of Humphrey Skinner and the mother of two sons: Abraham (b. 1840) and Washington (b. 1842). She arrived in Liberia in February, 1838, although there is no reference to her in the published passenger lists. According to the 1843 Liberian census, she worked as a washerwoman in Monrovia after the death of her husband. She was twenty-five years old when she married Peyton Skipwith. She probably met him through

her brother-in-law, Stocky Skinner, who was one of Peyton's apprentices. Nothing is known of her history after Peyton's death. On their marriage see *Liberia Herald*, May 31, 1845.

Monrovia Liberia   November 24th—49

Dear General

I drop you this to inform you that I would like to come over and spend a fiew months with you all as my father is dead, provideing you would arrange it so that I might come over in the next packet, should you make this arrangement I shall certainly come, if life are speared, and sickness do not take place.

Should you write for me, please arrange it so as I may be sent direct on to you as soon as I arrive in the States. Please send me a fiew things, to assist in prepareing me for the Voyage

My Brother in law[1] request that I should beg of you to send him on some books, such as you may deem proper, as he canot get any valuable Books there unless he orders a regular LIBRARY

I am most Respectfully your
Obedient Servant

Nash Skipwith

NB   Sister request that you would so kind as to write her concerning of her [and] my Grand Father Primus & Grand mother Betsey

Skipwith

Source: Shields deposit, Cocke Papers
1. Samuel Lomax, Matilda's husband. See also Matilda's letter of July 4, 1848 (p. 101, and n. 2).

Monrovia   May the 15 1851

Dear Sir

Your letter Came Swift to hand and I ware happy to Receave it and Ware Glad To here from you and your family and to here that you ware Enjoying Good helth   You Wished to know Wither I am a man of Bisiness   I am not yet   I have no more

to Tend to than Working at my traid and a Nother Thing You
Wished to know about Fathers Estate and What did he Leavin
his family   he left them Nothing   and you Wished to know
Wither father had enny Children by his Last Wife   he had non
by her and as for property She had non when She marred him
I am not marred   I am Still Working at my Traid   You
Wanted to know how much do I get per day   I will Tell you It
is but Verey Little   50 Cents and Some times 75 Cents pr.
day   You Wished to Learn from me how much Propity have I
made Earn by my o[w]n Industry about $15 dollars Worth or
more

You Wanted to know What did I get of father Estate   All I
got of father Estate Ware one Rifel and I would not got that if he
had not give It to me before he died   His Houce and his Lots
will be Sold and we will not Get Ennything[1]

Dear Sir Will you Please to Send me Some Trowells and
hamers   they are So hard to get hire that I thought it would be
best To Write to you and beg you to Send me Some.

And I would oblige you much if you ware to have murcy on
me and Try an help me along alittle and Send me a barrel of
Flower and Pork and Some other Artickles Which you think
you Could Spare to help the family along

Dear Sir I would not of ask you for nothing but Some Books if
I had no one to find but my Self, but I have all father Children
and Sister Matilday Too and Working Evry day of my Life To
feed and Cloth all theas Children and I beg you for God Sake
Pleas to have mursey on me and the family and Send us theas
things. And another Thing Dear Sir I would Like for you to
Send me about 12 Books Which I will menchun after While and
allso Some Writting Paper and Some Steel Pens and Some In
Velups with Gilted Edges   I will Call the names of the Twelve
Books which I wanted you to Send me

1 Large Dictionary, Webster first and 2d, 3d, 4 Volum of Alison History[2] and other Such Valubil Books as you think Will
Soote my Studdy   I would Rather have this book and To have
the other things for my Convientcy but I hope you will Send
them all for god Sacke

Yours
Nash Skipwith

Source: #5680, Cocke Papers

1. Liberian records reveal that on July 20, 1837, Peyton Skipwith was granted a quarter-acre town lot, No. 456, on the northeast corner of Perry and Carey Streets in Monrovia, and on May 5, 1839, he purchased another town lot, No. 225, on the northeast corner of McDonald and Carey Streets, and a farm lot, No. 3, of five acres. On April 7, 1852, the Skipwith estate sold another Monrovia town lot, No. 200, at the southeast corner of Mechlin and Carey Streets. The estate realized $112 from the sale. For evidence of additional land acquisitions by Peyton Skipwith, see Matilda Skipwith's letters of November 23, 1849, and July 24, 1858 (pp. 104 and 119). For the above references see "Miscellaneous Colonial Volume," folio 132 and folio 156, Liberian Government Archives (LGA); and Deedbook, Montserrado County, vol. 1, folio 305, LGA. I would like to thank Svend E. Holsoe of the University of Delaware for pointing out these references.

2. Probably Sir Archibald Alison's *History of Europe from the Commencement of the French Revolution in 1789 to the Restoration of the Bourbons in 1815* (4 vols.; New York: Harper & Bros., 1842–1844).

Letters from Matilda Skipwith

Monrovia Liberia   October 23rd/44

Miss[1]

I embrace the Oppertunty of writing You these few Lines hopeing they May find You in Good Health as they Leaves Me enjoy that Part of Gods Blessing   I was much Disappointed when the Govr. of Liberia arrived not Receiveing a Letter from You, I have nothing of Great Importance to write   You Requested Me to state to You how my sister Departed this Life.[2] I Can Just say that Her End was Peace and from the Time of her Conversations her Life was that as a Christian   I am trying to Live in that way as to meet her at the Right hand of God   I must say to you that I am Completely Left alone only Nash my Brother Since my sisters Death   Do tell my Dear Grand mother that I am yet alive and yet Expects to see her in this Life   Do write me about Uncle George Skipwith   I have not heard of him since I have Been in Liberia or Aunt Luvine Uncle Ned his Aunt Falitia Primous   I was very sorry to hear of the Death of Aunt Luvenias two Children   Erasmus has Left us and Gone to Philadelphia   I Believe I sent five Letters By him   I hope you all will Receive them   Write me word if any of you all is Comeing out.

Father is well and sends his Best Love to his mother sister and all Enquiring Friends   in a month or two from this I Expects to change my life   all of you must send me Something Nash sends his Love to his Cousin Ned[3]   Govr Roberts says that he saw the Genrl. and he said he intended to write But we Did not Receive any Letters from him   we was very sorry

I Remain Yours in Much Love
Matilda R. Skipwith

Source: #9513 "Bremo Recess" deposit, Cocke Papers
1. Sally (Cocke) Brent.

2. Diana (Skipwith) Moore died sometime in 1844.
3. Ned Washington, a slave at Upper Bremo.

Monrovia   July 4th 1848

To Miss S. F. Cocks[1]

Dear Miss

I now avale myself of the favourable oppertunity of addressing you with a fiew lines to inform you that I am well, and hope
this may finde you and all the family in the enjoyment of the
same.

Dear Miss   I hope that from our long silence, you have not
been induced to think that we have withdrawn our Communications, from you, if such have been your thoughts let me be-
seech you to do away with it as I am aware that I have not
written you as often as I ought, but such shall not be the case
again, that is whenever an oppertunity affords. I hope you will
not fail to write me by the first affording oppertunity as I am
very desireous to hear something from you all.

You requested of me in your last to say something about my
Marriage   I was wedlocked to a Young man by the name of
Samuel B Lomax[2]   he is a Young man who masters one or two
trades firstly a Cooper, 2dly—Printer 3dly Sea Captain and
Clerk—the latter he now turns his attention to princibly—as his
health has been quite bad for the past six or seven months, and
Liberia is a Country where it behooves every man to be up and
doing something for his feture prosperity.

I suppose you have long since heard of the Congoes that was
landed in Monrovia from on board of the Am. Barque "Pons"
nombers of them died from the fatigue of Cruel Imprisenment
on board of the ship before Captured. the surviveing ons are as
healthy a set of people as ever a person would wish to see.
several of which has embraced the religion of our saviour—and
making rapid improvements in Education. Tho I must say of a
truth that they are the most savage, & blud thirsty people I ever
saw or ever wishes to see. My Father's love to your father and
You   he would of written but is not in Town. he desires that
you fathr would be so kind as to send his Bro. on. also that he
would send him a set of Masons Tools   Please send me on

something for my Children as I have been the mother of 3 since my Marriage one of which I have lost the other two which is girls yet servives. Theire names are as Foulers: Eliza Adala & Lydia Ann Lomax. I must now close as I wishes by indulgence from You to say afiew words at the bottom to my dear Gr. Mother

I am with Respects Yours
Matilda R. Lomax

[*Enclosure*]
Dear Grand Mother[3]

I suppose you have thought from our long silence that we had forgotten you. May the Lord of heaven forbid that such ever should be the case. & I hope from this day henceforward to write you by evry oppertunity. I have written you several times & received no answer. Consequently I had almost come to the Conclusion that I never should hear from you again which I hope I shall do by the next oppertunity after this reaches you. we are all well and enjoying the blessings of our heavenly father, & it is our sincere wish that this may finde you in the enjoyment of the same. Please write us word about uncle George. Your dear son Peyton is well & would of written you but is out of Town. he Joins me in ascribing all manner of love to You and all the family. his love also to his sister Levenia & Uncle Nid. Nash my Bro. sends his love to you and also request that you should attend the same to Ned Washington and request that Ned should send him apresent & he will endeavor to return the same Conplements. My love to My Grand Mother Betsey & Grandfather Primus and all enquireing friends. My Husband Joins me in love to you all tho a stranger to you

I now close my dear Grd. Mother by subscribing myself to be your Grand daughter &c &c

Matilda R. Lomax

NB   Uncle Erasmus has been out to Liberia since you requested that we should give you some account of him. he is now on his way to the states & will leave for Africa again by the return of the "Liberia Packet"

[*In margin*] Please excuse all Errors as my husband was quite unwell when he wrote this. it was done lying on his bed.

Source: #5680, Cocke Papers
1. Sally (Cocke) Brent.

2. Samuel Barnaby Lomax (1823?–1850) was born a slave in Fredericksburg, Virginia, and, upon emancipation, traveled to Liberia in 1829 with his family: his mother, Roxy Ann Lomax Richardson; his brother, Thomas Asbury (or Watsey) Lomax; his uncles, Fountain Richardson and John Thomas Richardson; and his aunt, Martha Richardson. Lomax settled in Monrovia, where he initially worked as a seaman. According to the *Liberia Herald*, March 31, 1845, he married Matilda R. Skipwith on March 30, 1845, the Rev. Hilary Teage presiding over the Baptist ceremony. Samuel and Matilda had four children, all daughters, before his death in 1850.

3. Lucy Nicholas, Peyton Skipwith's mother.

Monrovia   R. P. Liberia November 23d—49

Dear General J. [H.] C.

As the Liberia Packet sails from this Port for the U.S. on the 24th Inst I hasten with a heart over burdened with grief to write you a letter in answer to the one by the packet to my Father, which was duly received, affoarding us all much pleasure in hearing from you and all. I shall now give you the sad and mellancholly news of the death of Father; who parted this life October 14th   his end was peace   he did not live more than two weeks after the arrival of the "Packet"   his complaint was that of the head and breast. he was taken sick on wednesday and expired on Sunday; he was perfectly sencible of his death. Mr Teage[1] visited him regularly during his illness, and questioned him from time to time concerning of his sole's salvation whether his way was clear from Earth to glory or not, which he would always answer in words like these if not the same, death is no dread to me my hope is anchored in Christ Jesus. a fiew days previous to his being taken sick, he was remarking to us what a kind and Effectunate letter he intended writing you and his mother, but before the "Packet" returned from Cape Palmas, he fell to sleep in Jesus Arms never more to have earthly communications with you all, but trusting to strike hands with you all in the *Fathers Kingdom* where parting shall be no more, and where we do all trust to drink of that stream that maketh glad the City of the New Jarusalem. You requested in your last to know of Father to whome he was married to, also whether his wife belonged to any denomination or no. She was a widdow, before he married her with two Children, also a Member of the M. E. Church in Monrovia   As regards his yearly income that I can give no statement of. I can mearly say that it was derived entirely from his trade during his life   Jack Faulcon I shall say nothing about as he has written you himself. Bro Nash has also written to you. he is not married, and still carries on the Masons trade, he is capable of taking under his charge fathers apprentice boys—and carry on the same as when father was liveing. Cousin Leander is not home   he has joined the States Navy as steward consequently I can not give you a correct account of his health, tho he was well when last I saw him. his Children are all well. Cousin Julia and Peter is both dead, and has been for more than two years. Father had acquired ten acres of farm land, & five town lots.[2] he had just entered in a good way of farming before his death. we ingenerally raised on our Farms—Corn, Potatoes, Cassado & rice, of the latter father had not entered or commenced its cultivation, befor his death.

Labourers can be hired in Liberia for 25^{c} per day—and at the outside from 3 to 4$ per month   a person may hire good Common labourers to work the ground to make it productive as that in the States comparitively speaking   My husband Mr. Saml B. Lomax who writes this, begs that you would receive his kindest regard and attends his respects to you and all the family trusting that you would keep up a regular corrispondance as ever, which he shall endeavour to give you every particular relating to Public as well as private affairs, taking great delight in so doing. I now close by begging of you to pardon all Grammatical and other Errors &c &c

Yours with much Esteem

Matilda R. Lomax

NB   Should it meet your approbation to send us on any thing please direct to Care Rev H Teage

Source: Shields-Wilson deposit, Cocke Papers

1. Rev. Hilary Teage (d. 1853), son of Colin Teage, edited the *Liberia Herald*, prospered as a merchant, preached in the Baptist church attended by the Skipwith family, and became a prominent political figure in the Republic.

2. See Nash's letter of May 15, 1851 (p. 98, and n. 1), for the only precise records of his holdings.

Monrovia   Sept 30th 1850

To Honorable John H. Cocke

Dear Sir

I lift my Pen to Embrace this opportunity to inform you that I am well, and Hope that these few lines may find you and all the families well as they leaves me and mine. this letter will inform you of the sad, the Heart broken intelligence of the death of my Dear Husband, he was Drowned about 90 miles from this Place, attempting to go on shore, when the seas was runing mountain High, this took Place on the 23 of July Last, leaving me with three small Children to provid for, in this New Country Where Every thinge is hard for a widow without sofficient means to take care of them; the Youngest Child is at the Breast. I Hope that you will give me some little aid by the next vessel coming to Liberia, for if I Ever, in all my life needed Help, it is now, for my father who, were he a live I might make out better, but he is also gone the way of the Earth leaving behind small children, who are Depending upon me to provid for them also, my youngest, and only bro. Nash, sends his love to you   Leander is in the U.S.S. Yorktown, and has been for the Last 10 or 12 months, all of his Children is well. you will be so kind as to write to my Uncle, and inform him of the Death of his Brother, Tell him he Departed this life on October Last   I mean his Brother George   I now write these few lines to Miss Sally F. Cocke[1]   Tell her I Received her letter, by the Packet before this, but did not get the things her agent sent, I heard from them, and that was all; if she should hereafter send me any thing Please Tell her to Direct them to the Care of Col Jas B McGill monrovia[2] and I will be sure to get them   Please Remember me very kindly to my Dear old Grand mother   Tell her I am well in Body, but are Buried in sorrow in consequence of my Great losses, of Husband and father, also Give my love to my other Grand mother Betsey, and all of my relations & friends Both white & colored   I have nothing more to say at Present, only Remain yours, &c

Matilda Lomax

Source: Shields-Wilson deposit, Cocke Papers
1. Sally (Cocke) Brent.
2. James B. McGill (d. 1859) was a wealthy merchant in Monrovia who maintained his own fleet of coastal trading vessels.

Monrovia   October 18 1851

To Genl. John H. Cocke
dear Sir:

I take this oppurtunity of writing to you hoping this letter may reach you. Some of the immigrants by the last trip of the Packet come direct from Lynchburg & I hoped to hear from you but did not. I am afraid my last letters did not reach you. You desired to know how I get along since the death of my husband & father. I am not disposed to complain: & I feel great gratitude in being enabled to say, that although I am now husbandless & fatherless, & have three small children to provide for in a strange land, yet the Lord hath not left me to want bread nor a place to shelter me. Yet I have to work hard, which together with the benevolent attention of some friends has furnished me with necessaries of life. Still, if you or any of your kind family, to whom I and all my connexions out here are already under so many obligations shall please to send any thing for me it will not be a misplacd charity. Please give my love to my grandmother Lucy, to Mother Betsy Randal & to all inquiring friends. Please say to Miss Sally that I have written to her once, & will write again; & I trust it will not be considered an attempt to [finger?], if I assure her that nothing could afford me more pleasure than to visit again the scenes of childhood & look upon those faces which were once familiar to me. But the hope of this is forbidden by circumstances over which I have no control. My Brother is not married—He lives in my father's house. My father married an American Woman. Mrs Falcon's people are generally well. R. Cannon is at this moment very ill—hopelessly so with the dropsy—Should you send any thing for me please direct it, as also all letters for me to the care of Mr H Teage—Monrovia

Your Obdt Servant
Matilda Lomax

Source: #5680, Cocke Papers

Monrovia   Jany 27 1852

John H Cocke Esq
dear Sir

I am again called to be the messenger of melancholy intelligence. My brother to whom you addressed a letter from Philadelphia on the 27 Oct last departed this life a few weeks after he received it   His illness was severe and of only three days' duration when it terminated fatally. It was occasioned by a strain in lifting a rock. I am thus bereft of my last near relative, excepting only my three small children of an age to be of no service to me as yet. In Nash's letter you said Miss Sally would probably write to me—but she probably did not find it convenient to do so, as I did not hear from her.

You stated in John Falcon's letter that you sent me some things in the Packet, but I did not receive them. The last articles I received from any of the family were brought to me from Baltimore by Mr H. Teage in 1849.

I am doing as well as a lone woman situated as I am could expect to do. By hard labor & the assistance of some friends I and my Children are kept from suffering. I can not therefore complain; but endeavour to content with such things as I can conveniently get. If Miss Sally should send a letter or any thing else for me you will do me a favor to ask her to direct to the "Care of Mr H. Teage for Matilda Lomax Monrovia Liberia."

Our people has just returned from a campaign at Trade town. Perhaps they had harder fighting than has occurred since the formation of the Colony. The loss on our part was greater than in any former battle being 6 killed & 25 to 30 wounded. The strongest & most populous native town on this part of the Coast was taken burned & the natives completely routed. The natives force is said to have amounted to 1500 men well armed & equipped. The war is supposed to have been excited by british traders on the Coast.[1] Leander is in the United States' service on board the Dale. Dianah[2] is here.

Your obdt. Servant
Matilda Lomax

Genl. J. H. Cocke

Source: #5680, Cocke Papers
1. Through careful diplomacy with the Vai and Gola peoples, President Roberts of Liberia opened trade routes to the interior. The Bopolo, or Boporo,

Matilda Skipwith Lomax's letter to John Hartwell Cocke, Monrovia, May 19, 1852. (From the Cocke Papers, University of Virginia Library, Manuscript Division) congeries of tribes, however, turned on Roberts and threatened to strangle the burgeoning Mandingo-Liberian trade by exacting tribute from caravans passing through their territory. When Liberia protested, a Bopolo chieftain named Grando surprised the Grand Bassa settlements, almost annihilating the new town of Lower Buchanan and slaying ten Liberians. The settlers drove him off, but the war stalled the Liberian advance into the interior. See Johnston, *Liberia,* I, 232.

2. Diana Sturdivant (b. 1828?), Leander Sturdivant's daughter.

Monrovia   May 19th 1852

Mr J. H. Cocks

i take my Pen in hand to inform you of my health   i am well al Present and hope you are the same   sir I Received Nashes Leter a Red it with the greatis Pasure   I Riting the answer to it and signed it to Mr Plney[1] and I hope you have Receved it the Leter you sent Nash he Received it and Didnot Live but 3 weeks after he Received it And was not sick but 3 days   I have seen Mr Eli Ball[2] and have converse with him   i have seen a great Deal of trouble since the Death of my People and all my hold hart is on the Lord   this is a very hard Country for a poor widow to get along and i have to Work one Day for a lone 25 Cts and men get $1.50 Cts per Day masons   i would be very glad if you could send me some things for me and my Children some Provisions and clothings   Sturdiv is well and Jack faulkin is well and sens his Love to you   i have a great Deal to say but time will not atnit   give my love to all inquireing friend   No more to say at Present

But Remain yours in Love
Matilda R Lomax

Source: #5680, Cocke Papers

1. Rev. John B. Pinney (1806–1882), a Presbyterian minister and former agent for the American Colonization Society in Liberia, held office as corresponding secretary of the New York State Colonization Society from 1848 to 1872.

2. Rev. Eli Ball visited Monrovia in 1852 to inspect missions for the Southern Baptist Board of Missions. He thought that the American Colonization Society coddled the emigrants and suggested that the Society release them sooner than the minimum six months' public assistance program allowed. He especially disapproved of the Society's policy of constructing houses for new arrivals. In his conversations with settlers he observed that the industrious and thriving persons spoke kindly of the parent society but that the indolent and indigent "never failed to complain of the society for what it had not done for

them." Some settlers wanted the Society to provide three years of transition
support rather than the six months then in practice. See *African Repository*,
XXVIII (1852), 229, 236–237.

Monrovia   April the 20 1853

Mr. J. H. Cokes
Dear Sir

I brace you these few lines hoping to find you & your Children are in good helth   I thank god that I am spared throug
life and still living in hopes it is true this Country is quite hard
yet I lives   it is true I am the only one living and sees a great
deil of truble   My Brother is dead & has been dead for a year &
six months and he died very sudden only three days dying & he
was dying preparing to go to war & since the deathe of him I
suffered severe hardship   I am a glad to hear from you all
Ann Sucky Faulkin have lately & has good helth thoug her
voyage was unfourtunate   She loss her daughter.[1] dear sir I
think this Country is improveing Evry day the more & more & I
think affter an alapse of years it will be a find couty   I am now
sending my children at chool and I try to teach them with the
best of my knowledge, & ability. I will now relate to you what
took place in the Vey Country. a stratagem of war. Bombo &
Dwahling-bey the former a chief of the gholah tribes the later
Vey they have been intruding upon the Republick and is fond
of abatrary authority, in stoping the mart from coming in & that
rose rouse the Cytizen & at last Cause the offercers in chief to
make a positive Conclusion and they went to war, hoping or
Expecting to have some fight but Bombo who have been
domerneering over Dwhalabey Came under submission & several times attempted to run a way but through no Excess he was
Erested took & Brought him up to monrovia & waiting for a
proper decision whether he shall be punish or noe.[2] is all at
pressent I have a great deel to Sey but time will not admitt

Yours affectunalee
Matilda R. Lomax

[*Enclosed with a letter of Matilda Lomax to Sally (Cocke) Brent,
April 20, 1853*]

Source: #5680, Cocke Papers

1. Ann Sucky Faulcon, mother of John Faulcon, left Hopewell with her daughter Agnes and her son George. They sailed from New Orleans in 1852, bound for Liberia on the ill-fated voyage of the *Zebra*. An outbreak of cholera on board carried off thirty-five emigrants, including Agnes. See Susan Falcon [Sucky Faulcon] to JHC, Sept. 27, 1853, #5680, Cocke Papers; and *African Repository*, XXIX (1853), 70, 71.

2. Boombo, a Vai chief near Little Cape Mount, was unwilling to submit to Liberian authority and antagonized friendly Gola and Dei tribesmen with periodic slaving raids in 1852 and 1853. During one raid he decimated the town of a Gola chief named Dwarloo-Beh. In an effort to expand its influence, Liberia sought to adjudicate all disputes among contiguous native tribes. In March, 1853 Liberian troops routed Boombo's party and captured him. At his trial in Monrovia, Boombo was found guilty and ordered to restore his plunder, to pay reparations, and to spend two years in prison. *African Repository*, XXIX (1853), 184–185, 245–246, XXX (1854), 100–102.

monrovia   April the 20 1853

Dear miss Sally[1]

I allso Embrace you these few lines hoping you are well to imforme you that Im well & hoping that these few lines may find you the same. I am very glad to her that you are well   It have been a good while Since I heard from you   I hope you are well   I have recieved you Present & am extremly oblige to you   Seem that god Seen my Suffering & cause you to Send it   I have some present to send to you but I cant make it convenient to send it to you   I fear If I send it you wont get it unless you sent me word how to directed it. I recieved the letter from you by the Ralf Cross & the present before shee got loss at Cap Palmmas   I was Extremly thankfull for them   I would have sant it than but I was convenent, & you mus give my love to all inquireing friend fare & nere   I think that it is a hight time for you to be looking out for a beau   I think I mus pount one out for you & it is my desire to See tham all once more   If I dont See them I shall to see them all in heaven, and please send me some garden seed of all description and if you send them so salt air wont get to them & I head that you father where going to send fifty people by mr Peices[2] in Columbia & If it is so I am very glad may bee some my kin may be with them, & Please to give my love to My Aunt Luvenia   I have a great many thing to say but time will not abmitte   I will ritee to you as long as I

can find a piece of paper   I hope the nex time I have time &
opetunity

Yous affectunate
Matilda R. Lomax

Source: #5680, Cocke Papers
1. Sally (Cocke) Brent.
2. Unable to identify.

Monrovia Liberia   Sept the 26 1853

Dear Sir

I now Embrace this favourable oppotunity of writing you
theas fiew lines to inform you of my Helth which is now Very
well and I hope that thees fiew lines my find you Enjoying the
Best of Helth   I Receaved your Daughters letter and it afford
me the greatis pleasure to Read it and was Glad to Heare from
you all and Pleas to give my Best Respects to all the family and
now I will try Indevr to tell them the state of my mind   now I
am left a lone in this Lon'sum Country Noe one to look up to
my Brother has bin Dead for this 2 Years and I have bin Suffering for to find my self and three evry since his death and I have
to work so hard evry Day and dont get but 25 cents pr. Day and
you know that is too hard for a poore Widder to get a long at
that Rate and have three Children to find Vitels and Cloths and
I was Very Glad to Receaved the preset from Miss Sally and this
Year it was hard to get Provisions and I beg that you will have
the pit on me and send me some Provisions out by the first
oppotunity and if you do send it Pleas to Direct it to Henry W.
Dennis[1] and write him that you have sent it out for Mrs
Lomax   there is so much Dificulty to get things when there are
sent out to us unless we have som one to get them when they
are landing   now I am trying to send my Children to school
and trying to bring them up in the fear of the Lord

I now will tell you about Aunt Faulkin is now over the fev-
vour and george[2] all so and he is gon up the river to farming
Jack falkin is quite well and stil Remain at his traid and pleas to
send me some seeds and nail them up in a little Box so that the
Sault are will not get to them   if the sault are get to them they
will not come up and some times I live in hopes to see you all

again and then again it seems that the way looks so gloomy and if I ar not see you now more in this world I expect to meet you in hevin   I have a great deal more to say but time wer not enough

I remain
Matilda R Lomax

[Enclosure]
Dear Aunt Lavinia

Will you pleas to send me one ribbin and a siftr to Remember you as I never Expect to see you all in this world but I expect to meet you in hvin ware parte will bee no more

Your
Matilda Lomax

Source: #5680, Cocke Papers
1. Henry W. Dennis was the American Colonization Society agent in Monrovia.
2. George Cocke, Ann Sucky Faulcon's son who emigrated with her on the *Zebra*.

Monrovia   December 10th 1853

Fluvania Virginia——
Miss Sarah Cox[1]

I take my pen to inform you that I am enjoying good health at present Hoping this may find you the same   I recd. your letter and was extremely glad to hear of your good health and also the rest of the family   I written to you by the shirley and sent you some seeds Coffee & sour sap & [illegible]—the largest seed were mangroes   the people that your father sent out are all well   they have went through the fever and now are doing well   I heard that your father intends to send out some more & I sincerely hope that he will send out some of my relation as I am alone now and would like to see some of them very much indeed   I suppose you have heard of the death of Mr. Teage He has been dead going on 7 months   you will gratify me much by giving my love to all my Relatives my aunt &c.   you will please send me out something by the next opportunity my children are doing quite well as they are going to school and are making considerable progress   I would like you to send me out some good Books for them   the Articles which you sent out by Mrs. Falkland I received two pieces   Studenfant is well & his family and he is still going in the man of war   I have such a Short notice of the opportunity of sending you this letter that I will close it hoping the next will be of more

Your Most Obdt.
Matilda R Lomax

Source: #9513 "Bremo Recess" deposit, Cocke Papers
1. Sally (Cocke) Brent, Cocke's daughter.

Monrovia   June 20th 1854

Mr John Cocks

Dear sir

this will inform you of my health which is good at Present and hope you are the same   for the Last 2 month I have Bin Sick But I am now getting Better and am Permited To write once more. I have writen 3 or 4 Letters and havnot Receive any answer from them I wrote By the Shirley and Sont you some seeds By Mr Sims[1]   the country is improving Verry well   the fever is not as Bad now as it was some years Back   Mrs falkon is through with the fever & george is now farmer   they are Doing well at Present   now my three Daughters is going To School   will you Please send me some Books for them   if you Please send me some Provision Say ½ Barrel flour & Pork   this Rains has Bin Verry hard times for Pervision

Sir   I would Be Verry happy To see Some of my Relation   I am Now Prepared To Received them   I have great Deal But time will not admit

Yours in christ
Matilda R. Lomax

[Enclosure]

Miss Sarah[2]

Dear miss   this will inform you of my health which is good at Present and hope you are the same   I have writen ofton But no answer have I Receive But am Determine To write until I Do Receve one   will you Please Send me some garden seeds By the first opportunity   give my Love To all your Brothers and

To my aunt. I Dont expect To See you no more in Life But Trust will See you in Glory   you must excuse my Bad writer   no more at Present   you must send me somethin   But Remain yours

Matilda R. Richardson

I am now married and have change my Name.[3]

Source: #5680, Cocke Papers

1. James Sims, a merchant in Monrovia who traveled to America in 1853 and returned to Liberia in May, 1854.

2. Sally (Cocke) Brent.

3. All evidence suggests that Matilda married James Richardson (d. 1860) in 1853 or 1854. Richardson was a house servant emancipated by the will of Dr. Cosmo P. Richardson of Georgia—according to Dr. Richardson's executor, James had been reluctant to leave America. He arrived in Liberia in late December, 1852, or early January, 1853. For information on his emancipation, see Richard J. Gibson to William McLain, Oct. 29, 1852, "Domestic Letters Received," vol. 128: 140, ACSP. I would like to thank James M. Gifford of Western Carolina University for this reference.

Monrovia   August 1857

Dear Sir

I am most happy to hear from you through a friend, and glad to find you are still well and that Sally is married at last   I have writen you several times and never received an answer to one   I do not know how it is unless I did not address right.

Solomon[1] arrived safe to Monrovia on the 10th of July, he has had but one slight attack of fever excepting that he has been well   he seems to like the place very much he said better than he thought he would   I think he will do very well out here. Sucky Faulcon is doing very well. she is staying at a boarding house. as for her son George he is at Cape Mount. As for Sturvent he is doing very well, and for Jack Faulcon he is doing very well at his old trade

And now about myself thank the Lord I am still spared to be able to write to you once more, since the death of my people I some times feel almost broken up and then when I look and think, I see that the Lord has not put on me no more than I can bare. I have been in the Baptist Church as a member for eighteen years, and I have member of Daughter's of Temperance for four years Sister's of friendship for five years. I hear there are some of my people are coming out here   is it so or not?   I would be most happy to see some out here before my eyes be closed in death, as for my Uncle George I wish you would try and do all you can in prevailing on him to come out here   my father before he died talked a great deal about his brother and wished he would come out here.

Please give my love to Aunt L. tell I was sorry to hear of the death of her son nedd   tell her for me that she must remember "that the Lord giveth and the Lord taketh away."

The fever is not so bad now as it used to be   the older the place gets and the more it is cultivated the better the fever is.

Mason's work is a $1 a day head workman $3 a day Carpenters $1 do. Monrovia is looking very finely now   we are improving in most every-thing. When shall I hear from you   I long to have a letter from you. This year has been very hard and I am afraid it will be still more so next in consequence of our people having to go to war so much with the natives and not having much rain this season   the sun has parched up mostly all the rice the fields so if you would be so kind as to send me out some-thing for myself and three children I would feel much obliged   any thing I do not mind what it is   I wrote to you last June but it was only a short one just to let you I am living.

Please give my love to your daughter Sally   I intend to write to her by the same vessel. Please give my love to all my friends and Believe me to remain your affectionate friend

Matilda Richardson

[*Enclosure*]

Dear Philip

I thought I would not let your father's letter go without sending you a few lines to say I am well and I hope you are the same   I thought you would have written me to let me know how your family are   I was glad to hear from you by Solomon. Please give my love to all my people and friends. I would be obliged if you would be so kind as to send me some flour   you must excuse this short letter. Good bye

Matilda Richardson

Source: #5680, Cocke Papers
1. Solomon Creacy (or Creasey), a former manservant to John Hartwell Cocke, Jr., and a member of the Hopewell community, received his freedom at

age sixty-five and embarked for Liberia on the *Mary Caroline Stevens* in May, 1857. He labored as a farmer and a foreman for a large absentee plantation, and, according to his letters in the Cocke Papers, expressed satisfaction with Liberia.

Monrovia   August 19th 1857

Dear Madam[1]

I was very glad to hear about you through a friend of mine   I was also glad to hear that you were married and I hope are doing well. I have written to your father and I thought I would just send you a few lines to let you know that I am well. I have writen you several times and have never received one from you   I wish I could hear from you. Please give my love to your brother Charles and I would be glad if you would send me some thing for myself and three children   please do not think hard, my asking you for some thing   I would not do it but really the times are so hard out here   please to ask Aunt Lervenia to send me some dryed peaches and to send my children some nuts & some dryed Aples. give my love also to Uncle Nedd and his wife and to all inquiring friends far and near. As I have such short time to write and have told you all the news in your fathers letter you must get that and read it. I[f] you do send me any thing please send to Mr. William Johnson[2] C. C. Monrovia and he will give them to me and if I should die before they gets here he will give them to my children. The person that send you these letters is the Daughter of Payten Skipwith now Matilda Richardson. I hope to hear from you before long much love to yourself: you must tell me how many children you have when you write.

Believe me to remain Your affectionate friend
Matilda Richardson

Source: #9513 "Bremo Recess" deposit, Cocke Papers
1. Sally (Cocke) Brent.
2. William Andrew Johnson (b. 1832) was a native of Liberia who later married Sarah Ann Roberts, the daughter of Joseph J. Roberts.

Monrovia   Febry 1st 1858

Dear Sir

I am truly glad to be able once more to send you a few lines and to thank you for the kind letter I received from you by my Cousin James[1]   he arrived here on the 25th December and he seems to like the place very well, he has had but little fever.

I have three children, one thirteen the next eight and the other one & they go to School every day.

Please give my love to Mrs. S. Brent and tell her that I am much obliged to her for what she sent me, please give my love to my Aunt L. and to all my friends. I expect most all the rest of the people will write to you. I am happy to be able to tell you that Solomon is doing very well at farming. I must now close my letter as I have told you all the news.

I remain Your friend

Matilda Richardson

[Enclosed with a letter of Matilda Richardson to Sally (Cocke) Brent, February 1, 1858]

Source: #9513 "Bremo Recess" deposit, Cocke Papers
1. James Skipwith, the son of George and Mary Skipwith. See his letters published below.

Monrovia   Febry. 1st 1858

Dear Miss Sally[1]

I have just closed a letter to your father and I thought I would send you a few lines with his, I was sorry to not to hear from you, your father told me in his letter that you were not at home   I hope you will not think any thing about these few lines as I have no news to tell you as time is so short   I hope you will excuse me as the packet will leave tomorrow morning. I must now say good bye as I have nothing more to tell you. Hoping you are well and I hope it will not be long before I hear from you.

I remain Your affectionate friend

Matilda Richardson

Source: #9513 "Bremo Recess" deposit, Cocke Papers
1. Sally (Cocke) Brent.

Monrovia Africa   July the 24 1858

Mrs. Sally F. Brent

I am glad that an opportunety is afforded to hand you a few lines which leave me and mine in good health and I hope may find you enjoying the Blessings of a favorable Providence   I were glad to here from you and the servents By Solmon letter for I ashore you that I am glad to here from you at any time and Beg that you would write to me By evry opportunity as it is a great treat to me to resive a letter from your hands   I am getting on as well as I can expect But not as well as I should like to do But I still look forde for a Better times and hope that time is not far of[f]   I hope to live to see the day when Africa this our dark Country shall rise Bud and Blossom as the rose of the garden of life   thir is nothing New at this time that is worth writing   my 3 children are well and gose to school and are lurning very fast to Read and write   Leander children are well and send love to you and all the Famely   Leander is not heir he is on board of amanofwar with Mr John Barroad[1]   we look for them every day   Cousin James is living with me   he is over the fever an is well Please with Liberia an wish to Be Rememberd to white and Colord   Solmon wish to Be Remberd also to all the Frends   Jack and his Mother are well and send love to all the Freinds   this is the Rany seons with us now and it is very dull at this time with us in Africa   it is true that I have Been to this Country 20 years an is true I have not got a Brick House But what is the case if my father Esate had not Been robed I Chould have had a Plenty to live no an to live well all my days But after my Father death I had no one to see to his Estate thirfore I got nothing from his Esate But 3 or 4 lots in town which is not worth nothing if tha ware sould   Please to Remember me to all the Famely   tell aunt Lavinia that I often think of her and tell her that she must write to me By the returne of the Packet and if we never meet in this world agane I hope to meet you on the other side of Jordan where we shall Be ever Presen with the Lord and ware we shall Pluck new lives from the tree of life and where Congregations never Break up and sabbaths have no end   I would like to say agreadel more But time will not atmit Just now   I must now come to a Close yours in the Bounds of christen love   Please to give my love evry Body

Matilda Richardson

Source: #9513 "Bremo Recess" deposit, Cocke Papers
1. John T. Barraud (d. 1860) of Virginia, Cocke's nephew by his first wife, was a lieutenant in 1858 serving on the sloop *Cumberland* of the African Squadron. In a diary and a letter which he circulated among members of the Cocke family, Barraud recorded several disparaging observations about Liberia and the impoverished state of Cocke's former slaves. He visited Matilda and was aghast at her decline in fortune, a condition he attributed largely to the lethargy of her husband. See John Barraud Diary (fragment), November 30– December 5, 1857, #5680, Cocke Papers; and Barraud to JHC, Nov. 12, 1857, #5680, Cocke Papers. Matilda's brief personal history in her letter was probably a response to the Barraud descriptions left with the Cocke family.

Monrovia Liberia
Febry. 22nd 1861

My dear Cousin[1]

I am sure you will be sorry to hear that Cousin James is dead   he went to Bassa last year and going all in the wet he got cold and gave him dirurhea and he had the Doctor to him but could do him no good   it lasted on him until January last when he received your letter he was sick in bed and it made him worst instead of better for he was expecting you   he wanted to see you but as you did not come you will not see him any more in this world but he said he was going to rest and hope that you all will meet him in heaven   he said that he hope that you will take good care of his children and bring them up in the fear of the Lord   when he came out here he came to my house and staid with me until he died and I don all that I could for his comfort and happyness but you must try and not let it go hard with you for the Lord giveth and the Lord taketh   you must try and look to the Lord and he will help you through all you troubles.

I hope it may not be long before I will see you out here   I must now come to a close as I have told you all the news   my husband died a year before James. Hoping that you are all well

I remain Your Affectionate Cousin

Matilda Richardson

[*Enclosure*]

My dear Cousin William[2]

I thought I would just send you a few lines to let you know that your Brother is dead   he was sick in bed when he received your letter. he talked a great deal about you all   he said that he hope you all will try and meet him in heaven for he said that he was going to rest in Jesus.

Please give my love to Berther Edwards[3] and tell him that I can not write this time but will do so another   I hope he is well   you can tell him that his Cousin received his letter also and was glad to hear from him   I must now close as I have nothing more to say   There are a great many of our people gon to war.[4] I want you to give my love to all the friends, I must say good bye

Your affectionate Cousin
Matilda Richardson

Source: Shields-Wilson deposit, Cocke Papers
1. Richard Skipwith, a son of George Skipwith and a slave of Dr. Cary Charles Cocke.
2. William Skipwith, a son of George Skipwith and a stonemason at Upper Bremo.
3. Berthier Edwards, a son of Ned Edwards and a ploughman at Upper Bremo.
4. In 1861 Liberia sent from three to four hundred men to Cape Palmas to quiet a disturbance between two tribes there. See *African Repository*, XXXVIII (1862), 84.

Monrovia   Febry. 23rd 1861

Dear Sir[1]

I thought as my Cousin was dead I would send you a few lines to tell you all about him. He went to Bassa year before last and took cold and it lasted on him until the middle of January he spoke about you all when he received your letter   he was down in his bed very sick   he was hopping to see his wife and as she did not come it made him worse but he spoke very cheerful about dieing   he said he was going to rest in Jesus and he hope that he may see you all there.

As for his prospects in life he did as well as could be expected in Africa and as about his Church affair he done well and perhaps he would have been a preacher if he had been spared but as the Lord knew best he took him to himself, as for his Mother and Father he talk a great deal about them.

As for Aunt Sucky she has been very sick but I think she is on the mend   as for all the rest of us we are well. There are right smart of our people gon to Palmas to war   them have been gon 3 weeks and have not heard from them but are expecting them the end of this week.

There was only a year and 3 weeks between my Husband and Cousin Jameses death.

Please give my love to Mrs. Brent   I have writen to her but have not received an answer   tell her that since I wrote to her I have seen a great deal of trouble and am now left all in the hands of the Lord. Please give my love to all my friends   tell them that I am still living and well. Please give my love to Aunt Levenia   Will you be so kind as to send me some seeds and let there be some hard head cabbage   I must now come to aclose as I have nothing more to say.

I remain Yours Respectfully
Matilda Ritchardson

Source: Shields-Wilson deposit, Cocke Papers
1. John Hartwell Cocke

Letters from James Skipwith*

Ala[ba]ma

Montgomery   Feb. the 11 1851

Master

I know take my seat acordein to your recest to let you know how I am getinon. I left Greensboro at 3 oclock and ative at Selma at 4 aclock in the afternoon   I stade in Selma a day and a half   I left Selma at 3 aclock in the morning and arive at Montgomery at one oclock in the afternoon   I went to Mister Farris[1] and he call me to miss Tilley[2] and he take me and Put me in the dincinroom & I believe he is very well Please with me so far & and I am very well Please with him so far   my health has been very good But I am getting very much consernd   the small Pox is very hot all over Town   sevel have died with the small Pox in Town. will you be so Please to give my love to Mother and Father   nothing more but Remaine your humbel Survant   I still hold on to my Pledge and will as long as I live

James Skipwith

Source: #2433-B Cocke deposit, Cocke Papers
1. William B. Fariss, a Virginia born planter living in Montgomery and a distant relation to the Cocke family. Fariss handled Cocke's business in Montgomery and supervised, with some difficulty, James's hiring out arrangements. He was a partner in the Montgomery dry goods store of Phillips, Fariss & Co.
2. Unable to identify.

*Ed. Note: Because his few Alabama letters are useful in understanding the tone and sense of his Liberian correspondence, they are included in this section of the book. Before moving to Alabama, James worked on Philip St. George Cocke's Belmead plantation in Virginia. James worked for eight years in a variety of jobs in Virginia and Alabama in order to purchase his freedom, but was unable to accumulate funds to claim his wife and children. He accepted Cocke's invitation to go to Liberia—the conditions of his manumission—and arrived there in 1858 without his family. He was only twenty-three years old when he settled in Liberia.

Montgomery Alabama
March 29th 1852

Dear Master

It is with pleasure I take this liberty in writing these few lines hopeing they will find you quite well. This being the third letter I have written without receiving any answer I imagine they must have got miscarried for I am sure you whould have written such as kind Master as you are. I am Enjoying as good health Thank God as I have only been sick six days since I have been here. I am living in the same place & am comfortable situated and like the place very well. I could have got better wages. Mr. Farrace thougt I had better not go on a Boat or Else I could have got $25 dollars per month. Otherwise I should have Booked Three Hundred dollars with good Health in the Year. I have put Twenty five dollars in Mr. Farraces hands and should have put more, but have loand out some and unfortunatly have not had the sucess in geting it againe. In case I get it, I will learn better another Time. All of my own honest and industrious making I have conducted myself with propritey & honesty Both to white & coulerd persons having no Enemies but plenty of Friends.

My Temperance pledge I have kept up to this day and continuing to do so beleiving it good both for my Body & Soul and with the Blessing of God may I stand to the Vow I have taken so to do. I was in hopes of seeing you out here past winter but I was deprived of the pleasure in not seeing you But I hope to see you next Fall.

you was speaking to me aboute my youngest Brother[1] living with me. I am now prepared and nothing whould make me more happy then having him under my charge. If you whould be so kind as to let him come, I could learn him somthing that whould be profitable to you & to him also. And be shure to give him a Book learning so that it whould make him Both industrious and good. Please to Remember me kindly to Mr. Charles & family and Miss Sally and my grandmother hopeing they and all my Friends are comfortable. My Bretheren & Sisters in Christ I am now come to close whould we never meet more in this world may we with gods mercy & goodness meet in the next. Now I pray God to bless you may you be prosprous and happy all your life is the prayer of your devoted Servant

James Skipwith

Source: Shields-Wilson deposit, Cocke Papers
1. "Little" George Skipwith (d. 1857) stayed with his parents. See also
George Skipwith's letter of April 15, 1848 (p. 169, n. 6).

Mobile   August 13 1856

dear Sir

I know take my seat to write you A fue lines   thes leave me
enjoyin good helth and I hope that thes may fine you the
same   I havenot herd from the Plantattion for sum time. mr
John Cocke[1] ware in town yeter day. he left for Green County
this morning on the Car   it is very Warme and dul in Mobile at
Present   we all think thir will Be Agreat deal of seckness in
town this summer   great menny of the Citizens of Mobile is
gorn north & well   I surpose the time is neare at hand for the
ship to sail for Africa and as I am determet thru you to make
Africa my Home and my Evry Prays is that God will Prived Evry
thing for the Junney   I hope that your mind is the same as
when I taulk with you in Montgomery and if so I hope I will Be
Ready for the Junney   thir is but one thing that I hate that is I
cant carry my Wife and Childreans yet I Belive that God in his
Provenodence will Remember the Poor in sperite and the Pure
in Hart   I will like to hear from you and at what time I must
leave for Virginia as I think that time is near at hand   nothing
more But Reamaine your humbel Survent untel Death

James Skipwith

Source: Shields deposit, Cocke Papers
1. John Cocke of Greene County, Alabama, Cocke's cousin and steward for
John Hartwell Cocke's Alabama holdings. See the Letters from Alabama, below,
for details of his affairs.

Mobile Ala   June 12 1857

dear Master

I know take my pen in hand to write you a fue lines to let you
know how sorry that I ware when your letter come for me I
never hatted enny thing so much in all my life Before   I did
not expet your letter untel you Reach home. when your letter
came I ware up the River and the watter getting very low which

made us a day or two latter then Common But I hope it will in
Abel me with God asistince to Be Better Prepard for the Junney
this Fauld if life last and it Be Pleasen to you which I hope it
will Be. I am still Employ as A steard on the steamer R L Cobb
and will Be Perhapes all the summer if my helth will Atmit   if
it will Please you I would like to come to Virginia this Fauld 10
or 12 days Before the steamer sale   thes lines leave me in good
helth and I hope tha may fine you the same But Better. Bepleas
to Remember my Love to all   Bepleas to write to me soon for I
want to hear from you very much
  derict my letter to Col Mings, Mobile ala[1]
  I Remain your Humbel survent untel death

James Skipwith

Source: #5685, Cocke Papers
1. Collin H. Minge was a longtime factor for Cocke's Alabama concerns.

Monrovia, Liberia, Africa
July 17 1858

Dear Sir
  I Now embrace this opportunity of writing to you as the Pack-
et will leave heir in a few days for the states   I resive your
letter By the packet & ware glad to heir from you & my
Friends   thees lines leave me in as good health as I can expect
& I hope thees will find you well & enjoyen good health   I am
glad that I can say that I am Better Please with Africa now then I
ware when I wrote to you By the Packet   Before now I see that
I did not know any thing about this Country But now I am
Better Please with Africa then I thought I ever would Be   I
now belive that this is the Country for all of my Race & god
grant that I may live to see the day when I will strike hand with
meny of my Friends in Liberia for with alittle help we can live
heir as well as we can in America   But I tell you that the
African fever is something that lay as a ded wate on the minds
of the Best men in Africa   I am told By the Dr that I had it very
light   in dead I ware more Frighten then I ware hurt   it is
true that anyone from the south do not suffer like one from the
north   thir is But little diffrence in this climant an south Ala
thir is nothing new in Africa now   the Wars is all over for a

while But it very dul times just now   Oen to the late War in the Country the Govement has Become much embrance But we hope that in a few years she will recover & hope that we will have a Country at last[1]   I have converce with the leading & Furst Men of this Republice sutch as President Benson[2] & President Robits which have enlight me & encorge me a gredeal as to getting a living in Africa & I have not the smals dout if I keep my health I can make a living in this Country   I cant say mutch about my Farm now But when I write to you agane I hope to Be Abel to tell you if thir is any verger in tilling the lands in Africa   the most of our Richs & independent Men of this Country is Farmes   you wish to her from thous People that went to the uppor County   the People at Carysburg do not suffer as the People that stop about monrovia & on the sea Board   But it is Better for any one to have the fever at once tha stande much better   Matilda and her children are well John an his Mother is well   as for George tha do not know waht has Be Come of him   Leander children are well   Leander is on boarde of amanofwar   I have not seen him since I arive hirr   Solmon is well an has compleated his house an living on his Farm   my Respect to all the servents   yours in the Bonds of Christan love

James Skipwith

Source: Shields deposit, Cocke Papers

1. The independent Cape Palmas settlement of the Maryland State Colonization Society clashed with local Grebo natives in 1856 and suffered a humiliating defeat at Sheppard Lake early in 1857. The colony appealed to Liberia for munitions and volunteers. Despite the low state of government finances following a recent campaign in the Sinoe country, the Liberian legislature authorized an expedition to relieve Cape Palmas, and the Liberian force helped to quell the Grebo uprising. Liberia's timely assistance encouraged the exhausted and vulnerable Cape Palmas settlers to petition Liberia for annexation, which occurred in 1857. See Penelope Campbell, *Maryland in Africa: The Maryland State Colonization Society, 1831–1857* (Urbana, 1971), 229–236.

2. Stephen Allen Benson (1816?–1865), a freeborn settler from Maryland, was president of Liberia from 1855 to 1864.

Monrovia, Liberia, Nov. the 12, 1858

Gen. Cocke
Dear Sir

it is with delight that I embrace this opportunity by the

United States Sloop of War which arive hier 4 days ag[o] with
the recoved Africans from Charlston[1] and will leave heir to
morrow so I Could not let this opportunety Past   thees lines
leave me well and I truly hope thees may fine you the same and
all the Friends   I have Be Come well Please with this country
and is more and mor incouage evry day   I Belive thir is no
Betty Cuntry Below the sun for any race Notwithstanding it is
very dul times heir and very little cand Be made heir But we
still hope for Better things and as thir is no Wars in the Country
now and a Plenty of Pervasion But very little Cash the President
says that the Govement will in a few mounts Be out of det and
at which time we hope to Be a happy Nathinon   I hope to
resive severl lettrs By the Packet which we look for about one
mont from this time   all my friends wish to Be Remeard to
you   Solomon is well an send his love to you   heis formind
and is very well and wish to Be Remembeard to all his frends
I am dooing as well as I can expect as times is very dull and
very little to Bemade   I am keeping A Bake Shop and I take in
about one dollar a day   I hope that I will Be Able to take in 2 A
day if I keep my helth   you must excuse Bad writing as it is
late soe I must Close

James P. Skipwith

Source: Shields deposit, Cocke Papers
1. In August, 1858, the U.S.S. *Dolphin* captured the slaver *Putnam,* also
known as the *Echo,* off Cuba with 318 "starving, diseased" Africans confined
below decks. Although the navy landed the recaptives in Liberia, a Southern
grand jury refused to hand down an indictment against the crew of the slaver,
and, after a judge forced a trial, a Charleston jury acquitted the crew "despite
the most damning evidence." See Howard, *American Slavers,* 144.

Monrovia, Liberia   Africa   Feb. the 11 1859
Dear sir
    I am glad that an opportunity is afforded to hand you a few
lines which leave me and mine in good health and I hope may
find you enjoying the Blessings of a favorable Providence   I
have not much But still something I think worth Communicating   since I wrote you last the Lord has Blesst us with good
health which I hope will Continue   we are under the empre-
sion that we shall have to Carry War with the Natives tribe at

grand Cape Mount But I hope that we shall be able to Com-
plemise with the kings for this is a Bad time with us to Fight
War with enny Country for this Government is much in need of
funds at Present.[1] I hope nothing will take Place to Pervent her
Progress   I am still trying to Farm But cannot see But little
Progress as yet   it is true that I have But little means and
cannot get surfishon tools   1 have 10 acres of Land for which I
Pade $6 an Acre   I am not disincorrige   I belive that I shall
make my Bread   it is well to Plant Coffee trees and it is well to
Plant Cotton   But it will Be severel years Before it will Pay
Sugar Cane and Pottaters ground nuts an Foulds of driffrent
kinds is Best   Natives Laber can Be obtane for $3 Per Mount
you can Buy Publice Lands for Fifty Cents acres   the Land that
I Bought is front Land on the st Paul River   no Better Land has
ever Ben found on James River   I hope that in a few years that
cotton will Pay us for making it in this Country But it will not
do it now   we are too Poor to trust alone on cotton   until
each Farmer can make from 2 to 3 Bales of Cotton no one will
Care to take it By the small   Solomon is well   he will write
you By this opportunity   all of my Friends is well and wish to
Be Rememberd to you and all   Jack is Marride and has one
dorter to Cormence with   Solomon is not Marrade But will Be
in short I think

I hope that Before menny years I shall see some of my Freinds
from Alabama in Africa   if you shuld send them to Africa
impress it aporne them to Bring with them tools for tha are few
an very dear in this Country   it makes no driffrence about the
kind all kinds will Come in Play   myself an Solomon Both
resive our Letters from the Church in Ala   I thank for your
kinnest   Farewell Very Respectfully yours in the Bond of Christian affection

J. Skipwith

Source: Shields deposit, Cocke Papers
1. A smoldering Gola and Vai dispute, exacerbated by French commercial
penetration of the region, almost erupted into war before the personal intercession of President Benson in 1860 quieted the several parties.

Monrovia Liberia   Aug the 20 1859

Dear Sir

I resive yours By the returne of the Packet from american & ware much Please to heair from you & my freinds   I am glad that an opportunity is afforded to hand you a few linaes which leave me & my friends in good health & I hope may find you enjoying the Blessings of a favorable Providence   I have not much (But still something I think) worth communicating

Since I wrote you last the Lord has in mercy visited the settlement & I have had the Pleasure of seen 31 hopeful converts Beside with christ in Baptism   Besides a number have Joined the Methodists[1]   the natives are more & more friendly   their confidence begins to awaken   they see that it is our wish to do them good & hostilities have ceased with them   we have daily applications to receive their children in to our church & sabath school   4 of the converts are natives of this country and are fild with the holy Goost   we have great write to look Back on the few mounts that Pass and thank God for the menny Blessing that he has Bestore aporne Liberia for when I look at menny things and the goodnis of god to this nathion I think that the time is near at hand when Ethiopia is to stretch its hands in Prayer and Praise to God   I have the Pleasuer of Returne you our thanks for the hansom Preasent of sabbath school Books which we resive By the Packet   as I am one of the Teachers of the sabbath I returne my thanks also and hope that the Lord will Bless you for the good feelings that you have for Liberia

Sir you wish me to say what I think of the little one becomeing a Thousand   hard hard indeed was the contest for freedom & the strggle for independence   the golden sun of liberty had nearly set in the gloom of an Eternal night   But sir all dangers is not death   our country stands at the Present time on Commanding Ground   Older nations with drifferent systems of Government may Be somewhat slow to acknowledge all that Justly Belongs to us But we may feel without vanity that Liberia is doing her Part in the great work of improving human affairs   there are two principles gentlemen strictly and purely Liberian which are now likely to overrun the civilized world which are, S. A. Benson & J. J. Roberts   thee light that led them this far was light from heaven.

I Belive that Liberia will yet stand with the eather Parts of the

Civilized world   O praise the Lord all ye nations   Praise him all ye people for his merciful kindness is great toward us and the truth of the Lord endureth for ever   paise the Lord

Sir   you wish me to say something about the high lands of the intur about Carysburgh   I have heard a greadeal But have seen very little   it is sed to Be very helthy & also that the land is & is fine table land   Carysburgh is improving very Rappit and in a few years will become the seat of Government   I intend taking a small Excursion in the country But cannot Promist when that will be as the rains has set in and I am desirous to get on with my fairm   I find that time is like gold dust with me   Just now I am now deviding my time   I go to Days Hope High School[2] & the Ballance of my time to my Plantation   I have found that a man must have an Edcation to be aman in enny cournty   I now regreat that I did not enprove my tallent when I warse young   I now see that what you tould me ware for my own Good   Please to tell my friends that think of coming to Africa try an master thir Book   I am truly sorry that I did not take your advice when I ware young But I have one hope what man has don man cando   I am Studing for the Ministry   I belive that is the Work that the Lord has apoint for in Africa   Solmon is quit sick and has Ben for sum time   he is a little Better now   he Expose him self & taken Could Matildas Husband is unwell & has Ben for sumtime   the rest of my friends is well   Jack will write to you   the tools for farming we use all the tools But the Plough   enny that you wish to send

yours truly

James P. Skipwith

PS   I have enjoyed som of the Privlige of a free man   I have surve my Curntery as Grand Jurry and as Pettet Jurry and also as Voting sumthing strong to me   one thing more that I must say this is one thing that I am fraid will Prove as a Curst on Liberia   Mr Cooper the oner of the Sugar mill is about to still Rum[3]   I am fraid it will Curst to Liberia

J.P.S.

Source: #5680, Cocke Papers
1. The 1858 religious awakenings of Fulton Street, New York, churches infected Liberians through the "bundles of tracts" and extracts of New York prayer meetings which Methodist missionaries distributed in Monrovia. The

religious fervor first gripped children, who, through their conversion experiences, communicated the enthusiasm to their elders. On New York see Timothy L. Smith, *Revivalism and Social Reform in Mid-Nineteenth Century America* (Nashville, 1957), 63ff, 72; and for Liberia see *African Repository*, XXXV (1859), 312–313.

2. Rev. John Day (d. 1859) was a black missionary for the Southern Baptist Foreign Mission Board. He founded Hope High School in Monrovia. The school was coeducational and had both primary and classical departments.

3. Reed Cooper (d. 1866) was a sugar planter, sea captain, and trader. He put up a sugar mill on the St. Paul River at the site of the future town of Coopersville. No evidence exists that he distilled rum there.

Monrovia   Liberia   May the 31, 1860

Dear Bertheer Edwards

Dear Sir

The arrival of the Bark Page Gives me an opportunity to hand you a few lines which I hope may find you in good health   nothing very interesting has taken place since I wrote you last only that among the last Emigrants that came out there has been some Considerable sickness But only two death   I know you wish me to write you a Great deal But I must plead the old Excuse want of time for I find that a man must work Both head & hands to make a living in this Country   our work is almost like Building the walls of Jerusalem   we have to carry our tools all day in our hands & our Bibles at Night yet Notwithstanding it is the Best Country for the Black man that is to Be found on the face of the Earth   God intended Africa for the Black Race

Please Give my love to Patesy & Children[1]   tell her that I did not write to her By this opportunitty   I writen to her a few monts ago By the Bark Benson & will write again By the Packet if nothing hapens   tell her to write to me By the first opportunity   I have not heard from ala for along time   when you write again tell me sumthing about them   I wish to write to them But do not now how to derit my letter to   Please Give me de rection

I must now come to a close as it is now late   my respect to Both white & Colored   Farewell very respectfully your

James P. Skipwith

PO   By the first opportunitty send me some of your Garden seeds as we cannot Get them heair   Cabage seeds Beens, Snaps

& as meny other kinds as you like and do not fail to write soon

J. P. Skipwith

Source: #5680, Cocke Papers
1. James's wife and children were owned by Dr. Cary Charles Cocke.

Monrovia   June 25 1860

H. W. Dennis Esqr
Agt A. C. S. Monrovia
Sir:

In december last you was kind enough as to inform me, that a box to my address had been landed from the M. C. Stevens at the Colonial Warehouse. On calling for it, it could not be found, nor have I received it, up to this time, [and] I am not informed of its Value not having received any information as to what the box contained, nor was there any bill of Lading for it sent me. As you seem to be certain that it was Landed for me & as I have not received it, I think the loss should be made good to me and I do hereby claim and demand thirty dollars of you for it, which I hope you will be good enough as to settle without further delay.

I am Sir
Respectfully Yours
James P. Skipwith

Recd Payment[1]
June 25 1860

Source: #5680, Cocke Papers
1. Dennis paid Skipwith's claim. See Henry W. Dennis to JHC, July 14, 1860, #5680, Cocke Papers, for details.

Monrovia   July the 10, 1860

Hon & dear Sir

I received your letter of the 16 of April 1860 & read its contents with much interest by the arrival of the Packet   I am glad to heare that your health is much Beter now then it ware last winter   thees leave me & freinds in as good health as can

be expect as the rains is now very heavy & the health in genreal
is not very good   I am Prode to hare of the great revial that has
taken Place amoung your servints   god grant that it may not
stop thir But it may cover the hold of america like the Water
cover the chanil of the great deep till all shall know the Lord
whome to know is life eternel & may the grace of our Lord Jesus
Christ may be with you with your families & with all you have
to do with   tell the Breathen to Be strong in the Lord & in his
mighty power for as much as we know that thir is a rest remaine
for the People of God a House not made with hands But eternel
in the Heavens   Since I writen to you last I have vissit Carysburg also Grand Cape Mount   it is a good healthy Place & thir
farm lands can be obtain about ten miles from the Cape up the
river   thir are 3 drifent rivers each have good table lands for
farmes   the People of Cape mount has now Cormence to turne
thir minds to till the Earth   thir is no Better farm land in
Liberia but your People must have sumthing to make astart or
they will not do well in no Part of africa

   the Settlement of Carysburg it may sute sum But it donot
suite me   it is a healthy Place   I belive it is an out of the way
place   in the first Place if the People makes more then they
want for themselves thir is no way to convate it to market
which is monrovia   thir is no other Place for them to sell such
things as they make for market But to live in Carysburg & to
have sutch things as you may wish to sell to have them Brought
20 miles to the river & 20 miles down to monrovia which is 40
miles   the Prophes is that is made is nothing so you see that
the People comes to this Country Poor & thay remaine Poor
Carysburg is not what it is Crakup to be   at last dear sir you
wish to have my advice about the Best Place for your People. my
dear sir do not give your servents all to girther to the society
do a little sumthing for them your self   when your six mounts
is up sick or well you must come out of that house   Evry man
that comes to this Country do not get over the fever in six
mounts nor twelve mounts   I must say as I think if you can
make sutch arangments which I no dout that you can that is to
settle your People on the road leading from the St Paule river to
Carysburg   it is good table land and good water and they can
settle from 2 miles to 5 miles on this road   this is the Best
Place for them   this land can be bought for 50 cents per acre
   I donot know of eny thing that could make me Happyer then

to see your People up by the side of eny People that has come to Liberia   I ware in hopes of seen sum of your People & my friends on Boarde of the Packet this trip   I ware sadly disorpiented but I Hopes to see them in shorte   now is the time if you wish to send your People to this Country   I know that it would be a great Pleasure to you to heare that your servents ware doing well in this Country now   settle your People on that road & you will have Pleasure with little Expence   I am glad to hear in your letter that they are doing Better then Ever as they has now come up to the mark that you wish them to come to   send them that thay may do sumthing for them selves the road to Carysburg is not compleat no Bridges on th[i]s road

mrs Faulcons People is heair & doing well as can Expect Leander the old man I have not see him as yet   he is on Board of the manofwar   his 3 Children is hear in Monrovia   the 2 girls is marread the Boy is working at the Carpners strade Jack & his Mother is heair   I will not say much about them you can Judge the Balence   no Cats & no gogs live worse a disgrace to our family   I do not ond them   they ought to be in the Back side of your cotton farm   mr Teirls People[1] is in Carysburg   I converse with sum of them when I vissit that Place   they told me of the great disavange in which they labers under

Matilda wish to be rememberd to you & freinds and says you have for goten her   you have not writen to her nor say eny thing in your letter about her   she will Be glad to resive sumthing from you By the returne of the Packet   I will write to you again in short at which time I will let you know sumthing about my farm & my prospect as for the Preaching of the Gospel   you must excuse this Bad writen letter as I am very nervis since I cormence this & now unto him that is able to keep me from falling and to Present me before the presence of his Glory with Exceeding Joy. Be Glory and majesty dominion and Power forever and ever aman

J. P. Skipwith

Source: Shields deposit, Cocke Papers
1. By his will James Terrell of Albemarle County, Virginia, emancipated almost ninety slaves. Sixty-eight of the freedmen and six who were purchased by the Terrell executor emigrated to Liberia in December, 1856, where most turned to farming.

PART II

LETTERS FROM ALABAMA
1847–1865

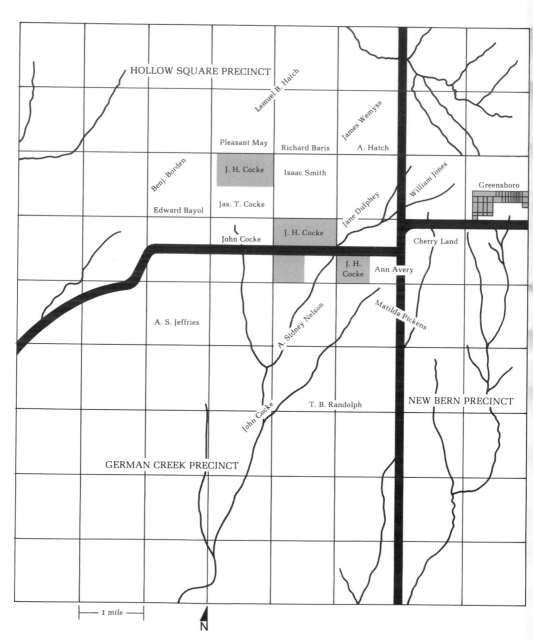

HOLLOW SQUARE PRECINCT

Lemuel B. Hatch

James Wemyss

Pleasant May

Richard Baris

A. Hatch

Benj. Borden

J. H. Cocke

Isaac Smith

William Jones

Greensboro

Edward Bayol

Jas. T. Cocke

Jane Dufphey

John Cocke

J. H. Cocke

Cherry Land

J. H. Cocke

Ann Avery

A. S. Jeffries

Matilda Pickens

A. Sidney Nelson

NEW BERN PRECINCT

John Cocke

T. B. Randolph

GERMAN CREEK PRECINCT

1 mile

N

Portion of V. Gayle Snedecor map of Greene County, Alabama, for 1855–1856, showing township twenty, range four east. Cocke's property, Hopewell and New Hope plantations, is marked by shaded areas. Ownership of nearby property is indicated. The numbers refer to section numbers; the heavy black lines indicate electoral districts.

The Driver

Wise planters never relaxed their search for talent among the slaves. The winnowing process of the well-managed Southern plantation sorted out the ambitious, intelligent, and proficient from the dull and the weak, and recruited the former for positions of trust and responsibility. These privileged slaves— artisans, house servants, drivers—served as intermediaries between the planter and the rest of the slave community, they exercised varying degrees of power, they learned vital skills of survival in a complex, hostile world. Knowing as they did the master's needs, and his vulnerability, they were the most dangerous of slaves. Given their adaptability and assimilation, they were also the most necessary to him.

None of these privileged bondsmen has been more misunderstood than the slave driver, the so-called policeman of the fields and quarters. To enforce discipline and guarantee performance in the fields, planters enlisted the support of slave foremen or drivers. On large plantations they worked as assistants to the overseers, and on smaller units they served immediately under the master. Generally, these men were of an imposing physical presence capable of commanding respect from the slaves. Armed with whip and outfitted in high leather boots and greatcoat—all emblematic of plantation authority— the driver pulsated with power. But physical coercion alone never moved slaves to industry. The drivers, therefore, were also elected for their intelligence and resourcefulness, sought out as men able to bargain, bribe, cajole, flatter, and, if need be, flog the slaves to perform their tasks and to refrain from acts destructive of order and harmony in the quarters.

On the whole, they were men who enjoyed the full confidence of their masters. Masters conferred with them on matters of farming and social arrangements and often deferred to their advice. Overseers as well were frequently governed by the driver's counsel, although the relationship between these two species of foremen was sometimes strained. A chorus of complaint came from Southern overseers that planters trusted the black driver more than the overseer and that in any dispute the planter favored the black over the white. The charge was justified. Planters considered overseers an expendable breed, and, indeed, overseers rarely lasted more than two or three seasons with any single master in the cotton South. The ubiquitous driver, however, stayed on as the master's man. Some drivers proved so skillful that planters dispensed with overseers altogether and entrusted the black driver with full managerial duties.

Cocke did so. Twice he elevated George Skipwith, the dark, secretive brother of Peyton, to sole control of his plantations. Regrettably, little is known of this elusive black man's early history; even his physical traits remain in doubt. We do know that he was a large man in physical proportions—and in ambition.

Cocke's first experience with George, who was sometimes described as clever and designing, portended later trouble. In 1830, George, aged twenty, replaced Cocke's overseer at the Upper Bremo place. Initially, as Cocke reported in a letter to his son, George was "a much more efficient agent than his predecessor," doubtless because of his leadership in temperance reform among the other slaves. George spent two prosperous, uneventful years running the tobacco plantation before succumbing to demon rum. After expiating for his sin, he was installed as headman on Cocke's Lower Bremo estate. In 1835, however, Cocke discovered George and several companions off the plantation at night without passes. During his examination George admitted to other breaches in discipline, including a second retreat from abstinence. Although George swore "never to indulge in anything intoxicating" again on pain of sale, Cocke administered "suitable" punishment and dismissed him from his duties. By 1840, George was restored to Cocke's confidence. In fact, Cocke entrusted him with the driver's duties at his Alabama plantation.

In 1840, forty-nine slaves, "of all sorts & sizes," set out from Bremo to Alabama, and thus inaugurated the Alabama experiment. No incident or sickness marred the seven-week march to

Cotton picking, 1898, in Alabama, similar to practices in the mid-nineteenth century. (Reproduced from the collection of the Library of Congress)

Alabama, and the overseer, Elam Tanner, sent back effusive praise of the devoutness and devotion of Cocke's children of Zion. The behavior of George and his daughter Lucy especially encouraged Tanner, who noted that they faithfully read five to six chapters in their Bibles nightly.

The several families arrived in Greene County, Alabama, in April. Tanner promptly hired out the slave artisans and set the remainder of the slaves to clearing land and planting corn. George registered displeasure with the hot, hard country, but the first year of the sojourn returned bounty rather than despair. The land yielded an abundant harvest, and no one died from the fevers of the Deep South.

In 1841, Cocke purchased a 320-acre half-section, intersected by two small creeks, near Greensboro. According to Cocke, the farm there was "in a shockingly disordered state," but he confidently expected that this land of periwinkle shells and marley clay would respond to careful husbandry. During the next decade Cocke added one thousand acres to his Black Belt estate, which by 1851 was complete and named, appropriately, Hopewell. In 1856, Cocke acquired another 480 acres of rich, virgin soil several miles north of Hopewell. He removed twenty slaves from Hopewell, including Lucy's husband, Armistead, to work the new plantation, New Hope. From 1858 to 1860, Armistead would run New Hope without a white overseer. The focus of Cocke's reform attention, however, fixed on Hopewell.

On a Sunday morning in March, 1841, after his first winter inspection of Hopewell, Cocke assembled his slaves and entered into an emancipation covenant. As Cocke relates in his journal for 1841, he addressed "his people" for two and one-half hours on "the high duty to their race and themselves devolving upon them." More to their immediate interest, he disclosed his emancipation plan. As soon as the slaves repaid their value, which Cocke calculated at $1400 including maintenance, he would free them, provided they had been throughout "honest & faithful," had forsaken all alcoholic beverages, and had not divulged his project to others. Cocke set forth the following five simple rules to govern their behavior at Hopewell: "No leaving the plantation without a written pass"; "No strange servants to be recd. without a pass"; "No fighting"; "Nor provoking language to be used one to another"; "Unconditional submission to the authorities I set over [you]." Each slave swore upon the Bible to observe the above regulations—a false promise as it turned out—and Cocke then "dismissed them to enter upon the Experiment."

The original slave force of forty-nine blacks grew steadily at Hopewell. According to Cocke's "List of Hands, Feb., 1845," there were fourteen men, thirteen women, five girls, and eleven children surviving from the original set. Twelve children had been born at Hopewell since 1840, although one died as an infant. By 1853 the slave force had increased to fifty-four blacks. Cocke's list of slaves for 1853 included seven mechanics and twenty-six working hands. The federal census for 1860 put the number of Cocke slaves in Greene County at seventy. Most of the slaves were prime hands in their twenties and thirties. Despite complaints of disease and trouble among the child-bearing women, the slave force continued to grow until emancipation. Generally there were about twenty to thirty working hands and between five and seven mechanics. The mechanics were especially valuable to Cocke because they were often hired out to other planters. Cocke relied on their earnings to offset losses from cotton production at Hopewell.

Cocke divided the management of his absentee cotton plantation between Elam Tanner, who survived an uncommonly long tenure of seven years, and his cousin John Cocke of Greene County, whom Cocke employed as a steward to regulate the overseer's activities and to market the crops. John Cocke served in this capacity until 1854, when Richard D. Powell of Columbus, Mississippi, who supervised Philip St. George Cocke's absentee Mississippi holdings, added Cocke's stewardship to his duties. Powell remained in this office through the Civil War. Ultimately, however, success in labor affairs and preparation for emancipation depended upon the genius and cooperation of the overseer and the driver.

Overseer Tanner, whom John Cocke thought "a little hair brained" and inexperienced, proved a weak match for the collective guile and wits of Cocke's slaves. Playing off the overseer against the driver and the master was an old game in the slave South, and the Hopewell slaves practiced it to a fine art. Among the slaves, for instance, Mike charged Tanner with cheating him on the cotton count, Janis ate dirt to render herself unfit for work, Frank stole and sold short to a white man in Greensboro, and Robert openly defied Tanner to whip him. To Cocke's dismay, each incident drew a more violent response from Tanner. This was sure admission of his failure to win respect.

Tanner's perpetual problem, however, was George Skipwith. Responsible for a separate slave force on land Cocke began renting in 1842, George limited Tanner's interference in his affairs. Clashes, however, were inevitable. Tanner related his side of the clashes in two letters he wrote to Cocke (April 9, 1843, and July 4, 1845). Checking up on George one Sunday evening, Tanner discovered a neighbor's slave visiting him without a pass. When he tried to correct George's guest, George "abruptly spoke," cautioning Tanner that he "had better be studdying about something that would profit" him. George informed Tanner that he "was not his master & had nothing to do there with him." Tanner had the driver "well lashed" for his insolence, but he feared that calm would never prevail as long as George controlled the rented place. Tanner despised George for his surface coolness and manly carriage, qualities he so desperately wanted, and he sniveled about how George "does just as he pleases & stand with his arms hugged up & look at me plane hard all day." To break the driver George, mused Tanner, was to win the whole game.

Tanner might have allied himself with George's enemies in the slave community. When drunk, George grew sullen and surly, and outraged or hurt one of the slaves. In an effort to loosen the driver's hold and to exact greater freedom for themselves—only ironically to wed themselves closer to the master—several slaves compromised George's reputation. In 1844, for example, Sucky whispered to Spencer, the blacksmith, that George had seduced Spencer's wife one wintry Friday night. Unluckily for Sucky, Tanner placed George at the cotton scale with him during the time in question. Fortified with this un-expected support, George challenged Sucky's tale, although he significantly relied upon black testimony to embarrass her repu-tation for veracity among the slaves. For two years Sucky had unsuccessfully contrived to revenge some past injustice, but her fabrication, plausible enough given George's later history of infidelity, fell short of the mark. It may, however, have sown further seeds of doubt in Tanner's mind. He initiated a closer review of George's private life, something sure to arouse the driver's ire. Sucky's invention also may have eroded George's standing in the quarters.

Whatever the case, Tanner had scant opportunity to exploit any advantage. This contrary, negligent man disgusted black and white with his constant complaints of some injury, real or imaginary. George hungered for Tanner's post and turned Tan-ner's many shortcomings to his own advantage. In 1842 for example, he attributed the low yields at Hopewell to Tanner's arrogant refusal to assist in the plowing and picking. In a letter to Cocke (March 13, 1842) Tanner rejoined that he worked "harder than any negro" in manual labor while Cocke asked nothing of George except supervisory duties. Cocke was un-convinced. He supported his driver. The tension between driver and overseer, however, eventually forced John Cocke's intercession in 1844, but the imposed peace proved shortlived.

However much master and slaves might allow Tanner his bawling and pretensions, they bridled at his sleeping with slave women. When Lucy Skipwith became pregnant with Betsey in 1844, blacks identified Tanner as the father. Complaints of Tanner's sexual advances became so loud they pierced Tanner's shell of distortions and falsehood. Tanner denied any sexual liaison, however casual, with blacks and insisted that Lucy had already acknowledged another man as the father. In his letters to Cocke Tanner tried to divert attention to the hapless girl, noting how she was "sorry that she has acted so contemtible" and was "fully aware" that Cocke had "lost all countenance of her." The perceptive Cocke commanded Tanner to do some repenting of his own and to find a white wife soon. Failing that, he must go.

Eventually, Tanner confessed to the crime. Throughout the controversy, however, he maintained that George had manufactured dark tales of barbarity and sexual improprieties in order to discredit him with Cocke. According to Tanner (Tanner to Cocke, July 4, 1845), George had tried for three years to persuade him to leave Cocke's employ, postulating how overseeing was a "poor calling." George conspired to drive Tanner off so that he could manage the place alone and "do as he pleases as he pretty much do now." When George realized that Tanner would not depart voluntarily, he invented the story of his paternity, confident that Cocke would "believe anything he said." In his letters to Cocke in 1844 and 1845, Tanner related other incidents in which George set him against Cocke and his steward with innuendo and false reports, and how, when ensnared in one lie, George would "tell a bigger one" by charging another slave with circulating the accounts.

Because of his profligacy, Tanner lost what little influence he had left among the slaves. Old Mary, George's wife, like any good mother, wanted her daughter Lucy wed and Tanner off the farm. In the rural slave society the loss of virginity constituted no great scandal; rather, marital infidelity and raising bastard children outside of a family unit violated slave community mores. If Lucy found a suitable husband, all would be forgiven and forgotten by the slaves. Tanner's letters also show the slaves' responses. According to Tanner, George ably summed up black feelings when he scolded him to "act like a white man and he [George] will do the negroes part."

Contrary to Cocke's directives, John Cocke did not cashier the overseer, because, as he reported to Cocke in September, 1845, he doubted George's ability to manage Hopewell alone. George's lackluster performance subsequent to Tanner's confession confirmed John Cocke in his prejudices. George refrained from corporal punishment and refused "to hurry up the hands" at picking time, contending that the slaves picked as much as they could and "none could beat him a great deal." In this, he was wiser than the steward, for George knew enough not to overtax the slaves' patience by demanding what could not be accomplished short of excessive coercion, if even then. George's retort to John Cocke makes explicit the driver's precarious position as mediator between the master's demands for what Eugene Genovese terms "clock-time work patterns" and the slaves' own seasonal, Nature–oriented work rhythms—a conflict, we learn below from George's letters, not easily resolved.

Tanner lingered long enough at Hopewell to witness the complete demoralization of the slaves. In 1846 the slaves took to their tasks with unwonted zeal, largely in expectation that the seventh crop, "the farthest time" before emancipation, meant that Cocke would fulfill his side of the bargain, but worms ate up the crop as well as any chance for an 1846 liberation. Morale and discipline disintegrated. Lucy and two other slave girls again carried children by white men, and several of the Hopewell men were caught sneaking off to carouse with slaves at John May's nearby plantation. George thus inherited an intolerable situation when he assumed sole control of Hopewell in November, 1846.

Cocke's failure to manumit any slaves in 1846, when combined with Tanner's removal, contributed to the delusion that the holiday season of 1846 conferred a license to extend freedom beyond the boundaries of the plantation. A restless lot, the slaves increased their nocturnal perambulations about the county. On December 29 at eleven in the evening, John Cocke surprised George with an inspection and learned that four slaves had slipped off to attend a quilting party at neighbor Dufphey's place. The discovery exposed George's tenuous hold as foreman, for he was accountable for a nightly cabin check. John Cocke warned George that if another slave stole out of the cabins after dark, he would suffer with the slave. John Cocke also threatend to take away privileges. This was a particularly effective means of dealing with men inured to violence and jealous of their few comforts. Another slave, Shadrach, for example, had been well willowed during the summer for his wanderlust, but, once penitent, was permitted to join George in singing, praying, and exhorting the slaves during devotions. Because of his December escapade, however, he forfeited his preaching privileges. The lesson of Shadrach did not escape George's attention.

Cocke entrusted considerable responsibility to George, as, indeed, he necessarily handed him awesome disciplinary powers. Through his driver, Cocke sought to inculcate proper standards of work and behavior in his slaves, who numbered about fifty in 1847, and he hoped to earn a fair return on his investments. Although the steward reviewed his work, George made all day-to-day decisions on farm management as well as meting out rewards and punishments. Whatever changes occurred in management, the daily tasks continued unbroken under the driver. He roused the slaves from slumber; determined the work pace for the several gangs; directed the marling, plowing, terracing, planting, and innumerable other farming operations; encouraged the slaves in their religious instruction; led devotions; and mediated family disputes—all of this and more. As such, George was at once the broker for the slaves' interests and the chief instrument of reconciliation of the field hands to the master's designs.

Power inhered in his office. To favorites he might parcel out extra rations or wink at minor indiscretions; to rivals he might act cruelly—and ruthlessly pursue every violation of the slaves' own code of conduct. But he wielded power only to a point, for when the driver's regime became tyrannical or overly dependent upon brute force, he ceased to serve his purpose for the master or the slaves. Planters like Cocke wanted stability and profits, not discord. Slaves wanted peace in the quarters. A factious slave population sabotaged farming arrangements, ran off, or dissembled in countless ways. To ensure his continued rule, then, the driver curried favor in both camps, black and

white. His justice had to remain even-handed, and his discipline be rooted in something more enduring than the lash—
namely community approbation. The driver was thus trapped
in the incompatibility existing between his swollen preroga-
tives on the one hand and the resistance on the other of his field
hands—at some physical cost to be sure—to his most extrava-
gant claims for deference.

In exchange for George's services, Cocke promised manumission. More immediately, he compensated George with
privileges, such as mobility and direct access to the master, and
rewards, such as superior housing and presents for his family.
Cocke also allowed his driver to sell the produce of his garden
in town for cash, which he could translate into greater material
comfort and status. Conspicuous consumption thus operated
for the driver, as it did for the master, to enhance his prestige
and to give sanction to his authority. George appreciated
Cocke's benevolence and the privileges granted him as driver.
In his first letter (May, 1847) written after assuming control
over Hopewell, George vowed again to remain vigilant in his
temperance, and he added, as if to assure his master that things
would run smoothly under his care: "my self and master John
gets on very smooth together."

Cocke demanded copious reports from George on Hopewell
operations. In an effort to demonstrate, de novo, his abilities
and to keep the master from excessive prying, George composed full recitals of the daily work routine. His letters, all
published below, provide rich descriptions of slave care and
scientific farming practices. In addition, the letters attest to the
immense store of practical farming knowledge possessed by
slaves, who took great pride in their accomplishments, and the
variety of work experiences beyond the corn and cotton culture
which were part of the slaves' work heritage. Most importantly,
the letters impart the feel and texture of Alabama plantation
life. On other matters George's epistolary vision was consciously narrow, discreet, and partial, but however unsatisfy-
ing in clarity, George's missives, through their interstices at
least, shed rare light on the driver's labor concerns and his
ambivalent feelings toward his job and the master class.

Cocke assiduously attempted to cultivate good relations with
his slaves and to create a *presence* among them by annual

winter visits and personal notes of praise and encouragement for exemplary performance. This was all part of the unwritten quid pro quo whereby the planter got his fields plowed, planted, hoed, picked, and the slaves' claims for autonomy and comfort were partially propitiated. The lack of runaways, of destruction of tools and property, of abuse of livestock, or of other traditional acts of overt rebelliousness among the slaves suggests that Cocke succeeded in convincing his driver and his slaves that his material interest was theirs as well. Besides George's commendations for his and the slaves' labors, there are appended messages to John Cocke's letters, not to mention those of Lucy, wherein slaves recorded their love for master and his family. How much of this was simply "puttin' on ole massa" in order to procure greater advantages we will never know, but the modest farming success at Hopewell, and later at New Hope, bespeaks something more than a gossamer fidelity on the part of George and the slaves.

Despite Cocke's studied efforts to civilize his slaves, slave contumacy at Hopewell surfaced during George's tenure as driver/overseer. In time, it led to the demise of his rule. One of the most revealing letters, which magnifies the ambiguities of the driver's disciplinary function and his need to retain his status in the slave community, is that of July 8, 1847, in which George recounts thrashing Robert and other alleged shirkers. By August 12, he could write that he no longer had reason "to complain about the behaviour of the people." To excuse his cruel treatment, he added that among "twenty or thirty hands there will be som times that a man will to spur them up." George did not forget the intervention of the preacher Isaac Taylor, a man who contravened his authority and undermined the plantation discipline which was so necessary for good crops and for good reports of managerial abilities. The driver moved with alacrity to undercut this rival for slave affections. The letter of November 18, 1847, nicely illustrates George's strategy and points up the driver's ability to eliminate undesirables from the plantation.

Despite George's suppression of information concerning slave affairs he considered outside Cocke's rightful purview, reports of slave malefactions found their way to the master, and a dispirited performance in 1847 further convinced Cocke to return to Alabama after a three-year absence. Cocke recorded his experience in his diaries for 1848 and 1849. He arrived in January, 1848, to find that George had transformed his experiment into "a Plantation Brothel." Venereal disease crippled the population, engaged as they were in a state of "almost indiscriminate sexual intercourse," and George had abandoned his wife and ten children to set up housekeeping with a young mistress. Worse, wrote Cocke, two of George's daughters cohabited with local "Southern Gentlemen," by whom each had borne bastard children. Confronted with these facts, George once more pledged temperance, constancy, and improved farm management. Cocke ordered all unwed couples living together to solemnize their union or risk sale, and in the case of one especially licentious slave girl, sale in Mobile proved the only remedy for her scandalous conduct.

All the Hopewell community suffered from George's lax moral example, for Cocke chose not to honor his manumission covenant. When Cocke outlined his plan of emancipation to the American Colonization Society in 1847, he explained that both the presence of illness among the slaves and the disappointing returns from cotton sales during this period of a downward price spiral retarded his emancipation progress, but that he expected twenty-five to thirty slaves would be ready to settle in Liberia. He promised that he would replace that number with a fresh contingent from his Virginia plantations and would continue the pattern until all his slaves were liberated. But his visit to Hopewell in 1848 opened his eyes to the appalling moral collapse among the slaves. In 1849 he lamented how none measured up to his standards of Victorian propriety and self-reliance. Few of them ever did. Only a handful of Cocke's slaves, ill-prepared for freedom he thought, ever realized the full promise of Hopewell.

Cocke demoted George to driver and brought Abram Perkins to Hopewell to monitor his activities. But, as George hints in his December, 1848, letter, reform did not ensue. In fact, George failed to end his drinking and frolicking, and plantation morality plummeted farther. When reports of miscegenation again emanated from Alabama in 1850, Cocke's patience evaporated. "Without remorse," as Cocke put it in his journal for 1850, he sold two of George's daughters, who were in his estimation "incorrigible strumpets." Cocke liked to believe that George professed satisfaction with the severe example he made of his "worthless Daughters," but the driver's growing addiction to alcohol and his indifference in the field argue otherwise.

The denouement of George's decline waited until Spring, 1850. Cocke's diary for 1850 tells this sad story. George and Spencer, both "drunk at a white man's House with whom they had been forbid to associate," became involved in a brawl. George got the worst of it, and he limped home so badly bruised that he was confined to his bed for many days. Informed of George's embarrassing circumstances, Cocke conceded his driver's irredemption. In the future Cocke would resort to the "exerable Overseer system" as the lesser evil. Cocke was distraught over his most trusted servant's long history of "perfidy, hypocrasy, & gross vice, added to drunkenness," but he consoled himself with the thought that with George's removal the prospect of "any more white bastards" among the slaves was greatly diminished.

Cocke blamed George alone for his daughters' vices and for the mayhem at Hopewell. Cocke's frustration was everywhere present in his diary entries. Unwilling to curb his tendency to enlarge his personal power, George created discord at Hopewell. He battened on the weak and helpless, and his disregard for his master's values was contagious. His quest for power induced fear and poisoned relations with other slaves. Morale declined. Cocke perceptively, if tardily, observed that power acted on George like strong drink. Unlike his brother Peyton, George preferred sure power to distant emancipation and indulged his own "libidinous and adulterous propensities," which, according to Cocke, he "vainly" expected to conceal by "practicing upon the fears & the criminal interests of the others, thus entering into a league of vice against themselves." The few slaves Cocke deemed in any way prepared for manumission and colonization included Shadrach, Robert and his wife, Champion, Becky Bird, and Sucky—none of whom had taken part in George's corrupting activities.

In 1851, Cocke renewed his manumission offer to the Hopewell community, who now included an additional twenty slaves from Virginia. To earn their freedom, the slaves must give evidence of honesty, "probity & good demeanor," and practice a "strict adherence to their temperance." Exasperated by what he labeled slave promiscuity, Cocke wryly commented in his diary for 1851 that he hoped the newcomers, "being more intelligent and virtuous than the original set," which is to say not privy to George's machinations, would inject a "good leven into the mass." To shield the slaves from George's "radical depravity," Cocke removed him from his "abused authority," and exiled him, Mary, and his young son, George, to Richard D. Powell's Columbus, Mississippi, plantation. There George struggled to conquer his drinking problem and otherwise lived in quiet obscurity until Reconstruction days.

Slave drivers have not fared well in our histories of the South's peculiar institution. The prevailing neoabolitionist historiography has limned a portrait of the driver as an unscrupulous, brutal, even sadistic, betrayer of his race—in a word, a diabolical Tom. George was nothing of the sort. While his behavior will not rehabilitate the image and reputation of the driver, it does show the ambiguities and paradoxes of the slave system and the driver's torn loyalties. George evinced recalcitrance and accommodation, deception and respect, as did other slaves. Cocke recognized this painful truth and bore George's lapses with resignation. Rather than disrupt clear lines of authority long established and carefully nurtured—for the complexities of the slave system could never be fathomed and resolved without the assistance of a functioning headman among the slaves—Cocke permitted his driver to remain in office after each lapse with the promise of a reversion to right ways. Only reluctantly did the master discharge his driver, since the training of a new slave foreman promised much effort, confusion, and suffering for slaves and master. To read the diaries and correspondence of other planters is to discern a dependence, sometimes blind, upon the driver and a reluctance to clog the social-control mechanism of the plantation. And to read the letters of other drivers is to observe similar blurred lines of loyalty and abuse of power, as found in George's writings, but it is also to appreciate, as with George, the fertile areas of discussion open to both races.

Letters from George Skipwith*

may the 11 [1847] green County Ala

Sir

I imbrace this oppertunity to write you a few lines. I Reseved your letter and should have anserd it before now but master John[1] was from home on busness and I could not write untel he returned wich was last Sunday. You told me in your letter that you was glad that I had the management of the farm my self, and you said that you noed that I was able to do as you and master John wish providing that I would not make use of ardent spirits, but I am convinced that it has been my greatest enemy and I shall consider it so as long as I live. We have not been able to do any thing towards marling our land[2]   our team could not be spared from farming except wet spells and it would be too wet for hauling, and master John thougt we could do as good busines by toating leaves to put on the poorest partes of the land by the spare hands and we put down two thousand and five hndred baskets full weighing from thirty five to forty, and thirty cart load out of the farm pen, and ninety óut of the horse lot. We have a very good stand of cotton, but it has been so cold that it does not grow but our corn cannot be beaten and about three days from now we will finish plowing our corn the second time and our peas. we will be then reddy to commence plowing our cotton the second time. it has been about a week since the hoes started over the second time. our oats crop hav been somwhat backward but we had a very fine rane and I am in hopes they will start to growing again. Lee[3] and archa[4] hav been working with us for sum time building a screw whiat looks very fine   I have not herd any thing from brother peyton sence you was out here   I should be very glad to hear when

*Ed. Note: Unless otherwise specified, all letters are addressed to John Hartwell Cocke.

you herd from him   We are all well and hav had no call for a docter this year and I hope that you will reseve this letter in good helth   my self and master John gets on very smooth together   he have not given me a cross worde this year. give my love to every boddy boath white and black and beleave me to be your umble servant

George Skipwith

Source: #2433-B Cocke deposit, Cocke Papers

1. John Cocke of Greene County, Alabama, was Cocke's neighbor and a distant relative. He was a planter of considerable means who also served as Cocke's steward for many years.

2. Marl—calcareous matter from marine deposits—was used to eliminate acid in the soil and to hold the properties of organic manures in the soil. Cocke experimented with marl on all his plantations. He established a marling corps among his slaves. At Hopewell they regularly dug marl and carted it to the fields. Cocke initially recommended applying 200 bushels of marl to the acre, later doubed the rate of application with little success, and finally settled on 300 bushels of marl per acre as the proper amount. Marling was only part of Cocke's effort to reclaim the fertility of the soil. He was also careful to include the application of organic manures to the soil and to practice crop rotation as key elements of his soil-enrichment program at Hopewell. By the late 1850s, Cocke's program took effect and significantly increased the crop yields at Hopewell.

3. Leander Creacy (or Creasey) was born in 1815 at Bremo, where he learned carpentry. When not employed at Hopewell, he hired out his time in the county. Leander lived with his children in Greene County through 1880.

4. Archer Creacy (or Creasey) from Virginia was Leander's younger brother by five years. He worked as a carpenter and also hired out his time during slack seasons at Hopewell. In 1857 he removed to Cocke's New Hope plantation with his wife Betty and infant son Jame. After the war he rented the plantation shops and local land and accumulated a small personal estate of $300 by 1870. As late as 1880 he continued to live among Cocke's former slaves near the Hopewell site.

June the 17 1847

Sir

I would hav written to you a few days suner but i was wating to see if you found any fault in my letter or not   I hav nothing perticulerly to say more than how we have spent our time sence i wrote to you. I mentioned in my letter that i could not write untel mas John returned but i signed no reason. I will now sign my reason   I wanted mas John to see my letters so that you may knoe that what I write is so. I hav ploued my cotten over the second time putting four furrows in a roe with the sweeps and we will finish in three days from to day   the hoes will also finish the last of this week or the first of next the third time in the cotten. then you may considder your cotten crop out of the danger of grass, tho we have had grass and a plenty of it and so has every boddy in green County for grass hav never growed so before. the Lice hav ingured the cotten cropes in our naberhood very much. they hav been very plentyful with us but hav not done us no great damage. mas John told me to chop it out in large bunches and that was all that saved it. it is now growing and ses it is the best cotten he has seen. I hav also ploued my corn the third time and hav laid it by and i dont see any thing to pervent us from makine an elogent crop of corn for it [is] much such a crop as we made the first year that we come into the country and it is praised by every boddy that speakes about it. there was about thirty acers of sandy land corn that was too thick, and mas John told me to thin it out and give it the second working over with the hoes and i hav don so and it is improve-ing every day. we expect rane every day and if we can get it in eight or ten days I shall not dought it for a moment. I Thought at one time that our oats would not be worth cutting but they mend very fast and I think that we will make a pretty good crope. I think that our last years crope will last us untel the new crope comes. our potatoes looks better this year than any we hav had since we hav been into this country   our muls stands well after hard driven and i can shoe them all with second sholders except too. I hav ten regelar worke muls but I hav been oblige to worke the three mares and the horse utill, but i can spell them in a few days. we hav six young coalts   amonge them are four horse coalts two of them which will be three years old this coming spring   they are boath very likely coalts. the other too, one is about ten days old and the other about a year old. we also hav two filies among them   one is two years old and the other is one year old, and the one at one year old is the finest colt I ever saw. I hav sixty hogs for this years killing. our fouls hav failed this year   we have hatched hundreds of turkeys and chickins but the Rats destroied them all so that we have not raised none. we are all well and hav had no sickness since i wrote except Spencer[1] he is got a risen hand, and i am in hopes that this letter will fine them all as well there as they are here. Lee and Archa are done ther Job at home (haveing Quitt cotton Prep) and are hierd out.[2] Remember me to the family boath black and white a[nd] Beleave me your servant

George Skipwith

Source: #2433-B Cocke deposit, Cocke Papers

1. Spencer Kellor (b. 1815?) was the plantation blacksmith and by 1858 was the recognized "head man" among the slaves. He was much affected by Rev. F. M. Crain's preaching and experienced a powerful conversion. During the war he added hog raising to his duties, but, much to the chagrin of the other slaves, he lost nineteen due to disease and carelessness. After the war he joined Archer Creacy in renting the Hopewell machine shop and several acres of land, and he prospered sufficiently to amass $250 worth of personal property by 1870. The 1880 census records reveal that he continued in his smithing operations and lived among the Hopewell community survivors.

2. Hiring out was a common practice in the Old South. The shortage of skilled workers in the South and the small farmers' need for labor created a demand for hired slaves in the rural areas. Planters with surplus slaves, or particularly skilled slaves, often hired them out to other planters or nonslaveholding farmers. The contracts for hire varied according to occupation and locale. In the rural South skilled slaves were often hired out to complete a particular job. Some were hired out for the entire year. The slaves turned their earnings over to their masters, but they generally were allowed to keep small amounts as rewards for good service. Surplus slaves were generally hired out on an annual basis. For a fuller discussion of the reasons for hiring out slaves and the mechanics of the system see Kenneth M. Stampp, *The Peculiar Institution: Slavery in the Ante-Bellum South* (New York, 1956), pp. 67–73.

hopewell   July the 8 1847

Sir

on the forth day of July I reseved your letter dated may the 25. I wrote to yo the 15 of June the second time giveing you a true statement of the crops, horses, hogs, and chickeins but I am sorry that I shall have to write yo princerble about other matters. I hav a good crop on hand for you, boath of cotten and corn. this you knoe could not be don without hard worke. I have worked the people but not out of reason, and I have whiped none without a caus   the persons whome I have correct I will tell you thir name and thir faults.

Suky[1] who I put to plant som corn and after she had been there long anuf to hav been done I went there and she had hardly began it   I gave her som four or five licks over her clothes   I gave isham[2] too licks over his clothes for covering up cotton with the plow.

I put frank,[3] isham, violly,[4] Dinah[5] Jinny[6] evealine[7] and Charlott[8] to Sweeping cotten going twice in a roe, and at a Reasonable days worke they aught to hav plowed seven accers a peice, and they had been at it a half of a day, and they had not done more than one accer and a half and I gave them ten licks a peace upon thir skins   I gave Julyann[9] eight or ten licks for misplacing her hoe. that was all the whiping I hav done from the time that I pitched the crop untell we comenced cutting oats. I put Shadrack,[10] Robert,[11] Armstead,[12] and frank to cutting. they comemince on friday, but they did not more than urn the salt in thir bread, but the next morning i went out there and staid untill a late breackfast, and i saw that the lick that they had then, they were about to do a pretty good days worke. I then leave them and went to the hoe hands, marking the last roe they cut while I was there. when I come to them at twelve o clocke, they had cut me nineteen roes, and it would not take them more than ten minits to cut one roe   as Shedrack was the ruler among them, I spoke these words to him. you do not intend to cut these oats untill I whip every one of you. Shedrack did not say any thing to me, but Robert spoke these words saying that he knoed when he worked. I told him to shut his lips and if he spoke a nother worde I would whip him right of[f] but he spoke again the second time saying that he was not afraid of being whiped by no man. I then gave him a cut with the whip. he then flong down his cradle, and made a oath and said that he had as live die as to live and he said that he did not intend to stay here. he then tried to take the whip out of my hand, but I caught him fast by the collar and holed him. I then told the other boys to stripe him and they don so   I then whiped untell I thought that he was pretty could but I was desieved for as soon as I leave him and went to the hoe hands, he come of to the house to our preacher[13] and his family becaus he knoed that they would protect him in his Rascality for he had herd that they had said that they were worked to death, and that they were lowed no more chance for liveing than if they were dogs or hogs. tho the preacher did not say any thing to me about whiping Robert neither to mas John but went down to the shop and holed about an hours chat with the negros   I do not knoe what his chat was to them but [he] ask Dr Weeb[14] what was good for a negro that was whipt albut to death, and he had much to say about it   Dr Weeb saw that his chat was calculated to incurage the people to rebel aganst me, and he went and told mas John about what he had herd and mas John took him and come up here to see if he was punised in the way that he had herd, but as soon as the Dr put his hand apon him, he told mas John that there was nothing the matter with him. mas John then ordered him to his worke and told him that he did not have what his crime was deserving him, and at som lasure time he intend to give him a good willering and then he would knoe how to behave him self. he rode over the land and saw what they had done and instead of finding fault of me he said I ought to have given the other three the same

we did not plant any ceaders last winter becaus we had a great deal of fencing to do that was oblige to be done for we have Joined fences with mr Smith[15] for he would not keep a good fence and his stork was often in our crops. mas John said that he would not be plaged with him no longer, to make my fence the whole line out and he gave me a half a mile of fence and was to hawl them at every lasure chance and the nearist rails was a mile and a half and from that to a mile and three quarters

I have not room to write you as I would wish. I will inform you in my next letter what fenceing I have done. then you can Judge whither I had any time or not. I have a nuf yet to write you to fill up another Sheat. permit me to say a few words to you in James[16] letter. we have our family worship every morning. Beleave me to be your servant

George Skipwith

Source: #2433-B Cocke deposit, Cocke Papers

1. Ann Sucky Faulcon (b. 1803) often vexed overseer Elam Tanner by her accusations and antics, but earned Cocke's confidence so that he liberated her in 1851. On her Liberian experiences see Letters from Liberia, above, and her letters in the Cocke Papers.

2. Isham Gault (b. 1810) was a field worker at Hopewell who had worked as a cowherder at Bremo. After the war he returned to his original occupation. He was the father of Hannah and the brother of Julyann and Mima.

3. Frank Randall, the son of Primus the driver at Bremo, worked as a brick mason, a ditcher, a field hand, and a marler. In 1842 he carried on a clandestine

courtship off the plantation, in 1844 he cheated a white man in a sale and resisted Tanner, in 1846 he left Hopewell without a pass, and on other occasions he was among those described as unworthy of manumission. In 1853 Cocke ordered him sold or hired out in Mobile because of his repeated quarrels with his wife Jinny and his refractory character.

4. Violly was a field worker.

5. Dinah was a field worker.

6. Jinny Randall, Frank's wife, was a field worker. With her husband, she was sold or hired out in Mobile in 1853.

7. Evelina Smith (b. 1821?) was a field worker who professed religion in 1853. According to the 1870 census, she lived with the Archer Creacy family and worked as a farm laborer after the war.

8. Charlotte (Morse) Lewis (b. 1834) was the daughter of Charles and Kessiah Morse and the sister of Albert, Cain, Carter, Charles, Jr., Frederick, and Matthew. In 1844 she married Robert Lewis, and in 1857 they went to New Hope plantation to live. After the war she scratched out a living as a farm laborer in the Greensboro area.

9. Julyann Cault, the daughter of "Old" Hannah and sister of Isham and Mima, was a field worker.

10. Shadrach Cocke (d. 1855) was a prayer leader and exhorter among the slaves and the driver after George's downfall. In 1842 he wrote Cocke asking permission to marry a woman on another farm, but Cocke refused. According to Tanner, Shadrach spoke "very bad" about the master's decision and, rather than give up the girl, he asked to be sold to her master. Tanner wrote that he ran "mad for 2 days" in disappointment. He involved himself in other scrapes in the next few years, but by 1850, probably as a result of his conversion, he mellowed and won Cocke's confidence. He died suddenly in 1855 of a "disease of the heart." On Shadrach's marriage difficulties see Shadrach Cocke to JHC, March 27, 1842, Cocke deposit, Cocke Papers; and Robert Elam Tanner to JHC, June 1, 1842, May 8, 1843, Cocke deposit, Cocke Papers.

11. Robert Lewis, husband of Charlotte, "cut up a few skins" in physically resisting Tanner in 1844, the only evidence of stubborn resistance prior to the affair described in George's letter. In 1856 he was whipped for feigning illness, and in 1862 he stole swine from Capt. John Cocke's farm. Still, John Hartwell Cocke considered him a likely candidate for freedom. In 1857 he joined the New Hope community.

12. Armistead Hewitt (b. 1814) was a field worker and carpenter at Hopewell and the driver at New Hope after 1857. In 1846 he received a thorough willowing for sneaking off the plantation, and, later, he had numerous falling-outs with overseers, particularly J. W. Carter. For a good description of one of the schemes Armistead and his fellow travelers employed against Carter see William K. Scarborough, *The Overseer: Plantation Management in the Old South* (Baton Rouge, 1966), 80. He married Lucy Skipwith, George's daughter, in the late 1840s or early 1850s. There is no positive record of more than one child by the marriage. Lucy's eldest daughters, Maria and Betsey, were fathered by white men, and the father of her daughter Dinah is unknown. Lucy's liaisons with white men and her attachment to Cocke may have been the causes of her unhappy relations with Armistead. She left him after the war (see her letter of December 7, 1865). Armistead married a second time after the war.

13. Rev. Isaac Taylor (1802–1874?), a Methodist minister hired by Cocke to live at Hopewell and to preach to the slaves of the neighborhood. He held a low opinion of the Hopewell slaves' moral values and particularly disliked George's

influence. See Isaac Taylor to JHC, August 17, 1847, Cocke deposit, Cocke Papers.

14. Dr. William T. Webb (1815–1883) of Greensboro provided medical care for the Cocke plantations in Alabama. He had a reputation as a skilled physician.

15. Isaac Smith, a neighbor.

16. James Skipwith, George's son, was then living at Hopewell.

Hopewell   August the 12 1847

Sir

I Reseved your letter a few days ago, and thir has been no sickness among us sence I wrote to you last. I told you in my last letter, that when I write to you again I would tell you what fenceing I done last winter so that you mought knoe what time I had to spare. I had to make a stob fence between me and mr Smith, a stob fence between the meltons and Sawyers track[1] the hole line out, a stob fence from the corner of the garden up to meltons, a stob fence from the house lot down to the widder Dufpheys[2] line, and the rails had to be hawled from the fence that devides mas John and mr may.[3] I had to hawl a hundred cords of wood for burning brick and the timber to hawl from mas Johns to build the screw, had to hawl twelve loads of lime rock between twelve or thirten miles, and this kept my team busy every hour that they could be spared from the farm. I hav been working with my forder nine days to day, and I shall finish it to day   I have put up thirty stacks and I think that there will be three or four more. the stacks are what I call duble stacks. I am now able to give you a true acount of my corn for it is the best crop I have made sence I have been to this country, and if my cotten turns out as well as my corn I know that you will be pleased and I have every reason to beleave that it will. you shall be no longer disapointted about the marl for thir shall not a nother sun set before I commence about it. I do not knoe how long I shall be able to worke at it, for I am expecting to be cawled of every day to worke the rode, and we will have to worke there a week, and after we worke there a week there will be no more time for Jobs, for our cotten is opening in spots now, and when we commence on that we shall have no more time to spare wet nor dry, for in bad weather we are gining, packing and geting trash out of the cotten.[4] I should like to knoe whither you reseved my second letter or not, which I wrote in Jun   I wrote princeble about the stork and if you have not reseved it I shall be compeled to write you again. I have no reason to complain about the behaviour of the people in this letter. thir has none violate from thir pledge to my knowing. I know that you manage your afars with a very littlo fighting, and I trioo to patern after you, but you knoe that amoung twenty or thirty hands there will be som times that a man will to spur them up   I Remane your servant

George

Source: #2433 B Cocke deposit, Cocke Papers

1. John Melton and Rev. J. E. Sawyer, neighbors to Cocke.

2. Jane Dufphey (1803?–1862), originally from North Carolina, owned a modest plantation adjacent to Hopewell. On several occasions the Hopewell slaves visited slaves on her estate.

3. John May, a planter living nearby.

4. Picking cotton in the South began in late summer or early fall and lasted into January. Weather conditions and the stamina and dexterity of the individual worker determined the worker's pace and productivity. The Hopewell picking force averaged about five bales per hand, a good but not exceptional rate for Alabama. Reliable figures showing the picking productivity of individual slaves at Hopewell and New Hope are not available.

It is difficult to gauge the productivity of the slaves. Cotton planters generally planted cotton according to the size of their picking force. The quality of the soil, climate, topography of the land, and particular strains of seed all varied from place to place and affected the size and quality of the crop, but in Alabama a full-grown field hand was expected to cultivate between three and ten acres of cotton. Cocke originally planned to put in three hundred acres of cotton at Hopewell, or about ten acres per prime field hand. A string of poor crops, partly due to the vexatious managerial problems at Hopewell, led Cocke to reduce the total cotton acreage by half in 1855. By 1860, however, he had increased the land planted in cotton to 270 acres. He also had eighty acres of cotton planted at New Hope in 1860.

Cotton prices fluctuated wildly throughout the 1840s and 1850s, but until the mid-1850s prices tended to go down. Cocke struggled with low yields and low profits. The worst year was 1847, when Hopewell produced only thirty bales of cotton—a bale weighing about 500 pounds. Yields were erratic. Late planting, worms, drought, excessive rain, and poor management all took their toll. Indeed, between 1846 and 1855, Hopewell did not have a single one hundred bale year. The poor performance cut sharply into profits. In 1848, for example, Cocke earned only $2000 from cotton sales at Hopewell. Against this small sum, he had to pay for all his plantation expenses. Conditions improved in 1856 and continued to do so thereafter. Prices rose, and Hopewell produced higher yields. But it was too late to salvage the Hopewell experiment. The slaves had not earned enough to purchase their freedom, and Cocke's commitment to his emancipation goals sagged over the years.

hopewell Sept the 8 1847

Sir

Yours come to hand too days ago dated august 28 and I was glad to hear that you all were well. we have som six or eight sick since I wrote to you last   the greatist part of them was atacked by the fever, but mas John attended and give medicin him self, and have got them up again without the help of a Docter.

my horces are improveing very fast and I have loosed none, and I think that we will have three more coalts by our mares next spring. the coalt that we got from the mare gusty that you drove out here is a fine coalt and there is no dought about it he is a dark bay and not a white hare about him. his legs are black and he has a very fine tale. we have fifteen cows intended for milk cows. we hav nine calves about a year old and three come this week, and four work oxen. this is the stork of cattle that we have on hand. my hogs are small   we burnt upwards of a hundred and fifty thousand brick but we are not called apon for them often   I hav sold eight thousand three hundred and fifty   we hav had worms in our cotten from the 15 of august untell now, and they have alreddy ruined our crops about that time that I wrote to you last mas John rode over my crope and he said that he thought that we would make as much as we could pick out   it is true that the worms hav not eaten the leaves as they did last year but they confine them selve to the bowls   I should not hav been out of hart altho the worms had done such great ingare I had old bowl anuf to make me a tolerble good crope, but the hole of august hav been wet cold damp weather   there have not been too fair days togeather since I wrote to you last and my cotten being very large instead of opening it mildews and rots. for the greatist part of my crops you cannot see Daniels init not five steps from him   I do not noe how to make a calculation about my crop for in som places there is not a bowl on a stork six or eight feet high, and in other places yo will find a stork of the same hight haning with bowls. I hav been fearful that we would not make no more than we did last year but I am in hopes that I may be deseved by my cotten being so large   I commenced picking the 2[8?] of august and hav geathered forteen thousand and too hundred. we hav commence apon our marl pit and as soo as we can get our cotten tolerble strait mas John says that he intends to put a cart to hawl it out. we menured our corn land instead of the cotten

I am very much obliged to you for your kindness to me towards James and tell him that I reseved his last letter.[1] I shoed mr Taylor your letter before this and he told me that he had wrote to you. I remane your servant

George

Source: #2433-B Cocke deposit, Cocke Papers
1. James, George's son, had returned to Virginia briefly, although the circumstances of his trip are unknown.

Hopewell   oct the 20 1847

Sir

I would have writen to you before now, but I hav been waiting for an answer to my last letter but I hav not reseved one yet. There has been a great deal of sickness among us since I wrote to you last but mas John Docttered them all except one case which the Docter made three light visits. the naberhood is very sickly and there has been a great many Deaths boath black and white, but ours are all well except too who are complaining a little. you must not expect nothing but a short crop of cotten, for I am convinced that we shant make no more than we did last year, for this is the case in every farm in our naberhood. mr John may who put in his crop for three hundred bags, I am told that he will not make more than sixty   the widder Dufphey pitched her crop for a hundred and fifty wont make more than thirty. I dont knoe what mas John and mas Thomas[1] turn out will be, but I am told that they will make short crops. I have geatherd fifty thousand weighg of cotton   I have packed sixteen bags. I have geatherd three forths of my corn and it turns out very well   I hav housed five hundred and twenty barriell. I have geatherd about too hundred bushells of seed peas and there will be a handred and fifty bushell more than we shall want and they will fetch us a Dollar a bushells from any boddy that will buy them next spring   we have not had a killing frost this fall   it is yet summer weather and if it continyo so too or three days longer I shall be able to fattne me hogs on peas. we were called a pon to day for fifteen hundred brick but I find that the brick want more than half burnt

I think that you will be pleased at the order of my mares when you come out this winter for the sorell filly looks better than I ever saw her. give my love to my mother   tell her that I am well and that I have not had a half of an hours sickness since you was in alabama. beleave to be your servant

George Skipwith

Source: #2433-B, Cocke deposit, Cocke Papers
  1. James Thomas B. Cocke (b. 1826), brother of John Cocke of Alabama, was a planter of some means near Hopewell.

Hopewell   Nov 18 1847

Sir

yours come to hand a few day ago, and I am sorry that you complain of not hearing from me once a month. the fault must be in the male for I have wrote to you every month sence I wrote my first letter   it is true I always wait som too or three days to see if I can get a letter or not but I always low my self time anuf to write you the same month

I did not give you any understanding about the marl when I wrote to you last, but you need not take it for granted that I have givein the Job out. it is true from our short cotten crop that we could have spared som hands about the marl, but we thought it was to your intress to put it off a while and imploy the hands another way. we knoe that fodder is always worth from six bits to a dollar a hundred and we thought that it was best to imploy the spare hands poling hay, so that would enable you to sell the fodder, and we are able now to spare you half of our fodder or little more   I have geatherd the balance of my corn which amounts to one hundred and twenty barrells   I have hawled up all of my fodder and have restaked it puting too stakes in one and I have now seventeen very large staks   I have paked twenty eight bags of cotten and they will avrige over five hundred and I have hawled the last load to the river to day and I think that there will be nine or ten more in the field   I have commenced digeing my potatoes but was stoped to day by the rain   I have diged four hundred bushells of eating roots besids the cut roots and seed, and I think there will be upwards of a hundred bushells more of eating roots excuseing the seed

I think that I have got too hundred bushells of seed peas, and master John was up here monday and we hav made our araing-ement and there will no Job come next before the hawling of the corn storks in to the farm yards and the marling. I knoe sir that you thought strainge of my not writeing to you about the minis-ter who we had with us but as I could not say any thing that would pleas you about him I thought that it was best to say nothing. I knoe that you always did think hily of ministers and christians   I cant say that mr Taylor was not a christian but he aked very comical the time he was with us   master John gave orders for a mare to be turned into the yard and after he knoed that it was master orders for it to be don he said that she should not stay in here and he turned her in the woods   master John toled me that after we had geatherd our corn that there was nothing to be turned in the field but the fattening hogs and the three mars   mr Taylor said that his mare should stay in there and he keep her in there   master John toled him also that he did not want him to interfear with the horces at the time of worke but if him or his family wanted a horse to go to church that he could get them at any time when they was not at worke but he was not to carry them of[f] of the land without his know-ing of it but he took one of the mares three diferent times and rode up to his plantation which was about eightteen or twenty miles and the last time he leave her up there a week at a time   I knoe sir that mr Taylor has don more harm amoung our people than he has don good for he says that we are treated worse than any peopel in the world and if there is any in the world treated any worse he has never herde talk of them and this he says he will tell to every boddy that ask him any thing about us. he has spoken very free about the matter and master John saw that he was doing more harm than he was doing good and he turned him off   I have writen you now the truth sir and you can Judge for your self

we are all well and there has been none married sence you was out here. I have done the best I could and I knoe master John is a man of truth and I shall be sattisfied with what ever correction he gives me   I would be very glad sir if it sute you as well to bring william[1] with you   I want to see him very bad   there has none profest religon sence you was out here   I remane your servant

George Skipwith

Source: #2433-B Cocke deposit, Cocke Papers
1. William Skipwith, George's son, was working as a stonemason at Bremo.

Hopewell   December the 26 1847

Sir

I wrote to you the 20 of last month and there has been no sickness amoung us since I wrote to you last   frank has put up Brick chimneys to all of the houses in the yard. he is now got a smal Job for mr parker[1] but he will finish it in a few days. Lea and Archa hav been hierd out for severl months. I hav been imployed all of my Lasure minits in search of the marl and I find it betwenn three and four feet deep   the stuff that I am now hauling hav every apearance of lime with a mixture of shells init   it is tolerble hard but when it is exposed to the sun it becoms very soft   I hav also been haulling corn storks into the farm yards   I started my plowes to brakeing up grown about a week a go   I hav killed twenty too of my hogs   it made me three thousand weight   I hav twenty eight more to kill which I shall kill in a few days if it keeps cold a nuf   one of the coalts hav died since I wrote to you but he has been lingering a long time. there has been a great storm in the Joining county and it don great damage   it blowed down gin houses Dwelling houses killed people and severl mules. give my love all boath black and white. I Remane your servant

George Skipwith

there is nothing like marl to be found on the sandy land   I hav tried beter than five feet but it can be found on the post oak land   I do not know whither you reseved my last letter or not but i hav writen to you reaglar every month   let me knoe when you hav herd any thing from brother peyton

Source: #2433-B, Cocke deposit, Cocke Papers
1. Unable to identify.

Hopewell December the 26 1847

Sir; i wrote to you the 20 of last month
and there has been no sickness among us since i
wrote to you last frank has put up brick chimneys
to all of the houses in the yard he is now
got a small Job for mr parker but he will
finish it in a few days. Lea and Archa has been
hired out for several months. i has been imployed
all of my Lasure minits in search of the marl
and i find it between three and four feet deep
the stuff that i am now hauling has every
apearence of lime with a mixture of shells in it
it is tolerable hard but when it is exposed to the
sun it becoms very soft; i has also been
haulling corn storks into the farm yards
i started my plowes to breaking up groun
about a week ago i has killed twenty two of
my hogs it made me three thousand weight
i has twenty eight more to kill which i
shall kill in a few days if it keeps cold
a nof one of the coalts has died since i
wrote to you but he has been lingering a
long time. there has been a great storm
in Joining county and it don great damage it
blowed down gin houses dwelling houses killed
people and several mules. give my love all
both black and white i Remane your servant
George Skipwith

George Skipwith's letter to John Hartwell Cocke, Hopewell, December 26, 1847. (From the Cocke Papers, University of Virginia Library, Manuscript Division)

Hopewell   april the 15 1848

Sir

I would have written to you before now but mas Thomas told me that he had written to you a few days ago and I was very busy and I did not write before now   I finished planting my cotten to day   I hav planted the cut that we menured when you was out here with the seed that come from Dr Withers.[1] I planted the pettygulf seed on the right hand side of the road from the marl pit down to the old horse lot. I hav cleared the half an acker that you said that you wanted cleared at the marl pit. I hav put marl on all of the places that you spoke about which amountted to fifteen ackers all at a dubble rate but three. my first cotten is up and I cannot ask for a better stand and I shall commence to morrow in my corn with all hands, and it is the best stand that I ever had except a few wet places. the first field of oats looks well and the others are improveing. I see som few of the oranges seed that are up som of the last that were planted   we hav had one or too hard rains since you leave and have filled up every Ditch that Frank cut down on the low side of road. the married people gets on very smooth togeathear and keeps themselvs and thir rooms very clean   Lea and Archa thoughted that they had timber anuf to moove them houses but when they come to pull them down there was so much more timber rotten than they calculated they had to go in the woods to get more but they will commence about them in a few days.[2] I hav attend the coalts and they are out of all danger. the Bull of mr Bordens[3] died the sundy night folering after you leav with the cholic   the Balance of the stock are all thriveing.

uncy[4] is sick at preasont and have binn for four or five days the Balance of the people big and small are all well. Lucy is dutiful to her intfant school and she says martha[5] and my little george[6] are the too smartist ons about learning   I have nothing more to say at preasant but remane your servant

George Skipwith

Source: #2433-B Cocke deposit, Cocke Papers

1. Dr. Robert W. Withers (d. 1854) was a physician, mill owner, and planter. He had a plantation near Hopewell.

2. For hygienic purposes, Cocke instructed his overseers and drivers to relocate the slave cabins periodically.

3. Benjamin Borden (b. 1802), a wealthy planter whose property was near New Hope.

4. Unable to identify.

5. Martha Skipwith (b. 1837), George's daughter, became a house servant at Hopewell and married Albert Morse (or Moss). In 1870 she and Albert and their three children lived near the Hopewell site.

6. "Little" George Skipwith, George's youngest son, was several times recognized as a strong student. In 1851 he removed to Mississippi with his parents, but he later returned to Hopewell to continue his education. His work as a coachman and wagoner allowed him to jockey between Hopewell and the Powell plantation in Mississippi. He died in 1857 after a fall from a building. Apparently, poor medical attention hampered his recovery.

hopewell   may the 6 1848

Sir

I have worked over my corn with the hoes and plows since I wrote to yo last and I have started over my cotton to day with my plows the seccond time I have been over my cotton down here with my hoes and I will start monday at meltons and I have got a good stand at boath places except about ten ackers that I marled at a dubble rate that is a dredful bad stand. my corn is as good as it was last year and my oats is far better. there is a very few of the sedars that you planted in the yard is liveing but the Locost is doing very well   there is a few of the fig trees liveing in the garden. the orange trees that you sat out in the garden is doing very well but the seed that we planted first have never yet come up. the last that we planted is doing very well

Lea and Archa have got up the boddy of the house and boards for covuring   they are now waiting for an oppertunity to get lumber from the Landing   in the mean time they are getting timber in the woods of difernt lenths   I have planted about too thirds of my potatoes patch and i have slips enuf to plant the next season which we expect every day. I have not fed up too staks of fodder since you leave us   the corn that I calculated would last me the year will not be half out until next month the mare that you rode when you was out here has proven to be with fold as well as the bay mare but we will get nare a one from the old sorrel mare and I thought it is best to give her the second trial and see if I could not get som worke out of her and after hitching her to the plow she refused to move one step for severl hours and I thought it was best to try her every way and I made one of the Boys mounted her and she started of[f] and she has never givein me a quater of an hours trobble since and she workes as well as any thing in the land

the people all are well and gets on very well. mas Thomas red his letter to me the other day and I am very glad that there is som probility of geting mr perkins to live with me.[1] the people are inquireing mightly about utill and if we had his pettygrees to show with his form and his acttions he would soon blow out robbins Browns and Sun Beems light which is called the too best horces about here.[2] I have nothing more to say at preasent but remane your servant

George Skipwith

Source: #2433-B, Cocke deposit, Cocke Papers

1. George's disingenous statement conceals the fact that Abram Perkins (b. 1785) of Virginia, a friend and agent for Cocke, was coming to Hopewell to check George's propensity for mischief. Earlier Perkins had helped to choose the Hopewell plantation site and, with Elam Tanner, managed the 1840 move from Virginia to Alabama. He intermittently served Cocke's Alabama interests, but finally departed for Texas in the 1850s.

2. Cocke's horses enjoyed local reputations for speed; indeed, one of his horses figured prominently in a celebrated escape story during the first months of Union occupation in Alabama. According to local legend, a Confederate veteran who murdered a federal soldier in Greensboro sped away to safety on a Cocke thoroughbred mare. For the account see William E. W. Yerby, *History of Greensboro, Alabama from its Earliest Settlement* (Montgomery, 1908), 52–58.

hopewell   June the 8 1848

Sir

since I wrote you last I have plowed over my corn the seccond time and plantted my peas. I have also been over my cotten the seccond time with boath hoes and plowes and my plows will finish plowing over my cotten down here the third time to morro   the next day we will commence the third time at meltons   I commence going over with my hoes down here the third time monday and I think that I shall be able to finish with my hoes this week and start at meltons monday with the plows. there has none of our crops of corn been as flourshing this year as it was last year. there is a great manny of our nabors that have not had any rain to do any good for four or five weeks but I have had three as good a seasons as I would ask for and my corn have taken a start and I am no ways doughtful of a good crop   I have got som latter corn in the slew that I shall have to give a nother workeing but I do not think that I shall be compelled to plow the balance the third time but this I cannot deside untill I get mas Johns opinioun. my cotten crop is as good as any man can shoe on sandy land and I knoe that there is nare a man in alabama can shoe a cleaner crop than I can   I shall have to cut one feelde of my oats next week   my mules stands up better than they did last year

Lea and Archa have finish the house and have been workeing at the marl carts   old Agusty has got a fine horse coalt and we are looking for a nother one from the mare that you rode when you was out here   old and young are all well and I hope that all there are injoying the same Blessing   Lucy have mad[e] seventy five cents afer the things that you leave with her   I have nothing more to say at preasent but remane your servant

George Skipwith

Source: #2433-B, Cocke deposit, Cocke Papers

hopewell   July the 4th 1848

Sir

yours came to hand a few days ago and I had written to you a few days before it came to hand, and I would have answer it but I was about to undertake an extry Job and I thought that it was best to wait untell my ushal time and then I could give you more sattisfacttion concerning my opperrasions   we have had a dry and a backward spring and our corn did not look promising, and mas John was fearful that our corn would fall short, and he told me that the best thing that I could do was to rush ahead with my crop and plant the hold pasture in peas and if I could get them planted in june I would be able to turn my hogs in, in august, and I would be able to fatten them without any corn. our stork kept our pasture graised down very close and mas John was afraid to put the marl down without somthing for it to act apon and he says that the peas would fatten the hogs, and left the vines for the marl to act apon and I have planted the peas and they are all up and would have finished brakeing out the backs to day but was pervented by the rain, and this is the way that I planted them. I runed one furrow in between the old cotton beds with the seater, and drop them one step apart and too furrows with the same plow coviers them and too furrows with the turning plow breakes out the backs, and mas John says that next fall he is going to have a deep furrow and have the vines put in to it and have the marl scatterd over that and then bed on for the cotton and he thinks that the land will be good as ever it was

I think that we shall be able to finish laying by my crop down here this week, and mas John says he was in this country before this land was cleared and he never did see a better crope on it and thir is now, and all that the crop need now is dry weather and I think that we will finish laying by next week at meltons I knoe that it will not need no more plowing. perhaps I may have to sweep it over. I do not knoe which place is got the best crop on it   I do not think that thir has been five days but what we have had a rain since I wrote to you last, and my cotton is growing almost too fast for it is as large now as it was when we made our largist crops when the frost fall. the cotton looks well whencever we marl it at a single rate. that where we marl at a single rate looks as well as the dubble even where we put the leaves. I walked over my corn feield to day and I am safe for as good a crope as ushal. I think that I shall be able to commence at the marl the last of next week or the first of the week after apon the land that we had oats in, and no more bother untell picking out cotton. we are all well   I remane your servant

George Skipwith

[Enclosed with a note from John Cocke to J. H. Cocke]

Source: #2433-B Cocke deposit, Cocke Papers

hopewell   auggust the 8 1848

Sir

yours come to hand to day and I am glad to hear that you are well but I am sorry that you complain of not hearing from me once a month   I have written to you every month since you went away. it is true that some of my letters was som too or three days after my ushall time but it was not throgh niglect but

I knoe that I would be able to give you more sattisfacshion about my matters. this letter is a few days behind now but if it was a week later I could give you more sattisfaction concerning my crops than I can now. my last letter to you was on the forth of July and I gave ya an acount of my crops at that time. I have finished poling my fodder and my corn is a pretty fare crop, and I have more oats than I have ever made yet. my crope of cotton is as good a one at preasant as any man can shoe on sandy land thoe I cannot say with saftity what the turn out will be yet, for the worms have been aponn our cotton some six or eight days ago, and they are working faithful, but I am no ways Disincurageed yet. there is but one thing now that I am afraid of and that is a spell of wet damp weathor but if we can be Bleesed with dry hot sons we will make a crop in fiance of the worms but if thir bo a wet spel now the worms will commence cuting and Boing holes in the old Bowls and they will rot but if we have dry weather they can do the Bowls no harm, and I have Bowls a nuf at preasant to make a better crop than we have made for several years. it is raining at preasent but it does not apear as if thir will be a long spell but you may considder that we will commence picking cotton the first fare day that comes if it is to morro. we have started our marl carts and mas John thinks that thir is so much trash that we had better put it at a dubble rate   we have paid our best attenshion to the sedars and the stork hav ingured but a very few of them   we are all well and we hav had no sickness of much acount since you leave   Lucy is attentive to the intfant school   the married people are geting on very smooth togeathear   they have been disposed to act contrary with one another but mas John has got them all to rights again. thir is but too roes of the orange that did come up   we have planted our hold parster in peas and they are all up and we have plowed them three times and worked them twice with the hoes and they looks now like they will make us a very fine crop   I will now come to a close   I Remane your servant

George Skipwith

[*Enclosed with a note from John Cocke to J. H. Cocke, August 8, 1848*]

Source: #2433-B Cocke deposit, Cocke Papers

hopewell   Sept the 1 1848

Sir

    I wrote to you on the 8 day of auggust and I have not got much to say now. we have had but a very little good weather for picking out cotton untell about now   I was called out to work the road with all of my men forse and worke there a week since I come of[f] of the road I have picked over my cotton the seccond time down here and I started at meltons the seccond time yesterday and I picked yester day three thousand four hundred and ninety eight pound   we shall be able to pick betwenn three and four thousand every day at meltons untell we get over this time, and if the weather keeps as it is now I think that we will get over it four or five days   in all that I have picked is thirty four thousand. the worms have been aponn us all in this naborhood and a great many are fearful that they will not make as much as they did last year   I do not knoe what sorte of a calculation to make about my cotton but I knoe that I shall make a better crop than I did last year   I keeps Daniel[1] and howel[2] at the marl pit and with to day worke they have put marl over twenty ackers. the carpenters are at worke at home puting up the new corn crib. I have ussed but very little over half of my last years corn   the land that we marled is not got any better cotton than the rest   the people all are well at preasant and we have had but very little sickness this year. our Bacon holes out better this year than common   we have a nuff yet to last thre months or more   I must now come to a close   I remane your servant

George Skipwith

PS   the new married people gets on very smooth at preasant

Source: #2433-B Cocke deposit, Cocke Papers
  1. Daniel, Virginia born, was one of the original Bremo group to settle at Hopewell, where he labored as a field worker and marler. In 1857 he removed to New Hope with his wife, "Red" Nancy.
  2. Howell Skipwith (b. 1830), George's son, was a field worker and marler at Hopewell. In 1853 he married Polly Brown, by whom he had four children. He lived in the area at least until the 1870 census.

hopewell   oct the 2nd 1848

Sir

I wrote to you the first day of Sept but was unable to give you sattisfaction concerning my cotton, but I now have it in to my power to make som shoe calcrelation about it. I shall be good for eightty or ninety Bags, and if it dont come a frost in a short time I shall be sure for a hundred. it will take me the Balance of next week to finish the third time down here and the field is as white as I would whish it now and my Melton field is also very white. I shall have another picking after going over the third time. there are a great many Bowls that are not open   I have had elogant weather for picking cotton ever since I wrote to you last but thir have been more sickness among my hands since I wrote to you last than thir have been this summer. thir is Robert Sharlott and Harriet[1] that I have not had picking but very little of last munth beside others that have been sick. I have picked one hundred and thirteen thousand   I have not packed but twentyfive Bags yet   I have twelve or thirteen more gined that I shall pack tomorro   I have been compelled to stop my marl carts but if I can get over Meltons the third time I shall start them again and more help with them

the paster that we planted in peas made us a pretty fare crop   I turned my hogs in them yesterday. we hears of Deaths in our naborhood sometimes too or three a day boath Black and white, but mas John manage all of our caces without a Doctter my married people gets on very smooth togeather, and if thire is any thing Between them they keeps it concealed to themselve   my stock of all kind is well and fat   I have too as fine a coalts as any man need to look at from old Agusta and the mare that you rode when you was out here. the coalt that mas John turned out is going to make a splended horse   I have nothing more of importance to say   I will now come to a close   I Remane your servant

George Skipwith

PS   when I wrote my last letter I could not see any Diference in the marled land and the other but thir is all the diferance in [the] world   it is better made and larger plumper Bowls and the hands can pick more cotton in that than they can the other. pleas sir to give my love to my mother and my children,[2] and tell James that I reseved his letter and will an[s]wer it as soon as I can

George Skipwith

Source: #2433-B Cocke deposit, Cocke Papers
1. Robert and Charlotte Lewis, and Harriet, who was a field worker at Hopewell.
2. George's children in Virginia included Richard and William.

hopewell   nov the 1st—48

Sir

I reseved your letter dated oct the 16 and was glad to hear that you and all were well and I have got my cotton picking very strait at last, and I have packed out 45 Bags and my gin has binn runing twenty days and I ought to have forty more gined, and I have twenty thousand picked out that is not gined   I do not knoe rightly what the twenty thousand will turn out but I think it will over go ten Bags and if my gin has gined as common I have already got nienty five Bags

we have Just had our killing frost this morning and I do not knoe what our turnout will be in the field but I think that we will be good for a hundred Bags   Daniel and Howell has been back to the marl pit about ten days. the land that I am puting marl apon is the oats patch that was behind my house, and I am puting down at the rate of twoo hundred Bushells an acker. Howell and Daniel keeps the carts runing   Daniel loads and Howell drives the carts and when they did not had to hawl too far they marled an acker a day. they have got down behind the garden now and they do not hawl quite so much. master John was up here to day and he informed me of his araingement for a nother year, and he says that the Bowling field and the pea field will have cotton in them next year and he says that the pea field being a small field we will have to put cotton behind my house to help it out and he says that thir is so much trash on the ground that too hundred Bushells to the acker is none too much and that he intended to put it so through the field. I do not think that thire is any danger of the marl giveing out for it is as firm and as fresh in the pit as it was when you was out here. I have been gearthing my seed peas for three days   I commence

diging my potatoes to day   I think that they will rise very
well   Lucy atends to the school as you request   I have not
geatherd my corn yet. we have one end of our crib full of old
corn yet and the other end full of oats but the carpenters are at
worke on the crib behind the garden and I am in hopes that it
will not be long before we will able to geather. the people are
all well and I hope that this letter may find all thir in good
health   I have nothing more to say at preasant but remane
your servant

George Skipwith

Source: #2433-B Cocke deposit, Cocke Papers

Hopewell   December the 1st 1848

Sir
   I wrote to you november the 2 and I have herd nothing from
you nor mr perkins since I wrote last. I have geatherd my corn
and I made seventy wagins loads and thirty Bushells to a load,
and I have got twelve dubble stacks of fodder. it will take me
about one more day to finish picking out my cotton   I have got
seventy seven bags packed out   I have hawled fifty of them to
the landing and the seventy seven Bags wayed forty five
thousand five hundred and forty five pound and I yet think that
we will make our hundred Bags. my marl carts have been constant runing except in bad weather   we are about finishing the
field behind my house. the next field that we commence apon
will be the pea fielde. I think that we will get a plenty of marl
we have got the pit about fifty foot wide, and thir is a Boddy of
marl six foot deep before me now but below the six foot it is
inclined to be sandy but is good on boath sides of the pit   we
have not commenced scattering the marl yet. mas John thought
that it was better to let it stand for fear of hard rain washing it
away but we will commence plowing and scatering it in next
week
   Frank is putting up chimneys to the new houses   he has put
up three and I think that he will finish them all by christmas
with fair weather. I think archa and Lee will finish the new corn
house in about too more days   I have forty hogs for this years

killing but som of them are right small. I was in hopes that you would hear a good acount of us all the hold year out but I cannot write any thing concerning our matters that will be pleasing to you, for the state of things at preassant are such as I have never knone here before   I remember the last discorse that you had with me at the gate and I have kept it daily before me and I have done as I promased you to do, and I have found it Just as you told me that it would be   you told me that no fals reports could condem a man if he went right. they have raised reports apon me once, but missed thir ame but here is the second one but master John says he will leave it for you to deside me and master John have talked on all of the difernt cases and he says that he intend to write to you forthwith and tell you of all of the cases. we are all well. I remane your servant

George Skipwith

Source: #2433-B Cocke deposit, Cocke Papers

hopewell   oct the 12th 1849

Sir

I reseved your letter several day ago and was glad to hear from you

I knoe that you would wish to here from us in mr perkins absents, but as I was not aurtherised I did not knoe what to do. Mr perkins told me in his absents to repote to mas John every Sunday and I done so, and I had no dought but what he was writing in Mr perkins place. our cotton crop is a very short one   I think if I can get fifty Bags waying five hundred it will be the end of my crope. I have packed out eightteen Bags, and they will go five hundred and a few pounds over. our pea field that we marled has failed, but I donot charge that to the marl altogearther, but I am convinced that we beded up our land too high altogearther, and beding apon so menny pey vines that it cost the squares, the best peace of cotton we had in that field was that we beded up with one horse. the field behind my house done very well where we got the first stand, but where we replanted there is none. this makes me knoe that your Mode of early planting is a wise one, altho we may get caught by the frost som few year

when I reseved your letter mr perkins was in the act of writing, and I thought that I would wate and write between his times

sir   I think mr perkins is the very man that you take him to be. he is kind to the people and whipes none bethout a suffishent cause. hen thinks that the horse will make some six or seven hundred dollars, and they are comeing in to us now like it was the first of the spring. Mr perkins have sold nothing of the land but what could be spared and he have bought such as was neadful, and they are oweing us now about ninety or a hundred dollars. Mr perkins is Busy now burning of his brick and I think that he will be able to bloe out about sattursday night or sunday morning. then my hands will all be togearther and my next Job will be to gearther my corn, and I wish that you could be here to see with your one eyes the difernce of the corn on the marled lands for there is better corn on the marled lands than any other parts of its. there is som sickness amoung us but non dangerus. we have losed none of our stock since you was here

we hav been trying to reduce our cattle but I beleave that one comes for every one that we kill. we have had seven young calves since you was out here   I have turned out Eight young stearers and if you think them Eight is too many let us knoe in mr perkins letter. I have a hundred and ten hogs and I calculate apon killing fifty or sixty of them   give my love to every boddy white and Black. I remane your servant

George Skipwith

Source: #2433-B Cocke deposit, Cocke Papers

hopewell   August the 11th 1850

Sir

I have now got my crop laid by but I hardly knoe what calcalation to make about it   the cotton stacks is very small but generly is well loaded with bolls. the cotton in the gin house field is a very nice stand, and I think that the nicest peace of cotton in the field is that in the pond that we guanoed. the stand in the field behind my house is a very indifernt one but not withstanding I think that we will make a great deal more in that field than we did last year. I cannot tell yet which of the new kind of cotton is the best yet but it is all well bolled. I have a very good stand at Meltons and there is som very nice cotton amoung it. I have seen no apearance of the worms yet. I think that I can venture to say that our crop of cotton will be a better one than it was last year. I have bin pooling my fodder for six days and I think that it will take me about three more to finish it. my crop of corn is not as good a one as I have made but I will make anuf to serve us   we have had a long spell of hot dry weather   we have not had anuff rain to lay the dust since the early part of July. I prom[i]sed Mr perkins to cut a great deal of hay but the way that my cotton is opening I am afraid that I cant do much at it. Archa Lee Frank and Armstead have been about the shop ever since Mr perkins went aways   they have got up one room and the other one about two foot hie. we are all well at preasent but Becky[1] and one of Lucys children Dinah[2] has parted from the world after long sufering. give my love to all my friends. I have nothing more to say at preasent but Remane your servant

George Skipwith

PS   I think from the appearance of the weather that we will have rane to day or in a very few days.

G S

Source: Shields-Wilson deposit, Cocke Papers

1. Rebecca (Becky or Becca) Bird (b. 1822?) was one of the original Bremo group to travel to Hopewell, where she was part of what was known as the house gang. She had a sufficiently strong constitution to survive several illnesses and childbearing mishaps. She married Champion Morse (or Moss), but he left her after the Civil War.

2. Nothing else is known of Dinah Skipwith's history.

Hopewell   oct the 14 1850

Sir

I will again write to you to let you see how we are geting along. the carpenters have got the corn crib up and covered on one side and I shall tomorrow commence gearthing my corn and it will take me all of the week to get in my corn and my

fodder. I have som cotton down here that I shall have to pick
over with the hands that are not gearthing corn. then I shall
pick over my dry peas   by that time my cotton will have a
pretty good start before me again   I have got now sixty two
thousand picked. all of our crops will fall short in this naberhood. I have twenty two bags packed out, and I have five more
that is gined, and I have Enough picked out to keep me gining
several days yet   when I come to get all of my cotton in thire
will be but a very few that will have more to the hand than I
will. I have had Daniel and his boy[1] cleaning of the marl pit but
they hav not done any hawling yet but I shall commence as
soon as archa fix one of my carts

we have not had any rane since I wrote to you. the weather
have taken a little change   it is a little coulder but it is very
pretty weathor   the people all have behaved very well in mr
perkins absents. there has bin no disspute between man and
wife. mas John was up here yesterday and he found no fault.
tell mr perkins the people all behave mighty well since he has
bin gone. there is no sickness amoung the grown people
Becky is mending very fast. the children are all takening the
Hooping cough   give my love to all of my relations   I have
nothing more to say at preasent but remane your servant

George Skipwith

Source: Shields-Wilson deposit, Cocke Papers
1. Unable to identify

Hopewell   nov the 10 1850

Sir

I will write to you again to let you see how we are geting
along. I have written to you every two weeks since you wrote
me words to do so but I do not knoe whither you resieves my
letters or not. I have not heard from you but twice since mr
perkins went away   the carpenters have bin at worke on wag-
gon wheels since I wrote to you   archa have bin hired two
days to mr Benden[1]   Frank have bin hired two days to mr
Bayall.[2] I have out Eighty thousand weight of cotton. after this
week I shall take all of my hands and go to worke down at the
low place. I have my marl carts runing. we [have] to take of[f] at

least four feet of earth before we get to the marl   I have twenty
Eight Bags packed out   by the time that I write to you again I
shall be able to tell you how manny Bags that I shall make   I
think that I shall make about fifty. the grown people are all well
Except Becky   the children all have hoopingchough very
Bad   mr Benden wife have bin very sick but she is now better

 I have diged my potatoes but they are the poorest crop that I
ever made. we have not had any rane since I wrote to you   we
had a little sprinkle last night but it did not more than lay the
dust   I have nothing more to say at preasent but remane your
servant

George Skipwith

Source: Shields-Wilson deposit, Cocke Papers
1. Perhaps Joseph Benton of Pleasant Ridge precinct, Greene County. He was
a small planter.
2. Edward Bayol (b. 1808), originally from Pennsylvania, was a small planter
with a farm near Hopewell.

The House Servant

Household slavery showed the least change over time and revealed the most striking contradictions which were inherent in slavery. Of all the slaves the house servants experienced the most constant exposure to white charity and fury, and recorded the most ambivalent attitudes toward their masters, their conditions, and themselves. Some planters who maintained unusually large slave populations of fifty or more attempted to isolate a distinct, self-recruiting caste of house servants—the faithful retainers who appear with unjustified frequency in the literature on slavery. Few planters had the resources or interest for such lavish display and rigid division of labor. Most house servants, like the drivers, occupied a shaky middle ground between the white and black communities. Masters enticed the house servants to identify with their interests by sharing confidences, extending privileges—which in time the servants claimed as proprietary rights—and in feeding, clothing, and sometimes sleeping them better than the field hands. But the domestics' daily attendance on the white members of the Big House also exposed them to the more unlovely aspects of white temperament—to every petty and real tyranny of the petulant, the spiteful, and the mean. From planters' diaries we know that even favorites were boxed, cuffed, kicked, willowed, and flogged. The fine clothes of the house servants too often concealed grim reminders of their tenuous grasp on "privilege."

Where physical punishment failed, the planter withheld privileges or, for the incorrigible, reduced them to the field for flagrant contraventions of duty. Actually, few house servants escaped some experience in the fields. Planters pressed them into service during emergencies and assigned them regular responsibilities in the garden. As one recent writer has observed, rarely did the house servants find opportunities to cultivate airs. Nor did they choose to do so. Most house servants, after all, had a large emotional investment in the fields and the quarters, generally larger than that to the Big House. They found their family, suitors, and friends among the other slaves, and in living arrangements generally sought out the privacy of the quarters. Lest any domestics forget their place in the world, the beck and call of the master's household reminded them of their servile status.

Since many house servants enjoyed the measured confidences of their masters and mistresses and since many were "indulged" as favorites, it was not unusual to find house servants who could struggle through a page of a newspaper or scratch out a note with their own hands. Many letters describing life in the Big House survive, although they are often less revealing than those of the more independent and self-assured drivers and artisans. This, however, is not the case with the Lucy Skipwith letters published below.

The important collection of letters left by Lucy Skipwith of Hopewell adumbrate, as sharply as any of the genre, house servant attitudes and assimilation of white values. Although Hopewell was an absentee plantation, white overseers lived there, and Cocke made more frequent and prolonged winter visits after George's departure. Cocke delegated to Lucy the responsibility of maintaining his house in his absence and of waiting upon him during his residence. She also served as plantation seamstress, weaver, nurse, and most importantly, teacher—all positions she held for a quarter of a century. Once rebuked by Cocke as the "vilest sinner" on the plantation, the gifted and comely Lucy repented of her abandoned youth to become for Cocke "the Christian Matron" of his "school for ultimate Liberian freedom." He respected her warm Christian devotion and, as he explained to his son Cary Charles Cocke in 1858, he consequently valued her more highly "than any other on the place." It was a reciprocal trust, which Lucy used to her own advantage to safeguard her family from the menaces of the whip and auction block and to seal friends and family in their positions of influence on the farms. For her part, she acted as a counterweight to the white overseer and was expected to report his activities to Cocke. She also functioned as a vehicle for the transmission of Cocke's evangelical Protestantism and his puritan work ethos, values she shared. In 1855, for example, he instructed her to read *Pilgrim's Progress* to the slave children. The letters place in bold relief, as much as is possible, the degree to which Lucy, like other house servants, looked to her master for approval and direction and made his interest her own.

Lucy's efforts toward accommodation cost her the unquestioning trust of her fellow bondsmen. This appeared, for example, in her efforts to run the Sabbath school and administer family prayers daily in the manner Cocke prescribed. Some slaves "prayed their own prayers," which discomfitted Lucy enough for her to complain to Cocke and the overseer, actions which labeled her a tattler in the quarters. The label partially fit. In 1856, according to R. D. Powell, Lucy informed him that her husband Armistead, the headman at New Hope, was plotting to undo the overseer by destroying the cotton crop. These were, however, sporadic, desultory excursions into the interior lives of the other slaves—actions which were prompted more by personal jealousies than by an unblinking subservience to Cocke's interests—and in time the slave community forgave her for them.

Lucy's principal concern was the direction of the plantation Sabbath, and the infant and night schools. Indefatigable and inventive, she enlisted a local preacher to help instruct the children in mathematics, she adapted the Decalogue to rhyme for easier digestion, and she persevered in her educational enterprises despite censure and threats from local whites. Sometimes her labors with the children brought joyful progress. The children loved to work on the slate—indeed, some made letters very well—and Lucy gushed with maternal pride over the arithmetical powers of her daughter Maria. But, like her tutor Mrs. Cocke at Bremo, Lucy learned that student indifference, exhaustion, and the competing demands of the harvest often interrupted her efforts. The disappointments in education and religious upbringing, however, she blamed on whites, not blacks, for the white persons at Hopewell, she wrote, "takes no intress in prayer and it makes the people very backward indeed." She added that with the support of even one white Christian "every thing would go on better" in morality and education.

Lucy's Christian purpose formed the leitmotif of her letters.

Church near Greensboro, Alabama (possibly the one attended by Hopewell freedmen and women). (A 1930s photograph reproduced from U.S. Department of Agriculture, Farm Security Administration files, Library of Congress)

Indeed, her epistles reiterate and reaffirm the unflagging quest for personal salvation among slaves. Because of her special trust with the schools and her extraordinary commitment to Christ, Lucy wielded influence with the master. Cocke responded to her guarded pleas for more forceful preaching in the plain style and for shielding the plantation family from the abuses of overseers or intemperate, un-Christian whites. By scoring the evangelical fervor of the plantation and itinerant ministers, she strengthened the hand of divines who suited her own tastes. Rev. F. M. Crain enjoyed exceptional popularity with Lucy, especially after he dissuaded overseer J. W. Carter from "stomping" her for writing to Cocke behind his back, and he won similar admiration in the quarters after he chastised Carter for harshly treating two slaves. Crain's pulpit exhortations in Cocke's brick plantation chapel moved the slaves to raptures of holiness. On one occasion, Crain wrote to Cocke, several black penitents from nearby farms grew so agitated that they gave "undue vent" to their "anguish of mind." This caused "some uneasiness" among their eavesdropping owners.

Lucy recorded other religious outbursts. In 1859 she observed the "prettyest revival" which spread to the white inhabitants of Greensboro. Earlier she boasted of a contagion of conversion in the county that owed its inspiration to a revival at Hopewell, especially among her Sabbath school pupils. The tide of religious enthusiasm swept over the black people during the Civil War. Interspersed between complaints of minor slave derelictions in his letters were R. D. Powell's comments about "the great interest" among the slaves for the "way of salvation," an interest which ebbed and flowed with Confederate war fortunes. Although no direct linkage between slave religiosity and the prospects of liberation exists in Lucy's letters, or elsewhere for that matter, still one wonders. Whatever her secret desires, the religious awakenings at Hopewell underscored Lucy's compelling Christian example and no doubt reinforced her influence with Cocke.

Lucy employed her power of the letter and the Word to the detriment of white rivals at Hopewell, and they knew it. L. L. Singleton, an overseer for whom the slaves had only contempt, strongly objected to Lucy's epistolary habits. Other white residents and overseers also opposed her in this and demanded the right to censor her mail. Lucy successfully resisted these attempts to limit her power, although her correspondence was occasionally disrupted and compromised by white strictures.

Lucy particularly disliked overseer William Lawrence's wife who corrupted the plantation by her disgusting habits of taking snuff and using laudanum "by night and day." Lucy also disapproved of Mrs. Lawrence's disciplinary policy for the Lawrence children who remained "spoilt as bad as ever." Mrs. Lawrence "whips them to day and humors them tomorrow and so her whipping them does them no good atall." Not only do Lucy's comments outline acceptable correction standards among slaves, they also reveal Lucy's attempt to discredit the overseer through the ill-reputation of his wife. When Lucy and Mrs. Lawrence clashed over Lucy's letter writing, Lucy proved anything but submissive in the confrontation—clear proof that accommodation and a willingness to accept the congenial aspects of the master-slave relationship did not breed docility.

Lucy's inveigling succeeded. Cocke discharged Lawrence, partially to satisfy her, and replaced him with a young man more to Lucy's liking—for a time. If nothing else, the inexperienced new overseer, R. D. Powell's nephew Smith Powell, seemed more malleable than his predecessors. Lucy established a close acquaintance with young Powell, whom she democratically dubbed "Smitty," and exercised a remarkable influence over him. Powell assisted her in the plantation schools, encouraged slave religiosity, and permitted Lucy to visit her father and mother in Mississippi.

Lucy's accommodation to Cocke's interests paid handsome dividends on two occasions that threatened the sale of her two daughters, Betsey and Maria. In 1859 Betsey was caught stealing money from a neighbor to whom she had been hired out. Earlier, Lucy had begged Cocke not to allow the girl to leave Hopewell and warned him that the neighbor Borden family neglected to instruct the girl in either the three R's or Christian precepts. Lucy's missive of June 9, 1859, pleading Betsey's case, repudiates the glib assertion that slave parents passively accepted family fragmentation, as it also illustrates the resistance tactics of a loyal slave. Cocke acceded to Lucy's delicate promptings, and a grateful mother wrote to justify his wisdom in restoring the wayward girl to her mother's care. Lucy reported that among those "crying aloud for mercy" during the 1859 revival was her Betsey, who came "a stranger to God and a stranger to me" but was now rejoined in fellowship with Father and mother. Unhappily, Betsey later slipped back into her errant ways, bore two children by white men, and after further scandals was sold in 1863 to a friend of Cocke's from Mobile who moved to Hopewell during the war. Indicative that the Hopewell slaves had rewoven Lucy back into their social fabric, others rallied to her support in the crisis. Charles Morse, a respected slave artisan, dashed off a note to Cocke protesting Betsey's sale. He assured Cocke that the girl, then betrothed to his son, would no longer engage in licentious conduct. Betsey stayed on the plantation throughout the war, assisting her new mistress, Julia Dorsey, and her mother in the weaving and housekeeping operations.

Lucy had better luck with her other daughter, Maria. When R. D. Powell asked to purchase the girl during the Civil War, Lucy reported to Cocke the sad history of Betsey's downfall, which she blamed on Betsey's absence from home, and implicitly laid the onus for Maria's future corruption on Cocke, should he endorse the sale. Lucy's letter of May 30, 1862, persuaded Cocke not to sell or hire out Maria unless Lucy approved without equivocation. Maria was to remain with her mother for the duration of the war as Lucy craftily dragged out negotiations with Powell. Rather than chance the loss of affection of a dear and faithful servant, Cocke again yielded to her wishes. Accommodation had its rewards.

Whether by contrivance or indifference, Lucy remained conspicuously reticent on the great issues of the day. Her white neighbors buckled on swords and raised hue and cry after secession while she discussed the family gossip of whites, local romances, the declining vitality of preaching, and her weaving. With R. D. Powell's inability to retain white overseers after 1862, Cocke insisted that Lucy devote more attention in her letters to farming news. It was an obligation she met with mixed success. Lucy tried harder after 1862, but her lengthy list of obligations prevented her from expanding the scope and depth of her letters.

Except for Powell's distant, almost random, oversight and the presence of Mrs. Dorsey after 1863, the Hopewell and New Hope slaves were spared contact with white overseers for many months of the war. Yet Powell generally applauded the slaves' good behavior, save for Robert who stole some shoats and Betsey who presented Lucy with a white granddaughter. Lucy's war letters intoned the rural monotony of unremitting toil from sunup to sundown, a pattern seemingly broken only by bouts with the whooping cough and revival spasms. On the face of it, the Hopewell family lived in an untroubled retreat.

Superficially, the language of her letters also leaves the impression of unquestioning submission and contentment with Southern norms and conditions. During the war, for example, Lucy incorporated the term "Yankee" into her vocabulary, freighted as it was with murky foreboding and malignancy. Her easy adoption of pejorative Southernisms, however, probably reflected less a dislike of Northern principles than a typical slave's ingrained, provincial mistrust of any interloper. Besides, the Yankees merited such suspicion. They riddled those she knew, and in some cases loved, with injury and suffering—witness, for example, her commiseration for John Cocke's forlorn search for his son and for her master's broken heart after the suicide of his son Philip. This empathic Christian woman, who wept with white mothers in 1856 at the funeral of their infant dead, did not, indeed could not, segregate her charity and compassion from whites. In fact, through its very privations and horrors, the war brought forth from slaves everywhere in the South the most baffling responses of generous pity for the misfortunes of those with whom they had endured an often turbulent lifetime.

On a second level, Lucy and the slaves showed a consuming interest in the war. They could hardly ignore it. Evidence of a disintegrating civilization was everywhere—in the ingratiating gestures of the once inflexible steward, in the lamentations over fathers and sons lost in combat, in the shrill command to shut the plantation school, and in the embittered master's erratic correspondence and diminished influence, for Cocke, who had recanted of his antislavery convictions after the successive shocks of civil war and his son's death, never returned to Alabama after the secession winter. For the less acute observers, there were more visible proofs of some impending cataclysm. The Cocke slaves planted less cotton and more corn, they watched the flight of Mississippi families from the Union armies, and they fell prey to Confederate labor requisitions, which left men dead or nearly so and evoked uncommon and considerable ire from Lucy.

After Appomattox the Hopewell and New Hope blacks betrayed to whites only a restrained enthusiasm for the idea of freedom. Smith Powell, who resumed his overlordship at Hopewell and New Hope after the war, feared local white brigands more than his black charges. In December, 1865, Armistead and Archer foiled two cotton-stealing forays by white toughs. Cocke's farms invited plunder, for they had escaped the war relatively unscathed, except for the systematic raids of government tax collectors and foraging Confederate soldiers and banditti. Hopewell had sufficient food for a season, livestock, and crops in the ground—all of which induced the freedmen and freedwomen to tarry in Cocke's employ.

By early 1866, however, the once-hesitant former slaves began to feel their freedom. Several had joined the migratory jubilee of Alabama blacks, while those who continued at the farm voiced increasing discontent over the Powell stewardship and their onerous labor arrangements. The octogenarian Cocke only grudgingly acquiesced to the new order in the South; indeed, the very suddenness of the collapse of slavery in Alabama left master and slaves unprepared and confused. Through R. D. Powell, Cocke attempted to lock his laborers into long-term contracts and thus perpetuate the old modes of labor until the blacks could be repatriated to Africa. With the first year's harvest, however, the Hopewell freedmen refused to abide further Cocke's degrading labor policy which bound them to gang labor, corporal punishment, restricted mobility, and a meager one-sixth share of the crop—in a word, the *profits* of sharecropping and the *wages* of slavery. In his letters to Cocke in the fall of 1865, Powell whined of unmanageable "servants" and insisted that nothing short of Cocke's presence would mollify them. In the prostrate postwar South impersonal economic forces further disordered Cocke's paternalism. Powell counseled Cocke to dispose of his unproductive land and to turn the blacks "out to get their livings."

Offering them a one-third division of the 1866 crop, Powell persuaded most of the Hopewell community to try him for one more year, but several blacks, led by Champion the driver, parted company with the Cocke enterprises. None of the blacks, however, gave Cocke's postemancipation offer of transportation to Liberia more than a curt no thank you, final proof of the distance that master and former slaves had traveled apart. If Powell's purpose was to hold the blacks on the farms, share-cropping functioned tolerably well, but the former slaves manifested little inclination to plant anything but corn and vegetables. Cotton, after all, smacked too much of the old order. In a May, 1866 letter the ever-pessimistic Powell urged Cocke to let a family representative assume personal management of the Alabama estates before the independent-minded blacks rendered the property worthless. He hoped that Cocke would thereafter "hire such hands as will work & no others."

Fate cruelly fulfilled Powell's petition for a renewed Cocke presence at Hopewell and New Hope. With John Hartwell Cocke's death in July, 1866, a family member finally ventured to Alabama. In 1866 Philip B. Cabell, Cocke's grandson, journeyed to Hopewell to claim his inheritance, a one-half interest in Cocke's Alabama lands. He also agreed to manage the property in conjunction with the Powells.

Cabell found conditions at Hopewell in a "pickle," and convinced himself that no one had dug a ditch or split a rail since the war. Furthermore, as he wrote to C. C. Cocke, the forecast for the 1866 crop was "well calculated to dishearten" the most resolute true believer among the black croppers, who already chafed under the garrison conditions imposed by the Powells. The former slaves, "pretty much dissatisfied with everything," complained "most bitterly" to Cabell about past injustices and warned him of their intention to leave after the harvest because of their universal and "utter abhorrence" of the Powells. In his letters to C. C. Cocke in 1866 and 1867 Cabell reported new problems. When Cabell retained Smith Powell at New Hope, every hand bolted "like a parcel of birds under a dead fall." Finding neighborhood plantations wholly without laborers and noticing blacks departing from the county "in great numbers"—a temporary and illusory phenomenon as it turned out—Cabell negotiated a contract more satisfactory to the blacks in 1867, and he divided his holdings into tenant parcels for his croppers. Albeit dismayed at the small monetary returns in cropping, the blacks preferred the share system to any other available to them, since it allowed them a large measure of privacy and self-direction.

Crop failures in 1867 and 1868 hardened Cabell's heart, and he threatened to "show no quarter" to any laborer who rejected his proposed division for the 1869 crop. The blacks would have none of this bluster. By 1870 most of the former Cocke slaves had drifted off the Cocke lands, although their roots were too deeply imbedded in Greene County to wander far. The 1870 census reveals nine former Hopewell families, including George and Mary Skipwith, huddled together in homesteads about the David Key property near Greensboro and Hopewell, an area heavily populated by blacks. Self segregated in their Baptist church and in their tenant community, some would remain there at least through 1880. The rest, alas, are lost to history.

The former slaves quickly learned the hard lessons about the limitations of their freedom and freed themselves of any illusions of economic autonomy, for the census reports and tax lists suggest that emancipation failed to increase occupational opportunities for blacks in Alabama. Although Cocke's former slaves on the average fared better than the mass of Alabama freedmen, the Hopewell community continued to know only hard labor. Several artisans amassed small personal estates of $150 to $350, but few others climbed into the propertied classes of Alabama. Fewer still, if any, had the leisure to participate in politics. Amid Ku Klux Klan terrors of unusual virulence near Greensboro from 1868 to 1870, Alabama Reconstruction follies, and the bullyrag of "Redemption," the former slaves silently eked out their livings as farm laborers and croppers, managing as best they could to keep the families together and to minimize white intrusion into their lives.

Sadly, despite Lucy's prayers and preachments, the former slaves were an unlettered lot. According to the census, illiteracy yet shackled many to ignorance, and even George Skipwith no longer acknowledged a writing aptitude. Perhaps the white census taker intimidated them to renounce their learning, or, as is more likely, they had no opportunity to refine old skills. Save the handful of American Missionary Association schools—the nearest in Greensboro—and some extramural coaching by black preachers, there was little regular instruction for blacks going on in the area. The former slaves had to content themselves with a solitary plantation school administered by local whites.

The educational backsliding among the Hopewell blacks strongly suggests that Lucy was no longer among her people. As she spurned Armistead after their unsuccessful marriage, so Armistead had her excommunicated from the local Baptist church, her very lifeblood. Shamed, she planned a retreat to Mississippi to reunite with her parents, but she gave up the notion when they left R. D. Powell to settle among old Hopewell comrades in Alabama. At least until 1870, George and Mary Skipwith, working as farm laborers and unpropertied, lived in a cabin adjacent to son Howell's family on the Key land. After that date, the Skipwiths too drop from sight. For Lucy, we know nothing beyond her sobering letter of December, 1865. Whether she continued her teaching in the face of local white animosity, left for the Cocke lands in Mississippi, or, after Powell ordered Maria off Cocke's property in 1866 for receiving visits from a white paramour, followed her daughter on some new hegira, is all conjecture. The records are silent.

Wherever Lucy elected to go, she would not go hungry, for Cocke had bequeathed to her an annuity of twenty-five dollars, "in addition to the other allowances she has been accustomed to receive yearly." And, as her letters to "Dear Master" attest, she had the instinct, savvy, and mettle to survive, if not prosper, in any environment.

As long as the planters of the antebellum South had to live among their slaves, they had of necessity to come to terms with the minimal psychological, material, and spiritual demands of their people. As Eugene Genovese has suggested, paternalism of the Cocke stripe was pernicious in that it siphoned off true political resistance from the enslaved black masses by separating them according to tasks and favors, encouraging a divisive hierarchy which set slave against slave, and bribing them with tawdry goods and limited privileges. To excel, to rise within the system, the slaves were encouraged to adopt the master's *Weltanschauung*, an impossible goal really. However, slave accommodators paid a dear price for their advantages. To become "fit slaves," safe to turn loose on the world, they erased their African past, or at least disguised it. The letters of Lucy, like the

Letters from Liberia, above, gauge the level of surface acculturation among privileged bondsmen who practiced a clear obedience to the master's social values.

Planters like Cocke sought total dominion over the blacks, if only to uplift them. They generally did not get it. Lucy's letters testify to that fact, for her chaste epistles to a beloved friend and benefactor remind us that even the assimilated slave was not wholly defenseless. Cocke's admonitions to religion and good conduct also fixed the standard by which he, indeed all whites, would be judged. Lucy's missives trace the lineaments of her disappointments with Cocke's hirelings and, obliquely, with the master himself.

Heroic defiance, such as Lucy's clash with Mrs. Lawrence, only occasionally defined her and the Hopewell slaves' principal strategy of defense; rather, they survived by keeping together, by forging a separate collective identity exclusive of whites, or nearly so. The syncretic black-white culture of the slave South, after all, did not extinguish the desire for cultural autonomy among blacks—witness the exodus of the Hopewell blacks after the war. The pressures to conform to white modes, although often too powerful or alluring to resist totally, heightened the desire for privacy among the slaves. A tenacious secrecy about their interior lives and the shared experiences of two generations of living and suffering together created and sustained a community among the Hopewell blacks. It was at once part of and yet apart from Cocke's world. By her proximity to the master and her fuller assimilation of his values, Lucy shuttled back and forth between the two worlds. Tragically, she seemed an anomaly in the South—someone without a sense of place. Almost. With the collapse of the planter regime, Lucy, who twice rejected manumission offers during the Civil War, cast her lot with the black world.

If there is nothing sublime in the commonplace, there is continuity. Lucy's letters, like those of other articulate slaves, celebrate the cycles of history for all rural folk—birth, growing up, courtship, family building, and death. Although jolted by her wrench from Virginia, family fragmentation, conversion, and war, her world retained a fundamental continuity—that of community survival and God's forgiveness in the end. And that made all the difference.

Letters from Lucy Skipwith*

Hopewell   august the 17th 1854

my Dear Master

I received your message in mr Singletons[1] letter and was very sorry that I had to be reminded of your orders to me. It is my desire and my determanation to do whatever you commands me to do, and I can do it now with more pleasure than I ever could before, but as I could not give you the sattisfacttion that I wish to give you, I refused to write to you attall, but as you have called upon me I will speak the truth to you. I have been trying to carry on Family prayers by the plan laid down by you but som has thought propper to pray their own prayers at times, and as you did not say that this was to be done it makes me feel uneasy, and it is always done unexspecting to me. every man heard your words, and those that do not obey I hope will stand for themselves   I tries to do all that I can in this matter. I know that I will be blamed by some of the people for mentioning this to you, but I am bound to speak the truth when I do speak, with the help of God   I have Just mentioned the matter to mr. Singleton and I hope that in future things will go on Just as you say. I have read from the 15th of matthew to the 3rd of Luke since you went away. none of the people have improved enough to read the prayer as yet, but I hope that some will be able to do it before very long   my School Children that comes to school every day are improveing in learning, but the boys that do not come every day I fear that I shall never be able to do much with them, as it do not lay upon their mines as it ought. I hope that you will soon be here to help me in this cause for I needs your help very much. give my love to all my friends, and tell Birthier to write to me.

*Ed. Note: Unless otherwise specified, all letters are addressed to John Hartwell Cocke.

I would be very glad to receive a letter from you. I have nothing more to say at this time. I remane your servant

Lucy Skipwith

Source: #2433-B Cocke deposit, Cocke Papers
1. Lucian L. Singleton (b. 1823?), overseer at Hopewell, had worked for other planters in the area before his Hopewell tenure. He married Mary Holcroft, a local girl, in 1848.

Hopewell   november the 11th 1854

my Dear Master

I received your letter dated october the 11th and was very glad to hear from you and to hear that you expect to be with us this winter. this leaves us all in the injoyment of good health, except uncle Mike,[1] but he is better than he has been   every thing is going on as usual. I have read as far as the 4th chapter of John at prayers in the morning. no one have read the prayer as yet but some of them are trying to improve themselves to do it, and I hope that I shall have help after awhile. sometimes I feel very much disincuraged and then again I live in hopes of seeing a greatter improvement of reading in this land   I have my school regalur and my children are still improveing   I shall try to do all I can with them while learning is in their heads   I am in hopes by the time that this reaches you, you will be readdy to start to Alabama. mr Singleton and his family are well. master John and his family are well. miss Lucy was married last week to mr samuel Webb[2] and is gone with him. mrs Bagshaw[3] expects to leave shortly but I do not knoe where she is going   I surpose you have herd of the death of Dr Withers before this   he left eight children behind. his wife has Just got back home. there has been a great revival of religion at the Baptist Church in greensboro with Black and white. thirty six persons were Baptized last Sunday. there is a hundred and over been added to it this year. the revival started here with us and it has been going ever since, and I hope that it will continue to go untell the whole country shall be saved   I feel proud that I have repented of my sins and been forgiven and my name mingled with the people of God here below, and I feels that it is writen in the fair book of life. I feels that my religion will not

only make me fit for life, but for death and I feels to day that I
am on the way to heaven. this sinful world is not my home, and
if I never see you no more I hope to meet you in heaven where
we shall part no more. I will now come to a close   I remane
your servant

Lucy Skipwith

Source: Shields-Wilson deposit, Cocke Papers
1. Mike regularly reported debilitating afflictions and thus escaped much
plantation work. One wonders whether the other slaves, who had to take up his
tasks in addition to their own, appreciated his suffering.
2. Lucy (Cocke) Webb, a daughter of John Cocke of Alabama. Samuel Webb's
identity and circumstances are unknown.
3. Amelia Bagshaw was a teacher at the John Cocke of Alabama plantation.

Hopewell   May the 19th 1855

my Dear Master
I received your message in mr Powells letter and will take
this opportunity to answer it   this leaves us all in our usual
state of health and every thing is going on as usual. uncle Mike
has been very unwell for the last three days but is up again
I am going on with my school as usual, and my Children are
still improveing. as they are going on reading so well, I am now
Teaching them to write, and some of them can make letters very
well. I am inhopes that some of them will write by the time you
come out here   I keeps up a night school for the instruction of
the Children that work out in the Farm. they seem to improve
very slow in reading, but they improve makeing figures very
much and they seem to have a great love for it   I Think that mr
Eastman[1] done much good by haveing the Black Board made as
the Children all love to work on it. when you write to mr
Eastman, tell him that little Mariah[2] that he gave the slate and
book to, she has caught up with George and Albert,[3] and is
going by them. she never made a figure untell she was Taught
by him and she can now Add multiply and Subtract.
I learnt more in Arithmetic while mr Eastman was hear than I
ever thought of in my life, and I have a great love for it   I
would give any thing if I had any one to instruct me farther in it
as I am unable to go on with it. the miss Averys[4] have been here

once since you went away. three other Ladies came with them and got Books but I do not have their names.

give my love to Berthear   tell him I will write to him soon. I hope that you will come out early this Fall and spend a longer time with us. give my love to all my Christian friends   tell them I am striveing to meet them in heaven. my greatest desire in this world is to serve the Lord and to serve him with a perfect heart, altho I finds my heart prone to wander, prone to depart from God, but with his help I will try to subdue all unholy desires and to deny all ungodlyness and wordly lust and to live soberly righteously and godly in this present world, to take up the cross and follow Jesus through evil report as well as good. I would be very glad to receive a letter from you. I have nothing more to say at present   I remane your servant

Lucy Skipwith

Source: #2433-B Cocke deposit, Cocke Papers

1. Mr. C. B. Eastman was a preacher who ran a girls' school in Greensboro and also distributed tracts for the American Bible Society and American Tract Society.

2. Maria Skipwith (b. 1847?), Lucy's daughter and her favorite, was the leading student in Lucy's schools. She later became a house servant.

3. Albert Morse (or Moss), Jr. was the son of Albert and Martha (Skipwith) Morse and was Lucy's nephew.

4. Fanny Avery (b. 1836?) and Mary E. Avery were the daughters of Rev. John Avery, an Episcopalian minister from Edenton, North Carolina, who came to Greensboro in 1835, and Ann Avery (b. 1807), who survived him by many years. The Avery land bordered the Cocke property, and the Avery family frequently visited Hopewell. Fanny Avery later married Richard Hooker Cobbs, an Episcopal clergyman. Mary E. Avery became a teacher and in 1874 filled out the unexpired term of Philip B. Cabell, Cocke's grandson, as president of Greensboro Female Academy.

Hopewell   June the 17th 1855

my Dear Master

I again take my seat to write you a few lines to let you know how I am geting along. I have been expecting a letter from you but have not received one

we are all well at this time and doing as well as we can expect. at preasant there is nothing new to inform you of   every thing is going on as usual. my school Children are still improveing. they have learnt nearly all of the writeing letters and are begining to make them very well. I think that the new plan of saying the ten Commandments at Sunday School is a great improvement to the Children and when they do wrong, they are begining to understand which Commandment they have broken. I takes a great delight in explaneing the Commandments to them and trying to teach them to remember their Creator in the days of their youth. the old people do not improve as much as the Children, but they are still striveing, and I am willing to do my duty by them all as far as I am able.

mr Powell[1] is with us at this time and we all feels a great deal better sattisfied since we have been in his care.

we have got the new loom to work and I am very much pleased with it and when I get som good Cloth to put in it I think that I can weave as much as any one elce can with a little help

mrs Avery and her Daughters were here a few days ago and desired to be remembered to you. master Johns family were all well when I heard from them last

I wrote to Berthier more than a week ago and I hope that he has received my letter and will answer it soon. the weather here has been the coolest for the time of the year that I ever saw   it seems to be more like fall than summer.

I am still trying to do my duty to God and to man and to live a life that becometh a child of God and to keep my self unspotted from the world. I hope that the Lord will give me a greater desire to seek and to serve him in his own appointted ways. I must now come to a close hopeing to hear from you soon, and if I never see you again in this world I hope to meet you in heaven is the prayers of the unworthy servant

Lucy Skipwith

to Gen John H Cocke

Source: Shields-Wilson deposit, Cocke Papers

1. Richard D. Powell, born about 1800 in Brunswick County, Virginia, managed the Philip St. George Cocke property there from 1835 to 1844 and, after moving to Mississippi, the Cocke Mississippi lands through the Civil War. He purchased slaves and land near Columbus, and by 1860 he owned twenty-one slaves and an estate valued at $42,000. He also assumed the stewardship of the John Hartwell Cocke Alabama lands in the 1850s, a position he held through the collapse of the old regime. For a good brief summary of this remarkably successful plantation steward see Scarborough, *Overseer,* 191–194.

Hopewell   July the 20th 1855

my dear master

as the time have arived for me to write to you I now take my seat with pleasure to do so. this is my third letter to you since you went away. mr Powell informed me that you had received my first letter and I hope that the second has also been received which was writen June the 17th. there is no sickness worth speaking about at preasant but we have had some very sick Children, three which have died within the last three weeks. Marshas[1] Child have died Bettys[2] and Nancys.[3] Pollys[4] Child has been very unwell but is geting better. Pollys baby and Sister Marthas are all the babys that are here. there is but one Child here that has lived to be old enough to walk for the last four or five years. Sister Etter[5] keeps very unwell but is still attending to her busness   she is not confined as yet but will be very soon

mrs Singleton has her fourth Child which is a son   she has been very unwell but is better   I am still going on with my School and I can see improvement in the Children every day there is two of the little girls that I think will write very well by Christmas, and three of the Boys. I hope that the rising genera- tion will be wiser than the old set   I do not get on with my night School so well at preasant. the nights are so short and the Children are so sleeppy when they come from work, that I cannot keep their eyes open no time, and it will soon be picking Cotton time and when they get through with their Cotton at night it will be too late to keep them up, as they will have to rise very early. we still attends preaching at the Church   mr Dubois[6] has preached five times since you went away. mrs Averys family was well when I heard from them last.

one of our best mules died the other night one of the last ones that came from va.

mr Singleton got a letter from mr Eastman the other day   he was well as usual.

Arthur Creacy sends his love to you and says that he is doing very good busness. master Johns family and mr Bendens are well   mrs Joe Borden[7] has her third Child. we have a very poor garden this Summer, but it is now a little better than it has been. Mike sends his love to you and says that he hopes to live long enough to see you out here once more. he says that his health is no better since the above was writen I have received your letter dated July the 4th and was delightted to hear from you and to hear that you were well, and I hope that the Lord will keep you in health sufficient to visit us this winter. as far as I can learn the crop is in very good order, and the Cotton begining to open. all hands are working in it with the hoes. they will soon pull the fodder. six of the hands are in the house sick at this time, but I hope they will soon be well again

I will see the miss Averys before I write to you again, and deliver your message. I am sorry to say that family prayers are not regularly carryed on. if it is rather late the people will not stay to prayers. the white people that lives here takes no intress in prayer and it makes the people very backward indeed. I would give any thing in the world if there was one white person on this plantation that was a friend to God and to the works of God. I know that every thing would go on better.

I wrote this letter to send by mr powell but I heard that he is in va   I have more to say to you but as I have the opportunity of sending my letter to the office I must conclude hopeing to hear from you again before long. I remane your Servant

Lucy Skipwith

J H Cocke

PS   Sister Etter is confined and has a fine Son

Source: Shields-Wilson deposit, Cocke Papers

1. Marcia Johnson, one of the original Bremo group, was the wife of Qually Johnson. They went to New Hope in 1857 and lived in the neighborhood as late as 1870.

2. Betty (or Bettia) Creacy (or Creasey) had a bastard child in 1854 and again in 1855, although the last one died. She enjoyed the attention of several suitors, especially Pepe and Washington, but she chose Archer Creacy for her husband. Within a year of their marriage they left to live at New Hope.

3. "Red" Nancy, Daniel's wife.

4. Polly (Brown) Skipwith (b. 1834) married Howell Skipwith, Lucy's brother, in 1853. She could read and write, and she alternated between domestic and field labor during slavery. After the war she remained at home to care for her four children.

5. Isaetta Skipwith (d. 1863), Lucy's sister, was plagued by poor health. As a member of the house gang, she had responsibility for tending the garden. R. D. Powell thought that she was lazy and threatened to demote her to the field for sloppy gardening, but Lucy intervened on her behalf by praising her performance. Etta and Martha were Lucy's closest companions and confidantes at Hopewell.

6. Rev. John Dubois (1797–1884), at this time assigned to the Greensboro Colored Mission, served various Methodist pulpits in Alabama for over sixty years.

7. Frances Borden (b. 1833?) was the sister of John Cocke of Alabama and the wife of Joe Borden who owned a large plantation and many slaves. They had three children: John, Frances, and Walter.

Hopewell   aug the 28th 1855

my Dear Master

as I think that you are expecting a letter from me I will put off writeing no longer. we have had a great deal of sickness since I wrote to you last. the house has not been clear of sick people since I wrote to you last, eight and nine at a time and some times more. there is several sick at this time but they are geting better.

my own health is not so good at this time   I have had the palpatation at the heart for three weeks more or less. I am attending to my busness but feels very week at times. my worst time is after I go to bed at night. I thinks very often that my days on earth are few but I feels that when ever death comes I shall be able to say let thy will be done on earth as it is in heaven, and I feels that he who has been with me in life will be with me in death. I suppose that mr Singleton has writen to you about the death of Shadwalk   he died the 30th of July   he went to bed as well as usual and died about midnight. before he went to bed he had been reading the 20th chapter of the acts. he is a great loss to us all. Champion[1] is the head man since he died   he often spoke of you and wished to see you once more. he has been evil spoken of very much since you went away about the subject that he told you about when you was here, but he bore it all with patience hopeing to see a better state of things. him and myself have live here this year like strangers in a disstant land but I hope that there is an end to come to all of these things. I have not heard a word from you since I received your letter in July   if mr Singleton has received any letter it is more than I know

I have heard nothing from mr Powell since I heard that he was in va   I hope that he will soon return home and visit us

I have not seen mrs Avery since I wrote to you last. miss mary has been at the point of death for three or four weeks but is recovering her health again. master Johns family is well and mr Bendens   mrs Lucy webb is confined at her Fathers and has a fine daughter   I am going on as usual with my School   I have nothing more to say at preasant but remane your Servant

Lucy Skipwith

Source: #2433-B Cocke deposit, Cocke Papers

1. Champion Morse (or Moss) was born in Virginia in 1810 and was an original settler of Hopewell. He held the driver's post until 1860, when ill health forced him to share his duties with his nephew Cain Morse. He married three times: first to Jane, who died in 1845; next to Rebecca Bird, whom he abandoned after the Civil War; and finally to Emma, with whom he lived through Reconstruction days. He worked as a farm laborer after the war.

Hopewell   Nov the 18th 1855

my Dear Master

I have taken my seat to write to you to relieve your mind from the anxiety which I know that you feels to hear from us all. I received your letter dated Sep the 14th and it is not carelessness why it has not been answered for I always take pleasure in writeing to you, and I never feels sattisfied when I neglect any thing that you desire me to do.

my reason for not writeing to you is this man that lives here[1] he has such a great objecttion to my writeing to you. I thought that I would not write to you again while he stays here, but I know that you are expecting a letter from me and wondering what is the matter with me. he told me that I am never to write his name in a letter to you while I live. I told him that I would not write his name in any of my letters to you. after he received your letter he made it known that he would not live here another year. I heard that he is going to live with master John next year as him and his overseer has parted. when you write to him do not mention this letter to him. since the above was writen I have heard that he is not going to master Johns. mrs Stevens[2] is gone away from there and no one lives there but him and the little children. Mary B[3] is gone to Summerfield to school

mrs avery and family is well. I went to see them after I received your letter. they were glad to hear from you and desired to be rememberd to you   I expect that miss mary have writen to you before this. mis Fanny has Just returned from North Carolina where she has been for several months.

mr Powell has not been here since the last of Oct   we will
send for the new overseer in a week from this   we have 72
Bags of Cotton packed out at this time and they thinks that
there is enough to make out 100. they are going over the fields
the last time and expects to Finish before Christmas. the wheat
was sowed a week ago.

I am going on very well with the new loom and if it holds out
and do as it is doing now I shall be able to provide a plenty for
the plantation   I am very busy at this time trying to get the
winter Clothes all done before Christmas.

the sickly season is now over and we are all in very good
health. I hope that nothing will happen to pervent you from
comeing out next month. my school Children are improveing
that come to School every day, but I can do but little with the
others   since the Cotton season commenced we have family
prayers every morning regularly whether manny or few, for the
Lord has promised that where two or three would meet togeather in his name that he would be with them, and it shall
never be neglected if there is but one other besides myself.

give my love to Berthear   tell him that we are all well   I
have nothing more to say at this time. hopeing that you will
soon be with us I remane your servant

Lucy Skipwith

Source: Shields-Wilson deposit, Cocke Papers
1. The overseer, L. L. Singleton, who left Cocke's employ at the end of the
year, much to the delight of the slaves and the steward.
2. Unable to identify.
3. Mary B. Cocke, a daughter of John Cocke of Alabama.

Hopewell   May the 30th 1856

my Dear Master

a longer time has elapse than I intended should done before
writeing to you but as mr Powell wrote from here the first of the
month and mr Carter[1] wrote about the middle I put off writeing
untill the last. I have nothing new to inform you off   every thing
seem to be going on as it did when you was here. we missed
you a great deal after you went away and we are very anxious to
hear from you. mr Carter is expecting a letter from you every

day   he got a letter from mr Powell several days ago   he had been very sick but had got better. we expect him and mrs Powell and the widdow winston[2] down the last of next week. mrs winston will be on her way to Summerfield. mrs Powell was with mr Powell when he was down and she seemed to injoy her self here very much   they never got here untill nine oclock at night   mrs Powell never called on any one   neither did any one call on her while she was here. I saw mrs Avery not long ago   she and her daughters were well.

   master Johns family is well   I have seen mrs Lucy webb several times since you went away. she seems to be forgeting her trubles. she has been to Summerfield to see her sister mary. we have finished our summer Clothe and are making ready for the winter   my school Children have improved but little since you went away   the largest of them are out at work and those that I have every day are very small, Just learning their letters. I will do the best I can with them at night Schooll. Family prayers are regularly attended   Mike complanes as much as ever but he looks better and has a very good appetite. he has done nothing in the garden since you left. the plants in the garden looks very well. we have been eating peas and greens some time. several of the people are sick at this time but not dangerous. mrs Carter has been very unwell since you left. her baby is five weeks old. she is not able to leave her room. the docter came to see her a few days ago and said that if she is not very carefall she would be in bad health all of her life. she sends her love to you   we have been expecting mrs Walton[3] and mrs Dubois[4] for several days but I expect that mrs. Dubois is too unwell to come. I have nothing more to say   your servant

Lucy Skipwith

Genl John H Cocke

Source: Shields-Wilson deposit, Cocke Papers

1. J. Willie Carter (b. 1827?) served as the overseer at Hopewell for three stormy years, during which time the slaves conspired to destroy the cotton crop, pilfered, and embarrassed him sufficiently so that R. D. Powell had to remind him of his duties. Barely literate, his letters reveal little of Hopewell affairs.

2. Unable to identify.

3. Justina I. Walton of Greensboro.

4. Davisa Dubois, the wife of Rev. John Dubois.

Hopewell   July the 5/56

my Dear Master

I would have writen to you before this but hearing that you were absent from home I defered writeing untill I could hear of your ariveal. Mr Carter received your letter several days ago, and will answer it very soon. we were delighted to hear from you and to hear that you were injoying a reasonable share of health. may the Lord continue his mercyful kindness and his tender care towards you, and may he ever keep you in the hollow of his unerring hand. this leaves us in our usual state of health. Evelina has been very unwell for the last two or three weeks but the Dr has been called in to see her and she is now better. Mikes health seems to be the same no better nor no worse. he is still unable to work. Brother Howells little boy[1] has been very unwell but is now better. it is the little boy that was so Cross when you was out here. I think that it will be a hard matter to raise him. the weather is very hot indeed and we have had rain every evening for the last week which makes the grass grows very fast, but mr Carter thinks that he will be able to get through with it. mr Carter received a letter from mr Powell about two weeks ago but he did not say what time that he would be down but we are looking for him every day. mrs Powell did not come with him as she promased to do but she expects to come this time. I am sorry to tell you that mrs Lucy Webb has lossed her baby   it died the 23rd of June after and illness of four days. she seems to be in a deep destress about it. on the same night mr Joe Borden lossed his second daughter about four years old. the funeral of the Children took place next day at master Johns   it was preached by the Rev mr Wadsworth.[2] the two corps were placed togeather on a table untill preaching was over. then they were carried to old mrs Cockes and buried. it was disstressing to see the weeping mothers weeping for their Children. there was death at mas Joes three nights one after the other   two of his Colord Children also died and several very sick yet. master John lossed a Colord Child to day. his Children are all well.

mrs Carter is again restored to her usual health. her baby is well and grows very fast. Carters wife Jinney has been Confined and was deliverd of twins, but neither of them were alive. I am very much disincuraged with the pressant prospect of my school   it seems to be falling every day. in the week days I hardly ever have more than two Children and they are very small, and at my night schooll there is so many of them and I have them such a little while that it is little that I can learn them. my greatest Chance to learn them is on the sabbath. my sabbath school goes on very beautiful.

I was glad to hear that you had received my letter and would answer it soon. as I am at the end of my paper I can say nothing more. hopeing to hear from you soon I remane your servant

L S

Source: Shields-Wilson deposit, Cocke Papers
1. Berthier Skipwith.
2. Rev. Edward Wadsworth (1811–1889), a prominent Methodist clergyman and educator, preached at the Methodist church in Greensboro which had the largest black membership of any Methodist congregation in the county.

Hopewell   Aug the 29/1856

Dear master

I received your letter dated July the 14th and would have answerd it sooner but as I had Just writen you a long letter I thought that I would put it off untell this time. we have received no letter from you since the 14th of July, but have heard from you through mr Powell who was down here the 17th of July mr Carter got a letter from him a few days ago he was well. we have had a good deal of sickness this summer but no deaths. there is five down sick at this time with Chills and fever. poor Mike looks like he will never see another year he cannot walk without his Crutches. he has been trying to seek the Lord for the last four weeks, but it seems to be a hard matter for him to seek with his whole heart, for I do know that the moment he seeks the Lord with his whole heart he will be found of him.

I was in hopes that all our winter Clothes would have been finished by this time but the Cotton that was left in the Jin house was not half enough for the winter Clothes, so we had to wate for the new Cotton to open before we could go ahead makeing Cloth. the wool too had to be spun which takes a great deal of time as there is not many to spin it, but after all I will try to have the Clothes all done in time. I hope that another year there will be a plenty of Cotton left in the Jin house. the mulberys that you had planted in the garden are all dead   there is about two dozen of the Rose Cutings liveing. the young nursery of Fig and other slants that you planted are all alive

I heard from master Johns a few days ago   all were well but Willy and Johny[1] who has been very sick. master John and miss Lucy was expecting to come to virginia but they have given it out. they speaks of going to Arkansas this fall.

master Toms Family are all well. mrs Averys Family was well when I herd from them last. her son[2] has been teaching school at mrs Witherses all the summer. mrs withersses Family are all well. mr Bordens Family was well when I heard from them. miss mary Scott[3] has lossed her husband and has come back to her mothers to live. she has two Children. There has been but little improvement in reading this year. old and young seem to be learning but a very little. the people all sends their love to you and wishes to see you very much. Solomon sends his love to you and says that if you do not come out this winter you must send master Charles out but I hope that nothing will happen to pervent you from comeing out. The Top mare has a very fine horse Colt about three weeks old. george will go up to Columbus with her next week. give my love to Bertheer   tell him I hope to hear from him very soon   I will write to Brother William in a few days. give my love to all my Christian friends   tell them that I am determind by the help of god to meet them in heaven   tell them that it my greatest desire in this world to do the will of my Father which is in heaven, for he is my strength in weakness, he is my light in darkness, he is my all.

nothing more at preasant

Lucy Skipwith

Source: #2433-B Cocke deposit, Cocke Papers
1. Willy D. Cocke (d. 1864) and John Cocke, sons of John Cocke of Alabama.
2. William Avery (b. 1833?), who pursued teaching as a career for the remainder of his life.
3. Unable to identify, but see Lucy's letter of October 20, 1860 (p. 235), for another reference.

Hopewell   october the 13th 1856

my Dear Master

I would have writen to you before this, but when I have to write any thing that is displeaseing to you, it is always a berden to me to write. since I wrote to you last, their has been missbehaviour with some of the people. Armstead has had another falling out with mr Carter, and master John has been put to the truble to come here to have him corrected for his behaviour to mr C. uncle Charles has also rebelled against him. others have also done wrong but as the matter will not be investigated untell mr Powell comes down, you will then receive farther information.

Another thing makes me backward in writeing   I am not as far ahead with my winter Clothes as I wanted to get before writeing to you. Sister Etter has been very unwell of late, and I haves her busness to attend to which is a great pullback to mine. as no one can weave on the new loom but me, no one has wove a yard on it but me since you went away. I have yet 200 yrd to weave before my winter Clothes will be compleeted, but if I can stay at the loom it will take me but a very little while to finish as some part of it will be wove on the hand looms by Becky Bird.

It has been two or three weeks since we heard from mr Powell but we expect him down some time next week. mr Carter received your letter a few days ago and intends to answer it very soon. he had Just writen to you when he received it. miss mary Avery was here not long ago   she desired to be rememberd to you. the rest of their family was well. mrs walton and mrs Dubois and several other ladies from greensboro have visited the Cottage. mrs Harvey[1] had not returned home from Philadelphia when I heard from her last. master Johns family is well. master Toms also. mr Borden was very unwell when I heard from him. the neighborhood has been very sickly this fall and a great many Deaths bouth black and white. mrs Dufpheys soninlaw[2] while on a visit to her with his family from mobile died a few days ago, left a widdow and three Children. we keeps up family Prayers every morning. I does the best I can teaching the Children but I can never get more than two and sometime three little ones of week days. my little girl maria is begining to write very well and is very anxious to write to you   I haves a very little chance to teach her as she stays in the house with mrs Carter. miss mary Avery has been down again this morning looking for eggs and butter   we were able to furnish her with some. the health of the people seems to be geting better than it has been. the weather here is very warm at this time. it is not near as Cool as it was the first of September the Cotton fields looks as white as snow and mr Carter thinks that he will smartly overgo 100 bags. he has been to day and bought his rye from mr Smith. I have heard nothing from brother James since you went away. my little girl[3] at master Joes is learning but a very little as miss Fanny has been staying at her mothers ever since July, and the girl left at home to do mostly as she please. she cannot write atall, but reads very well. I will now come to a close hopeing soon to hear from you. I remane your servant

Lucy Skipwith

Gen John H Cocke

PS   mr Carter is got 58 Bags packed out. this is the 17th. I have Just had an opportunity to send my letter to the office   the weather this morning is very cool and clear.

LS

Source: Moore deposit, Cocke Papers

1. Sarah A. Harvey, the wife of John G. Harvey who edited the Greensboro *Alabama Beacon.*

2. Unable to identify.

3. Betsey Skipwith, who was hired out at age seven to Joe and Frances Borden in 1851. Cocke indentured her for a period of fourteen years and required the Bordens to teach her to read, to cipher, and to understand the basic precepts of Christianity. At the expiration of her term he would send her to Liberia with an outfit of $50. If she proved dishonest, drank alcohol, or smoked tobacco, she forfeited her claim to manumission. As related below, she did not live up to Cocke's or Lucy's hopes for propriety and Christian example.

Hopewell   may the 16th 1857

my Dear Master

   I hope that you have reached home safe and sound. long before this. and in good health. we all have been very unwell since you went away with bad colds and the sore throat   I have been very unwell for several days with it. but I am now better. old and young seem to be complaining with it.

Hopewell may the 16th 1857

my Dear Master

i hope that you have reached home safe and
sound . long before this . and in good health .
we all have been very unwell since you
went away with bad colds and the sore throats
i have been very unwell for several days
with it . but i am now better . old and
young seem to be complaining with it .
i have nothing new to inform you of .
every thing seem to be going on as it did
when you was here ; Mr Canter has written to you
giving you an account of his matters .
we are very anxious to hear from you . and
to hear whither Solomon is gone to Africa
or not . Mr Powell told me when he was down
that with your permission . when him and Mrs
bomes down the last of the month . that i may
go up with them to see Mother . i would thank
you very much to let me go as i will be done all
my summer work . before the end of this month
i have had no trouble with the loom since you went
away . i would be very glad if you would answer
this as soon as you can make it convenent .
nothing more at this time . i remain your servant
Lucy Skipwith

Lucy Skipwith's letter to John Hartwell Cocke, Hopewell, May 16, 1857. (From the Cocke
Papers, University of Virginia Library, Manuscript Division)

I have nothing new to Inform you of. every thing seem to be going on as it did when you was here. Mr Carter has writen to you giveing you an account of his matters.

we are very anxious to hear from you. and to hear whither Solomon is gone to Africa or not. Mr Powell told me when he was down that with your permission. when him and mrs P comes down the last of the month. that I may go up with them to see Mother. I would thank you very much to let me go as I will be done all my summer work before the end of this month   I have had no truble with the loom since you went away. I would be very glad if you would answer this as soon as you can make it convinent. nothing more at this time. I remane your servant

Lucy Skipwith

Source: #2433-B Cocke deposit, Cocke Papers

Hopewell   July the 26th 1857

mr Dear Master

It has been a long time since I have writen to you but it is not because I have forgotton to do so, but as Mr Carter and Mr Powell has bouth been writeing to you from this place, Mr Carter thinks it best for us all to write at diferent times

this leaves us all in our usual health. we have not had as much sickness this summer as we had last. the whole neighborhood seems to be more healthy than it was last summer. mrs Carters Baby has been in bad health this summer and has fallen off a great deal, but is now mending, but I hardly think that she will ever raise it. we heard from Mr Powell a few days ago. he was well and will be here by the 30th of this month. Mr Carter got your last letter, and we were glad to hear that you wer well. our garden has been very dry this summer and we have had a very few vegatables. all the Mulberys are dead. eight of the figs are liveing, and 7 Chestnuts. by this time you have heard of the Death of brother george. he had been Crippled 8 weeks before he died, but before he died he expressed his willingness to depart and live with god in heaven. we haves our family prayers regularly every morning. there seems to be a very little done here in the way of learning to read. it is seldom you can see any one with a Book in their hands. I haves my sabbath school regularly every sunday   Masters John and Thomases familys are well. Master John is gone to Rolley N C to carry miss mary to school. master Tom has a fine son called Thomas. Mr Bordens family is well   Mr Duboise fills his appointements a little more than he did last winter. I had the pleasare of hearing mrs Powells Brother[1] Preach while I was in Columbus   he is an excellent preacher and a worthy man   he says that he would like very much to come down to see you when you come out this winter   I will now bring my letter to a close as I intends writeing to you again very soon   your servant

Lucy Skipwith

Source: #5685, Cocke Papers
1. Rev. E. C. Hardy, a Methodist minister.

Hopewell   Aug the 31st 1857

my Dear Master

I would have writen to you before this but for eight or ten days I have been sick. I feels better at this time tho not well. Maria also has been very sick but is up again. mrs Carters Baby also has been very sick but it is now a little better. it has fallen off a great deal. mrs Carters health is not very good. the Children all seem to be suffering with very bad Colds. the old ones seem to stand very well. we have two very fine young Babies. one is Jinneys,[1] and the other Bettias.[2] Matilda[3] also had one but it died. I do not think that our sweet potatoe patch will make us many potatoes. they were planted so late I think that the frost will catch them. the Cotton seem to be opening very fast   they will start to picking it out before very long. the Carpenters are still workeing at the low place   mr Powell told Archa to try to get the Buildeings done by the first of November any how. mr Powell left this place on the 27th. he wrote to you from this place. you have heard I supose of his wifes sickness he expects to be here again the middle of November   Mr Bendon visited him while he was here. mrs Avery and miss mary

was here a few days ago   they were well. miss Fanny has not
yet returned from North Carolina. mr Ben Carter[4] is still liveing
with them, and expect to live there next year. the Topp mare
has a very fine horse colt. it is a very pretty Male. I am in hopes
that you will soon be makeing ready to start out here and spend
a longer time than ever with us, and should any thing pervent
you comeing I hope that master Charles will come. I send you
these verses which I have taken from the 10 Commandments. I
wish you would have them printed for me in a small track. I
will now bring my letter to a close   hopeing soon to hear from
you I remane your servant

Lucy Skipwith

The 10 Commandments

1st

Thou no god shalt have but me
This Command I give to Thee
love me then with all thy heart
Never from my words depart

2nd

Thou no golden gods shalt have
gods of silver do not love
Seek the true the liveing Lord
For I am a Jealous god

3rd

Thou shalt not take my name in vain
Sinful words thou shalt disdain
guiltless live before my face
And I will be thy hideing place

4th

Remember thou the Sabbath day
Never work nor even play
The god of Heaven will ever bless
The man who keeps the day of rest

5th

Honour thou thy Mothers words
Never break they Fathers laws
They who does their Parents will
Long upon this earth shall live

6th

Thou no murder shall commit
With the murders do not set
Lest thou learn his wicked ways
And live in Sorrow all thy days

7th
Thou no wicked deed shall do
Righteousness shalt thou persue
Let your actions all be right
And like the morning star be bright

8th
Thou shalt see by this Command
Honesty do I demand
Every human being should feel
That it is a sin to steal

9th
Thou shalt always speak the truth
To the aged and the youth
False witnesses do I despise
Ile drag them downwards from the sky

10th
Covetousness here thou see
Is a great offence to me
Thy neighbours goods thou shalt not crave
Thy neighbours goods thou shalt not have

Source: #5685, Cocke Papers
1. Jinney Morse (or Moss), the wife of Carter Morse, gave birth to Simon.
They removed to New Hope in 1857.
2. Bettia (or Betty) Creacy's child was named Jame.
3. Matilda Morse (or Moss), the wife of Cain Morse, lived on or near
Hopewell through 1880. She was literate.
4. Benjamin Carter, a farmer and occasional overseer.

Hopewell   May the 30/1858
my Dear Master
by this time I know that you are expecting a lettor from me,
but as mr Carter, mr Crain,[1] and Mr Powell have all writen to
you from this place, I have defered writeing untill this preasant
time   we were glad to hear from you through mr powell who
is with us at this preasant time, and I am glad to say that he
seems to be well pleased with the state of things here upon the
plantation. every thing has gone on very smoothly since you
went away. we are all in our usual state of health at preasant.
Champion has been very sick but is now better. we were glad to
hear that you were injoying a reasonable show of health   the
people are all delighted with Mr Crain. the people would not

have him to leave hear for nothing. he is indeed a kind hearted good man. Albert[2] sends his love to you and says that he thinks that god will bless you for geting such a man as Mr Crain to live here. the Chappel is in a much better state than it was when he took place. the people from all the plantations turns out most willingly to hear him and when he calls sinners to the Alter they comes in crowds. their has been several convcrsions since he took place. there is a great deal of differance in him and Mr Duboise. Mr Duboise has preached once since you went away I do not know whither he will give up his place to Mr Crain or not. Mr Crains health seems to be a little improven since he has been here. the sunflower seeds all came up and begining to bloom very pretty. the Fig trees planted in the Fence sine behind the depot are growing very pretty. the cuttings that you left in the little Boxes are all dead. the Lucern planted in the garden is growing very pretty. there has been no increace amoung the goats since you went away. the old Red goat was found dead in the Creek not long ago   we do not know whither she was sick or how she came to to be in ther. Mr. Borderns Family is well, also Master Toms, and Johns. since the above was writen Mr Crain have received your letter, and I received your message about writeing to you. he says that he will write to you in a week or two. he would write now but as Mr P and my self have writen he thinks best to put it off. I will no[w] bring my letter to a close hopeing soon to hear from you again. your servant

Lucy Skipwith

J H Cocke

Source: #2433-B Cocke deposit, Cocke Papers

1. Rev. Francis M. Crain (d. 1859), a native of Autauga County, Alabama, had been preaching about five years in the Methodist Episcopal church when he came into Cocke's employ as plantation preacher. Crain was the most successful white minister Cocke engaged, and several revivals occurred during his brief stay with the Greene County blacks. Although a weak man physically, he bellowed forth the Word in a powerful manner, and his genuine concern for the welfare of his black charges earned him the respect of the Hopewell slaves and the discriminating Lucy.

2. Albert Morse (or Moss) was born in Virginia in 1833 and worked as a field hand at Hopewell. He was the son of Charles and Kessiah Morse and the husband of Martha (Skipwith) Morse. After the war he continued to work as a farm laborer while residing among other members of the Morse clan on the Key property near Hopewell. He did, however, send his three children to school.

                                        Hopewell   Aug the 1st '50 [1858]
my Dear Master

  I received your letter several weeks ago and wrote in answer
to it but as I had not the opportunity of sending it to the office
when it was writen, I found it nessary that I should write again,
but as Mr Crain was about to write, I defered writeing untill the
presant time, thinkeing that it would be more pleasure to you to
have a little diferance in the times of our writeing. This leaves
the greatest part of us in the injoyment of good health. we have
had but little sickness this summer. Isham was quite sick a few
days ago but is now better. we had a little Child also that was
quite sick but is now nearly well. I am sorry to tell you that Mr
Crain has been confined to his bed for several days. I am glad to
say that he is a little better to day tho not able to set up. he has
suffered a great deal and has not been able to sleep for two
nights and days. we does all in our power to make him comfortable. I was glad to hear in your letter that your health was
good. I hope that you will be able to come out early, and spend
the fall and winter with us. several of the people at Mr Meltons[1]
are sick at this time. Mrs Melton is also sick but none of them
are dangerous. Capt Cocke has Just returned from his other
place with his family. they are well. they have been down there
all the summer. Mr Borden and the rest of his family is well.
Mrs Avery and her Daughters have Just returned home after an
absents of six or eight weeks. they are well. the old lady and Mr
Ben Carter have parted at last and he is going to live with Mr
Alfred Hatch.[2] she has one overseer at this time. the people
have all behaved themselves very well. I have heard no complaint from Mr Carter about them. they all Joines me in love to
you and wishes to see you very much. I often think of the time
when you will come to spend the winter with us, but if it be so
that we never meet again in this world, let us strive to meet
each other in that good world where parting shall be no more. I
often think that I shall never be able to get there, but the grace
of God has brought me safe thus far and I trust that his grace
will lead me home. As Mr Crain wishes to write a few lines in
this letter I will bring my letter to a close   hopeing that we
may soon hear from you I remane your servant
                                                    Lucy Skipwith
[*Enclosed with letter of F. M. Crain to J. H. Cocke*]

Source: #2433-B Cocke deposit, Cocke Papers

1. John Melton (or Milton) was a planter of the neighborhood. His wife's name was Eliza. Their son John worked as an overseer at New Hope in 1858; nothing further is known of his brief service.

2. Thomas Alfred Hatch (1841–1863), the son of Lemuel D. Hatch, worked "Arcola," one of the Hatch estates near Hopewell.

Hopewell   Sep the [?] 1858

my Dear Master

I again seat myself to write you a few lines to let you hear from us. we are all well at this time and hope that this letter may find you the same. Mr Carter received your letter a week ago. we were glad to hear that you were well. he also received a letter from Mr Powell   he was at the Springs in va but expected to be at home by this time. his wife was sick at the time he wrote. I suppose Mr Carter has writen to you about the Death of Godfrey[1] who fell from the screw in the time of packing cotton and died the next day. Mr Crain has been very unwell for better than a week. he has been confined to his room with a risor on his abdomen but he is now up again, and says that he will write to you in a few days. he is indeed a great comfort to the whole plantation and his dayly walk and conversation proves him to be a Child of God. he is doing all that he can at the Chapel, and many of them are Inquireing the way to zion. the people are all well at the other place. I understands that Mr Melton is very anxious to leave from there and is trying to get busness elsewhere, but you will find out more about it when Mr Powell comes. Mr Ben Carter has left mrs Avery and is liveing with Mr Alfred Hatch. mrs Averys family is well and she is got another overseer.[2] Master Johns family is well. his overseer has also left him. the rest of the family is all well. you will see by the papers the Death of one of mrs Witherses little boys. the plantation affairs seems to be going on as usual   I hears but a very little complaint   mrs Carter and the Children are well. as I have the opportunity of sending my leter to the office I must bring my letter to a close. hopeing soon to hear from you an see you I remane your servant

Lucy Skipwith

Source: #5685, Cocke Papers
1. Godfrey was a young field hand at the time of his death.
2. Unable to identify.

Hopewell   Nov the 8th 1858

my Dear Master

I received your letter dated the 12th of last month but as Mr Powell was here at that time and had writen to you I defered writeing untell this time. I was very glad to hear from you and to hear that you expected so soon to be with us. I hope that nothing will pervent you from comeing out next month   we are all in tolerable good health at this time except Etter who has been very unwell for a week with bleeding at the Lungs but is now better but is looking very pale.

We have the new overseer[1] with us at this time. he seems to be a very good man. he has a wife[2] and three Children. he went down to the other place to stay the balance of the year, but him and his family keept so unwell that he had to move back up here. he goes down every morning and stay all day. they live in one end of mr Carters house. mr Carter and his family are well. I do not know whither they will go away before you come or not. I do not know where he expects to go another year

I do not know hardly what to say to you about mr Crains health. he is one day better and the next day worse that it is hard to tell whither his health is improveing or not. he expects to start to Conferance next week if he is able, which will be held in Macon Miss. he would send you some message but he is not at home.

We have some very nice potatoes and will have enough of them to last all the winter. we have them cooked for the people every day.

we have had a very warm fall so far. it has not been cold enough to put on winter Clothes but we had a big frost last night and to day it is quite cold. The neighbours around us are all well   I cannot tell you how master Johns family is as they are all down at his wifes place   as you expects to be with us very soon I will add no more.

your servant
Lucy Skipwith

Source: #2433-B Cocke deposit, Cocke Papers

1. William N. Lawrence, the overseer at New Hope from 1858 to 1859 and at Hopewell in 1859, was engaged by R. D. Powell, who had some reservations about his firmness and intelligence.

2. Cocke referred to Mrs. Lawrence (d. 1863) as a "strenuous Mississippi tobacco dipper and opium Eater and withall a professed member of the Meth. Ep.—judge what must be a standard of Religion where such a subject is tolerated." See JHC to Cary Charles Cocke, March 30, 1857[9?], #6418, Cocke Papers. Lucy and Mrs. Lawrence did not get along. See her remarks below.

Hopewell   June the 9th 1859

my Dear Master

I received your message by mr Powell, also the one by mr Lawrence about not writeing to you, and I am sorry that you had to romind me of it. I would have writen to you before this but I have been waiteing to hear of your safe arival at home. as we had not heard a word from you we did not know but what you was sick on the road. we are much releaved by hearing from you and will try to let you hear from us as often as necessary, and keep you informed of our movements here.

I knoe that you will be mortified to hear of the troble that my little girl Betsey has got into at mr Joe Bordens by being perswaded by one of their servants to steal money for him,[1] and I lear[ne]d that this is the second time that he has made her do it. she says that she had no thought of it being so much monney   neither did he. he saw that she did not dress up like the other girls did and he tempted her with such things as he knew she wanted. I do not know what master Joe will do with the man. he belongs to mr Ben Borden but he lives with master Joe. he has a wife and four Children at master Joes. he also has Brothers and Sisters there, and I heard mas Joe say to day that they were good hands to work, but they would steal, and that girl is growing up among them and if she continue there they will bring her to everlasting destruction. her mistress has taken very little pains to bring her up right. the girl has had the raising of her self up. she has been left down there among those people four and six weeks at a time with not as much as a little sewing to do, and now they complains of her being so lazy. It seems to be almost Imposeing upon you to ask the faver of you to let the Child come home, but I would thank you a thousand time If you would do so. I want to give her religious instruct-tions and try to be the means of saving her soul from death. master Joe says he rather that she would come home. mr Powell says he thinks she had better come home and work in Williams[2] place and let him work out. I hope that you will not sell her if you can posuble do any thing else with her. if you do sell her, have you any objection of my trying to get mr Powell to bye her, providing he is willing to do so, as I think that he could make a woman of her. let me hear from you on the Subject by the first of July. if it was not for the grace of god I would sink beneath such a load as this, but I have a preasant help in the time of troble. I have not seen the girl but once in twelve months. We are all geting along very well at this time. the people are all well, and in good Spirits, and I hope that we may continue to do well. mr Lawrence still holds family Prayers with us every Sunday morning, and explains the scriptures to us. we have had preaching at the Chapple three times this year. we have mr Duboise and Dr Mears the school teacher[3] from greensboro. they will preach every second and fourth sunday in the month. we have Just received a letter from mr Crains sister. she wants his things to be sent to her by mr Powells wagon when it comes down after his goats next monts. we have seven beautiful little kids since you went away, and two very pretty Coalts. we have a very nice garden but every thing is suffering very much for rain.

I have seen nothing of the Japan plum seed in the flower pots nor the garden. only one of the Chessnuts have come up. I will write to you again soon. the people Joines me in love to you. nothing more at preasant from your servant

Lucy Skipwith

To Gen John H Cocke

Source: Shields-Wilson deposit, Cocke Papers

1. The letters of the victim, Joseph Borden (June 9, 1859), and of R. D. Powell (June 9, 1859) to Cocke corroborate Lucy's account of the $300 theft, although Borden's account relates the grim details of the whipping Betsey suffered. R. D. Powell recommended that Betsey return to Lucy's care at Hopewell, where "she can be better trained than to live under the influence of such negroes as I learn some of them are" at Borden's place. This was no act of charity on Powell's part, for in 1862, after Betsey had given birth to a white bastard child, he confessed: "I did not put Betsey with her mother to stop the sale of her but to better prepare her for sale." See R. D. Powell to JHC, Dec. 8, 1862, #5685, Cocke Papers. For further accounts of Betsey's tragic history see below.

2. William (d. 1863) was the "little yellow boy" who professed religion so powerfully in October, 1859. He remained at Hopewell employed as a field hand until 1863, when the Confederate government forced him to build fortifications in Mobile. He died there.

3. Rev. Joseph W. Mears of Vermont had earlier established the Mears English and French Institute for young girls in Montgomery before removing to Greensboro. He was a Methodist minister and teacher there.

Hopewell   July the 28th 1859

my Dear master

I wrote to you the 9 day of this month and hope that my letter has been received and answerd before this reaches you, and as I promsed to write again soon, I shall not wait to receive a letter from you before doing so. we are all well at this time except too of the women, but they are not dangerously sick. every thing seem to be going on very well. mr Lawrence has had no fuss with his hands attall. we all think a great deal of him for we can see in his daily walkes and in his conversation that he is a Child of god. the habits of his wife are the same as when you was here. she still uses the snuff and the Laudanum, by night and by day. she received your message in your last letter to mr Lawrence about the watch. her Children are spoilt as bad as ever she whips them to day and humours them to morrow and so her whiping them does them no good atall. I never saw such Children in my life. it is a pitty for such a good man as mr L is to have such a family as he is got for they all imposes upon him. mrs L health continues to be so bad that she is gone up with her children to spend two weeks at her Fathers. mr L has been very uneasy about his crop, but seem to be in better spirits at pre-ast   he says that he will write to you in a few days. the three little Coalts in the yard are very pretty and is growing very fast. we also have nine very promasing little kids. the old black goat has two very fine kids, and I think that she will raise them. our garden is still very good. we have a plenty of greens, and thousands of Tomatoes. there is five of the Chessnuts up at preasant, and I think that more will come up after a while. none of the Japan plum seed have come up as yet. I have heard no more about the monney scrape at mr Bordens. Capt Cockes family are all at their other place. I heard that mrs Lucy Webb and miss mary B Cocke are bouth to be married very soon. I do not know the gentleman, as they are not Alabamans   write to me soon and believe as ever your servant

L S

[*In margin*] mr melton is turned of from mr Jones,[1] and gone back to mississippi   we have had a plenty of rain since I wrote you last

Source: Shields-Wilson deposit, Cocke Papers
1. Probably William Jones, a small planter living near Greensboro.

Hopewell   oct the 2nd 1859

My Dear Master

I again seat myself to write you a few lines hopeing that they may find you in the injoyment of good health. Mr Lawrence received your last letter and we were very glad to hear from you and also to hear that you hope soon to be with us. I hope that nothing will pervent you from comeing out as we are all looking forward with Joy to the time of your ariveal here. This leaves us in our usual state of health with the exception of a few Chills once and a while, but we are all up at this time. I am rejoyced to tell you that we have had a most beautiful revival of religion amoungst us, and it is the prettyest revival that I ever saw in my life. we have 11 that has been converted within the last two weeks. there is not a grown person amoung them. they are all my Sabbath School Schollars. they have all professed that are large enough but two, and they are crying aloud for mercy and I hope that before this reaches you that those two may be brought to the knowledge and truth of our Lord and Saviour Jesus Christ. amoung the Converts is my daughter that came home from Mr Joe Bordens. she came home a stranger to god, and a stranger to me, but I thank the Lord that she is now able to say that she once was lossed, but now is found, was blind, but now she see. the little yellow Boy William also professed. he had a most powerful conversion. you would be happy to see them at this time and hear them talk about the goodness of god. there has none professed at the other place as yet, but some are seeking. it is indeed a great wonder to see so many young people all turn to the Lord in so short a time. I pray that god may dwell with us untill the last sinner may come. Mr Powell spent last sunday and monday with us. he did not write to you from here but said that he would write to you when he returned home the stork of all kind as far as I can see seem to be doing well. we have had no more young kids. the young ones seem to be growing very fast. I am inhopes that we will have more milch cows to the pail than we had last winter. we have very nice milk and Butter at this time.

we have had bad luck with our Fowls this year. the Rats and Minks destroyes them as fast as we hatch them. the Chickens now have a very bad stemper amoung them, a brakeing out about their head   we have a very nice Turnip patch indeed. we also have some very nice winter Cabbage coming on in the garden. The weather at this time is very fair and pretty for picking Cotton, and the people are trying to save it all. Mr Lawrence has twelve Bags packed up here, and ten at the other place. I cannot tell you how Capt Cocke and Mr Borden familyes are as they are not at home. as I have the opportunty of sending my letter to the office I must conclude   I remane your servant

Lucy Skipwith

Source: #2433-B Cocke deposit, Cocke Papers

nov the 8th 1859

my Dear master

I received your letter a few weeks ago, and would have answerd it before this, but as it was mr Lawrences time to write I have been wateing for him to write, but he is so long writeing I must let you hear from us. this leaves us all well but Sippio[1] who is very sick at this time. I have not time to write much as the boy is going to the office now and I did not know it untell Just now   mr lawrence has shiped som Cotton but I do not know how much Just now   surely he will write to you in a few days. I do not want him to know that I have writen to you, as it is his time to write   I will write again soon if he does not. our number of young converts at this time is 15   amoung [them] is

Spencer the Black Smith   I can say no more at this time as I am in a hurry

Lucy Skipwith

Source: #2433-B Cocke deposit, Cocke Papers
1. Scipio was a field worker at Hopewell.

November the 22nd 1859

my Dear Master

I received your letter yesterday, and was delighted to hear from you and to hear that you expect so soon to be with us. I am sorry to tell you my Dear Master that your letter caused me to see trouble. after reading it, mrs Lawrence desired me to hand it to her to read, and this I could not do, for I did not want them to know that I had writen to you unbeknowing to them, for they want to see every line that I write to you, and they would have been very angry with me to see that your letter was in answer to one that they did not know that I had writen to you. I told mrs L. I had rather no one read it but myself, that nothing was in it that conserned any one atall. she then desired her husband to make me give it up to them, and I then put it in the fire and burnt it up, and I would have rather taken punishment than to have given it to them. they abused me very much with words, but did not strike me. she insisted that her husband would give me five hundred lashes, but he has not done it. I have given neither of them a cross word about it. mr Lawrence has writen to you and I recond has given you an account of every thing, and as you expect so soon to be with us, I will say no more your servant

Lucy Skipwith

PS   I hope that you will have in mind what I said to you last winter about keeping up your own table in your house, for the way that mrs L acted in several respects last winter, it is actualy necessary that you should do so, and if you conclude to do so, get some new table Cloths as you come through Richmond you also need a dinner table. I am afraid to direct my letter to you. I will direct it to miss Sally or I will have it directed to Birthier

Lucy Skipwith

Source: Shields-Wilson deposit, Cocke Papers

Hopewell   Feb the 4th 1860

Dear master Charles[1]

I wrote to you tuesday as you desired me to do and will write
again this morning to let you hear from master. he still seem to
be improveing every day and I hope he will soon be restored to
his usual health again. the weather is now good again and he is
able to walk out every day as well as ride. his appetite is a great
deal better than it has been. we have heard nothing from Mr
Powell since he went away. we have seen nothing of master
Philip but I hope that he will soon be here, for it is necessary for
somboddy to be hear besides master, for I have had to dissturbe
him already about some of mrs Lawrences mean ways towards
him

Lucy Skipwith

Source: Moore deposit, Cocke Papers
1. Cary Charles Cocke, Cocke's son.

Hopewell   April the 28th 1860

my Dear Master

I hope that you have arived safe at home long before this, and
had a Joyous meeting with those who never expected to see you
again on earth. I hope that you had a pleasant trip and is now
injoying better health than when you went away. I feels very
anxious to hear of your health since your return home.

We are all well at this time and I hope that we are doing well.
the people are all in fine spirits and is trying to do their worke
well. they are very busy now choping out the Cotton. there is a
good stand of cotton and corn on boath places. we have had
copious showers of rain, which was very favourable for the
crops. since the rain we have had very cool weather. cold
enough to keep a fire all day. the Thermometer yesterday was
48 to day 50. The garden is looking very nice since the rain and
the cabage is growing very fast indeed. all the plants are looking well. Etter gets along very well workeing the garden. no

slips has come up as yet from the potatoes that Dr Brent[1] brought out.

Smith[2] is well and is very well sattisfied here with us. he is very well pleased with his School. he says that the the mares worked well from Marion home. we heard from mr Powell yesterday   he expects to be here the 3rd of May. he said he did not know whither his wife would be able to come down or not. uncle Charles has whitewashed the House and it looks much better than it did. he expects to go to Mr L Hatches[3] next week. he has whitewashed all the Houses at boath places. We have had three young kids since you went away but we have lossed one. Mr Nelsons[4] Buck goat has been carried home, and ours brought back. Mr Borden has sent them home that were at his house.

Maria is well and stands working out better than I expected
I have been reading the little Book in the medicine chest and find it a great help to Smith and my self about giveing medicine. are you going to try to do without a Docter. I shall soon be done the people summer Clothes and be ready to start on the next winters worke and try to have every thing done in good time. The little mulbery tree in the yard looks very nice and it has mulberys on it nearly ripe.

Cain[5] says the Oats are looking very nice

The people in the neighbourhood are all well   I will now bring my letter to a close   hopeing soon to hear from you I remane your servant

Lucy Skipwith

Source: Moore deposit, Cocke Papers

1. Dr. Arthur Lee Brent (1821–1871) married Cocke's daughter Sally and managed the Bremo Recess plantation.

2. Smith Powell, no more than seventeen or eighteen years old, was R. D. Powell's nephew and the overseer at Hopewell from 1860 to 1862. Smith Powell attended Southern University in Greensboro with R. F. Nickles, the young overseer at New Hope.

3. Lemuel Durant Hatch, a Presbyterian minister, devoted the last years of his life to a ministry among blacks in the Tuscaloosa Presbytery. He died in 1866. His son Lemuel D. Hatch, Jr. (1841–1905) operated the family home, "Roseland," at this time.

4. Sydney Nelson, a neighbor and planter with whom Cocke clashed over land titles and surveys.

5. Cain Morse (or Moss) was born in Virginia in 1828. He was another of the sons of Charles and Kessiah Morse. He toiled as a field hand before assuming the duties of foreman, along with Champion, in 1860. He married Matilda and

lived in the area at least until 1880. Cain was one of the Cocke slaves who knew how to read and write.

Hopewell   May the 26th 1860

my Dear Master

I received your letter dated May the 16th and was very glad to hear from you, and to hear that your health still continues to improve. Smith also received a letter from you a few days ago.

We have had some little sickness with us since I wrote you, but we are all up again.

I have nothing new to inform you of. every thing seems to be going on as when I last wrote. Cain will finish going over his cotton the second time in a few days with the hoes. the Plows are going over it the third time. the cotton grows very fast, and is cleaner of grass than I have ever seen it. the Cotton in the Lawn looks very nice indeed. the Corn Crop is growing very fast and looks promising   The Chinese Shugar Millet is looking very well, and I think that we shall have a very good Crop of that.

The garden still looks very nice. we have very nice Irish Potatoes, Cabbage, Peas, and Squashes. we have no ripe Tomatoes as yet but soon will have some. The Sun Flowers are in bloom and looks pretty. We have more than half of our Potatoe Patch planted over, and we are going to try and finish it next week. Sprouts has come up from every one of the old Fig trees   there was a dead one amoung them. they are all trimed up. The Crops at New Hope are doing well. there has been less sickness down there so far than we have had up here.

uncle Charles is Jobing about here at home   he has been off but a very little since you went away   the Children are all well at boath places and growing very fast.

Mr Powell was well when we heard from him last. he will be with us the first of June. his wife still speaks of comeing with him.

Smith is well and desires to be rememberd to you   he seems to be very well sattisfied here with us. the people seem to like him very much. he is growing very fast. he spends some nights down at New Hope. I have but ten young Turkeys as yet but soon will have more. the people in the neighbourhood are well   give my love to Bertheer   tell him that I have writen to him and hope that my letter has been received. Remember me kindly to master Charles when you see him   I hope that he will come out again some time. when you write again i would like to hear how master Charles little son has got.

Smith sends his love to Dr Brent and says that he will write to him soon. I will now bring my letter to a close   hopeing that your health may continue to improve I remane your servant

Lucy Skipwith

Genl John H Cocke

Source: #2433-B Cocke deposit, Cocke Papers

Hopewell   June the 25th 1860

my Dear Master

By this time you are expecting a letter from me, and I take my seat with pleasure to write to you. we are all well and have had better health so far than our neighbours around us. I have been very unwell for several days but feels much better this morning. I have nothing new to inform you of. every thing seem to be going on as usual. The Crops still seem to be in a prosperous state. we have had no roastingears as yet but I think that they are in the field. We have had several good rains of late, which fell in due season. I think that we will have a very good Crop of sweet potatoes as we have a very large patch planted and is growing very fast.

We have a very good garden and have had earlyer Cabbage and Tomatoes than any body in the neighbourhood. we have sent several messes to boath mrs Avery and mrs Borden. we are going to have a few Figs from the trees in the garden some from the old trees and some from the young ones. Smith desires to be remembered to you   he says that there is seven stacks of oats made this year. they could not get rain at the right time.

mr Beng Borden has been very sick but is up again. he brought us some very nice watermellons this morning   We get a letter from mr Powell a few days ago. he was well, and will be with us the 1st day of July. he expects to stay with us two weeks this time. his wife has not been able to come down to see us yet. we have been expecting her ever since you went away. Mr Lawrence has left Greensboro, and is liveing on the young Joness plantation 9 miles from Greensboro. his wife has been very sick this summer. The goats are all looking very well except the old black goat   she looks very bad. we have had no more young kids this summer.

we have preaching regularly twice a month at the Chapple. the Church seem to be in a very cold state. I am geting along very well with the people winter Clothse. I will now bring my letter to a close   hopeing soon to hear from you I remane your servant

Lucy Skipwith

Source: #2433-B Cocke deposit, Cocke Papers

Hopewell   July the 21st 1860

my Dear master

By this time you are expecting a letter from me. I have writen to you monthly and hope that all my letters has been received. I received your letter dated July the 2nd and was glad to hear that you had been benefited by your visit to the hot springs. I was glad also to hear of the improvement of master Charleses little Boys health.

We are all well at this time with the exception of a little girl who has been very ill for ten days, but is now a little better. the Dr has visited her twice a day for several days. she is a little girl five years old. Mr Powell has made his July visit to us   he stayed ten days with us, and was well sattisfied with every thing on the two plantation. the letter you wrote him has Just been received and is forwarded to Columbus. he will be here again the 1st cf august.

We are suffering very much with hot weather   it is the hotest summer that I have ever seen. we have not had a good rain since the 21st of June. every thing is very dry. if the garden does not get rain very soon every thing will be burned up. there is no apeareance of rain at preasant.

the Carpenters are at home workeing on the screw. The

young fig sprouts are growing very fast   mrs Avery and the young Ladies are well. mr Bordens family are also well. mr Borden and his wife visited mr Powell while he was down Cain desires to be rememberd to you. I will now bring my letter to a close   hopeing that it may find you well I will add no more   your servant

Lucy Skipwith

[Enclosed with letter of Smith Powell to J. H. Cocke.]

Source: #2433-B Cocke deposit, Cocke Papers

Hopewell   August the 25th 1860

Dear Master

I received your letter dated July the 18th and would have answerd it immediately, but as I had Just writen to you I defered writeing untill the preasent time. I was glad to hear that your health had been benefited by your visit to the hot Springs, and I hope that your health may continue to improve and that you will be able to come out early this fall. Doubtless you have seen in the papers the accounts of our once promaceing crops, but Him who doth not willingly afflict the Children of men, knows best what to do for us, and in adversity as well as in prosperity, we should say not our will but thine be done.

the Cotton since the big rain is growing but I do not think that it will yield any more. Cain will soon finish picking over his Cotton the first time. the Cotton that was open was damaged by the heavy rain. we commenced gining yesterday. what little we have in the garden is looking better since the rain. we have sowed Turnip Seed and they are comeing up very well. we have also sowed Spinage and kale, boath here and at new hope. we had a light rain yesterday which was very good for them. we have heard nothing from Mr Powell since his return home from here. several persons visited him during his July visit to us, Mr and Mrs Borden, Mr Robert Withers,[1] Mr Bawldwin[2] from Mobile and a young Minister from Greensboro.[3] the Carpenters are at home building a new Screw which they will raise to day. uncle Charles is also at home Jobing about. he has done a very little this year towards makeing money.

Smith sends his love to you. he is well but was very sick several days ago with the Colic. he will commence going to school monday week. we have had no preaching at the Chapple for nearly two months, but we expect to have some to morrow. one of the young ministers from greensboro[4] have been out and spent a night with us, and promased to come out again. we have family prayers every morning. I have my Sabbath School every sunday and I am happy to say that I can see a little improvement in some of my Scholars. Smith takes a delight in assisting me in the sabbath school, and is never absent from there. he is very good to learn any body any thing that he can. Mr Borden spent last Sabbath evening here with him   master John was here the other day. his family is well. nothing more from your servant

Lucy Skipwith

Source: #2433-B Cocke deposit, Cocke Papers
1. Robert Walker Withers, the son of the late Dr. Robert W. Withers, lived with his mother, Mary D. Withers, on the family plantation near Hopewell.
2. Probably Rev. J. D. Baldwin, a Methodist minister in Mobile.
3. Unable to identify.
4. Unable to identify.

Hopewell   Sept the 22nd 1860

my Dear Master

I have writen to you regularly every mounth and hope that all my letters have been received. This leaves us all in the injoyment of our usual health. we have had some little sickness since I last wrote but all are well again. I am glad to see by all of your letters that your health continues to improve, and I hope that you may be able to come out early this Fall. I have nothing new to inform you off. every thing seems to be going on as usual. I think that we are going to have quite an early Fall. the weather this morning is quite cool. the Thermometer this morning was 58. Since the late rains the garden has afforded us a few more vegatables. we have a very good Turnip patch in the garden. Cain is going ahead picking out his Cotton. he is also sowing Rye. our hands have been down to New Hope to help Armstead pick out some of his Cotton. The Carpenters have finishd their work here and gone off again. uncle Charles is still at home. Smith received a letter from Mr Powell the other day he was well and will be here the 2nd of oct   Mr Bordens and Capt Cockes familys are well. as Smith wants to say a few words to you I will say no more   your servant

Lucy Skipwith

[Enclosed with letter of Smith Powell to J. H. Cocke]

   Source: #5680, Cocke Papers

Hopewell   oct the 20th 1860

Dear Master

   We have been expecting a letter from you every day but have not received one for nearly two mounths. I hope that you are not confined to a bed of sickness.

   Several of the people are sick at this time but I hope that all will be well in a few days. Etter keeps very unwell but I hope that she will soon injoy better health.

   The garden is looking very well and we still have some vegatables to eat. we have very nice Tomatoes, and the nicest Butter Beans that we have had this summer. we also have winter greens and a very good Turnip patch in the garden. I do not think that our Crop of sweet potatoes will be very good. the vines looks well but the potatoes are small. they may be larger in some parts of the patch that we have not tried. Mr Powell left us yesterday after spending three days with us. he would have stayed longer but had to attend to some busness in Eutaw. Mr Robert and William Withers[1] dined with him while he was here.

   one of the Carrage mares was taken very sick while mr P was here   we came very near looseing her, but she is now a great deal better   The weather at this time is very cool. I do not think that we will have any more warm weather. we have had frost twice. it was heav[i]er at New Hope than it was here.

   there is a great many young bolls on the Cotton but they are two late to make any thing. our hands are going down to New Hope next week to help pick out Cotton down there a few days. Armstead thinks that he will make about fifty bales. uncle

Charles is workeing in greensboro at this time. Mr Banister[2] expects to leave Greensboro in two weeks   he is going to live in Huntsville Ala   aunt Kejiea expects to live with Mr John May of Greensboro. Mrs Withers wishes very much to hire her. Mrs Averys family was well when I heard from them   Miss Mary Avery is in Tennessee.

Mr Bordens family is well. he has had the carrage and mares several times. mrs mary Scott is to be married the 24th inst to a Mr Howard[3] of Gainsville Ala   Dr Grigg is married to one of Col Jamess daughters[4]   I will now bring my letter to a close hopeing soon to hear from you   your servant

Lucy Skipwith

Smith desires to be remembered to you

Source: #2433-B Cocke deposit, Cocke Papers

1. William Withers was the brother of Robert Walker Withers—sons of the late Dr. Robert W. Withers.

2. Rev. John M. Banister (1818–1907), an Episcopal minister born in Virginia, was the rector of St. Paul's Church in Greensboro (1850–1860) before moving to Huntsville, Alabama. He was a friend of Cocke's and visited Hopewell on several occasions. In 1851 he hired Kessiah Morse (or Moss) as cook, a position she held until his relocation in Huntsville. On her conditions of employment see her letters, Kissire Cock [Morse] to Sally (Cocke) Brent, June 1, 1851, April 9, 1859, #9513 "Bremo Recess" deposit, Cocke Papers. Her subsequent employment arrangements are unknown.

3. Unable to identify.

4. Dr. J. Beverly Grigg (b. 1821?), a Greensboro physician who occasionally administered to the Hopewell community, married Alice G. James, the daughter of a local planter named Francis James.

Hopewell   May the 1st 1861

my Dear Master

As there has been several letters writen to you from here I have put off writeing untell this time. We are not all well at preasant. I have been very unwell for two or three days but feels a little better to day. Mr S Powell has also been very unwell. he fell over a stump in the yard the other night and got his arm knocked out of place but he is nearly well again. The woman Sally[1] that was sick when you went away has not yet been restored to her health but is now walking about. the rest of the people are very well   Cain commenced chopping out cotton yesterday. it looks very well what part of it that I have seen, but they say that it has not come up very well in some places. the corn they say is doing very well, both here and at New Hope. our potatoes are coming up very well. we planted our first Saturday evening. the garden seems to be comeing on very well. we have but a very few Tomatoes plantes as yet but I think that more will come up after a while. we have had garden peas ever since the first of april. the cabbage is growing very fast. the peas that you brought out are planted in the garden and are all up. Etter and her Baby are bouth well. her Baby grows very fast. We got a letter from Mr Powell a few days ago. he was well but he did not say what time that he would be down. I saw Mr and Mrs Borden last Sunday   they were very anxious to hear from you   their family and master Joes are all well. mrs Averys family is well   I heard that Miss Mary is comeing home. we have preaching regularly at the Chapel. Mr Brame[2] took dinner with us the last time he preached at the Chapel. the people thinks a great deal of him. I will now bring my letter to a close hopeing soon to hear from you. your servant

Lucy Skipwith

Genl. John H. Cocke.

Source: Moore deposit, Cocke Papers
1. Sally (d.1862) was a member of the house gang.
2. Rev. Charles E. Brame (b. 1823?) preached at the chapel in 1861 and 1862 and ran the Greensboro Female Academy until 1863.

Hopewell   May the 30th 1861

my Dear Master

I wrote to you the first of May and hope that my letter has been received. I was sorry to hear that you were not very well but I hope that by this time you are restored to your usual health. The Crops I think are in very good order. the cotton that I have seen looks very well. we have our Potato patch more than half planted. the plants are all liveing and looks very well. the garden is looking better than it did a week or two ago. we will have a plenty of Tomatoes after a while. we have at this time Peas Snapps Cabbage Squash, and soon will have cucumbers. Mr Powell thinks that some one elce wold make a better gardner than Etter. he will decide when he comes here again, which will be the 4th of June. we got a letter from him to day   he was well. the people here and at New Hope are well. the woman that has been sick so long is now nearly well. Mrs Avery was very sick a few days ago but is now better. Mrs Joe Borden also has a very sick Child. I have not seen Capt Cocke since you went away. he stays up here but a very little. I am geting along with my house busness very well. the people have all got their summer Clothes boath here and at New hope. The weather at this time is very warm. two weeks ago it was cool enough to keep a fire all day. we are now haveing a fine Shower of rain. we have not had any rain before for three weeks. we have preaching regularly at the Chapel. I send you a piece that Mr Brame has had published in the Religious Herald about this plantation,[1] thinking that you may not have seen it. he made a little misstake in the number of people, but that makes but little difference. I am glad to see that he thinks so much of us. Mr S Powell is well and desires to be remembered to you. nothing more from your servant

Lucy Skipwith

PS   May [June?] the 4th   my letter has been in the office a day or two and it is sent back to me to be paid for with money. I have your letter dated May the 27th. I feels submissive to the will of God comeing my Brother.

Lucy Skipwith

Source: Moore deposit, Cocke Papers
1. The *Religious Herald* reprinted an article Brame published in the Tus-kegee *South Western Baptist,* April 25, 1861. Brame described Cocke's brick plantation chapel, remarkable in that it had a stove, and the pattern of the three monthly services held there for the neighborhood slaves. Brame put the figure of slaves at sixty for Hopewell and twenty-five at New Hope, but the 1860 census for Greene County lists only seventy slaves for Cocke. There were thirty-nine males and thirty-one females of all ages, although most were young men and women in their twenties and thirties. The census did not record the Cocke hands hired off the plantations.

Hopewell   August the 5th 1861

my Dear Master
    I received your letter two weeks ago, and was very glad to

hear from you, and as Mr Beng Borden expects to start to virginia in a few days I expects to send my letter by him.

we are all well at this time, and have had but little sickness this summer. I have heard of but very little sickness in the Neighborhood. I have nothing new to write about every thing is going on as usual. the people are very busy at this time pulling Fodder. they commenced three days ago. we have had a long spell of rainny weather, but for the last week it has been quite fair. last night we had a good shower. the garden is quite grassy this rainny weather. we still have a plenty of vegatables to eat. we have more Tomattoes than we can destroy. Mrs Avery and Miss Mary came here the other day, and got a half Bushell of them. they desired to be rememberd to you. Etter has a very nice crop of onions. they are all dried and I think that they will keep. the peas that you had planted in the garden has turnd out very well, boath kind of them. we have enough of Josephs Corn for seed another year. we are saveing sunflower seed and other different kind of seed we have a very few Figs on the Trees this year. the Mulberry Cuttings that were planted in the garden behind my Hen House is dead. one of the young Pomegranate Trees in the garden is full of fruit. We have Preaching at the Church regularly three times a month. we also have family prayers regularly every morning. We have not heard from Mr Powell since he went home from here the first of July, but we expect him here this week. I will do what I can at Clothing the people my young Turkeys are growing very fast I have 10 that are as large as a Hen, and 10 smaller size which are growing very fast I often think of you, and fear sometimes that we shall never meet again, but should we fail to meet again on earth, I hope that we shall meet in heaven where parting shall be no more remember me to master Charles, and to Berthier, and to all of my relations, and believe me as ever your servant

Lucy Skipwith

[Enclosed with a letter of Smith Powell to J. H. Cocke, August 6, 1861.]

Source: Moore deposit, Cocke Papers

Hopewell   oct the 28th 1861

my Dear master

I have writen to you every month and hope that my letters has been received. We have not received a letter from you since your letter dated September the 2nd. I hope that you are not sick.

We have had a great deal of sickness among the people both here and at New Hope, mostly chills and fever, but we are now much better than we have been. We have had more sickness up here so far than they have had at New Hope. there is a great deal of sickness in the Neighborhood at preasant, mostly Chills and fever, but I hope that the sickly season will soon be over. We have had a very pleasant fall so far. wo have had but very little cold. we had one very cold morning last week, and a very frost. We have had several hard rains since my last letter to you. mr Powell was down the 8th inst. and staid two days. he said he was well sattisfied with what work had been done in his absents. he said he had not received a letter from you for some time. he wrote to you from place giveing you and account of the birth of Betseys Child.[1] she has increased, to my surprise, and I see that she was in that way when she came home from Columbus. she has a fine child and a white one. We have preaching regularly at the Chapel. there is no revivals of religion nowhere in none of the Churches. we have our family prayers every morning. as master Smith is going to write I will say no more.

your servant

Lucy Skipwith

John H. Cocke

Source: Shields-Wilson deposit, Cocke Papers

1. Betsey's promiscuous carrying-on with white admirers disgusted Powell, who described her as "very ignorant" and "filthy, Lazy" with "but little sense." Because he objected to her "very white child," he recommended selling her. See R. D. Powell to JHC, Oct. 10, 1861, May 12, 1862, Cocke deposit, Cocke Papers.

Hopewell   Dec the 1st, 1861

my Dear Master

I ought to have writen to you before this, but I have been so trobled in mind about Betsey[1] that I could not compose my mind to write a letter, but I feel a little better sattisfied than I have been knowing that all things are in the hands of God, and he has said that all things shall work togeather for good to them that love him, and I know that I do love him, therefore will I trust his holy words. I want you to be sattisfied in this case let it cost me what troble it may.

we are all well at this time and the people are quite healthy again. Archa down at New Hope has been very sick but he is now much better. the rest of the people down there are well. The weather this morning is very Cloudy. we have Just had a hard rain, and are looking for more. we also had a hard rain day before yesterday. it is very bad on the Cotton as it is too wet to pick. Cain has packed seventy three Bags. he says that he do not think that he can get a Hundred. he says that he has worked on his Ditches since the rain and put them in good order. The garden is in very good order. we have some very nice winter Cabbage. our Turnips are not as nice as they were last year they seem to be rottening   We have had no weather Cold enough to kill Hogs. We had preaching at the Chapel yesterday by the Rev mr Brame. he gets here very often time enough to hold morning prayers with us. he seems to be a fine man. I have Just heard of the death of mr Alfred Witherspoon.[2] he died at his Residence the 29th of Nov.   he died of Consumption. Dr William Avery returned home from va three weeks ago in very bad health. he is now much better. his sister mary went after him. mrs avery and the young Ladies are well. as Smith is going to write I will Bring my letter to a close hopeing soon to see you an hear from you   I remane your servant

Lucy Skipwith

[In margin] Smitty is gone to the Landing to see the Soldiers take the Boat   I do not know when he will be back.

Source: Moore deposit, Cocke Papers
1. Lucy refers to the portended sale of her daughter.
2. William Alfred Witherspoon, a merchant of Greensboro and Mobile and a distant relation to Cocke.

Jan the 13th [1862]

my Dear Master

I wrote to you the first of December, and hope that my letter was received. We are all well at present and we have had but little sickness this winter. Carter[1] has been sick this last two or three weeks, but is now up again. Lee also has been very unwell but is geting better. I have heard of but very little sickness at New Hope. we have had two very fine Children Born lately, one here and one at New Hope. Carters wife here, and Archa wife at New Hope. The weather at this time is Beautiful and spring like. we have had a very few cold days this winter. we have preaching at the Chapel regularly by the same ministers. Mr Brame wishes to know if you want him to continue preaching for us this year   we will be glad to get him again this year. write to him on the subject.

I have heard with surprise of the death of master Philip. I hope that you may be able to say with Job, the Lord gave, and the Lord hath taken away. Blessed be the name of the Lord. I often think of his wife and Children. I hope that God will Comfort them in there afflictions.

I will now bring my letter to a close hopeing soon to hear from you. Your servant

Lucy Skipwith

[Enclosed with a letter of Smith Powell to J. H. Cocke, January 13, 1862]

Source: #2433-B Cocke deposit, Cocke Papers
1. Carter Morse (or Moss) was born in Virginia in 1835 and came to Hopewell with his parents, Charles and Kessiah Morse, in 1840. He professed salvation in 1853. In 1857 he removed to New Hope with his wife Jinney. After the war he lived among his brothers near Hopewell and labored as a farm worker. He accumulated an estate of $250 personal property by 1870. Jinney was not with him at that time.

Hopewell   Feb the 11th/62

my Dear master

We received your letter about three weeks ago, and was glad to hear from you, and to hear that your health was good. I have been very unwell for a week but I feel much better to day. Sister martha has been sick for nearly a month   she has not been confined altogeather to her bed, but she has been unable to do any thing. she is now much better   Cains wife Matilda has been a little unwell   she has a very fine Child two week old.[1] she is now doing very well. The rest of the people are all well both here and at New Hope. We have not had three days of clear weather since I last wrote to you. We have done but little gardening yet, but I hope that the weather will fair off and then we will commence. we have different kinds of seed sown in the Hot Bed. We have our Prayers regularly every morning. we also have Preaching at the Chapel regularly by the same minesters. mr Brame is very anxious to know whither you want him to continue Preaching for us. write to him on the subject. I will say no more as Mr Powell is going to write

L Skipwith

[Enclosed with a letter of Smith Powell to J. H. Cocke, February 11, 1862]

Source: #2433-B Cocke deposit, Cocke Papers
1. Matilda Morse's child was named Sandy. He grew to manhood in the neighborhood of Greensboro.

Hopewell   mar. 31 1862

Dear master

I would have writen to you before this, but as Smith wrote to you after receiveing your letter I thought that I would wait untel the present time. Smith left us the 24th inst for the War. he went from here to Mobile. we have hea[r]d nothing from him since. mr Powell has sent another young man down to take his place. his name is Sterling N. Hardy, nephew of mrs Powell.[1] he seem to be a very nice young man. he intend going to the College as Smith did, but not untell mr P comes down the 5th of april   Cain is still planting corn   he commenced up at Meltons this morning. the whole of Meltons is to be put in corn. they have planted the Rye field and Evans field in corn. The weather is now beautiful for Farming and gardening. Etter is geting along very well gardening   she has very nice plants in the Hot Beds   she has Peas and other vegatables up.

the people are all well at New Hope. they are planting corn down there. mr Powell intend planting but very little Cotton. none of the people [abrod?] here intend planting much   they intend planting the house field and the Lawn in cotton.

I surpose that mr Powell has writen to you about Robt. at New Hope stealing Capt. Cockes Hogs. it was a very bad act in him to do so, but mr P has setled with him for it.

mr Borden was here two days ago. he says that he received your letter and he intends answering it very soon. his family is well.

Capt Cocke is not up here at this time. we are looking for you to come out here in april, but as you did not say any thing about it in your last letter I fear that you are not comeing. our neighbour mrs Dufphey is dead. she died the 2nd inst. the people all Joines me in love to you. your servant

Lucy Skipwith

Source: #2433-B Cocke deposit, Cocke Papers
1. Sterling Hardy attended Southern University in Greensboro; he quit Cocke's employ within a year.

[April 26, 1862]

Dear master

It is not yet time for me to write to you, but as mr Hardy is writeing I thought best to say a few words to you

I wrote to you the 2nd or 3rd of Arp, and hope that my letter has been received

I have nothing new to inform you of. every thing seem to be going on as usual.

I am geting along very well with the people summer Clothes. I have a great deal of weaveing to do, but I am inhopes to get it all done in due time. I am puting up another hand Loom, and I think I shall be able to make every thing at home   I am sorry to inform you of the death of my Sister mary[1] up at mr Powells. she died the 6th of april. she is a great loss to mr and mrs Powell, also to my poor mother and Father, but I trust that they are able to say with me that the Lord gave, and the Lord hath taken away, blessed be the name of the Lord.

The last time that I heard from mrs Averys family they were well, mr Bordens also   I saw mrs Withers not long since   her family was well. I will now bring my letter to a close hopeing soon to hear from you. I remain [your] servant.

Lucy Skipwith

J H Cocke

[Enclosed with a letter of S. N. Hardy to J. H. Cocke, April 26, 1862]

Source: #2433-B Cocke deposit, Cocke Papers
1. Mary Skipwith died of measles and pneumonia. While at Powell's plantation, she endeared herself to her master as a good seamstress, dining-room attendant, and, according to Powell, "in truth a Lady." Mary's death occasioned Powell's desire to hire or purchase Lucy's daughter Maria as a replacement.

may 30th 1862

Dear master

I received your [letter] written the first of may, but as I had Just written to you, I did not answer it. I was very glad to hear from you, and to hear that you were well   This leaves us in the injoyment of our usual health. we have had very little sickness this spring. The weather has been very good since I wrote to you last. we had a good rain last night which was needed for the Crops. I am geting along Clothing the people very well. I hope I will be able to keep them from Suffering. Etter is geting along very well with the garden. we are going to have a plenty of Tomatoes, pepper, Cabbage, and different kind of vegatabls   We have not heard from mr Powell very lately, but we expect him down next week. he told me when he was down here that he had written to you to hire Maria, to take the place of sister Mary. I am willing to part with Maria for the sake of my mother, as she is old, and has no child of her own to help her, but when Betsey is sold, it will be hard for me to give them both up.[1] mr Powell wrote us that master Charles would be out here very soon, but we have seen nothing of him as yet. I would be very glad to see him. Miss Fanny Avery is married to the Rev. mr Cobb, pastor of the Episcopal Church in greensboro. he is a son of the old Bishop. There is twenty one Fig trees in the garden that are bareing, and nine out in the fence corners. I will now bring my letter to a close

L Skipwith

Source: #2433-B Cocke deposit, Cocke Papers
1. At this time, Lucy's parents, George and Mary Skipwith, were living on Powell's plantation near Columbus, Mississippi.

[July 25, 1862]

my Dear master

I Again take my seat to let you hear from me. We are not all very well at present. I am sorry to inform you that we are in the midst of sickness and death, but we have a right to be thankful that we have escaped so far. Sallie died this morning after an Illness of four days. she was the woman that was so sick the last winter that you was out here. I have been quite unwell for the last day or two but I feels much better than I have been. I Am not geting along with my busness very well at present. so much sickness is seting me back. mr Powell saw your message to me about maria liveing with him, but as his wife did not receive the letter you write to her, he said that he would not take her untill he can hear from you again. Mr Bordens family is well. I have not seen none of mrs Averys family very lately. The Garden is looking very dry. this dry weather has nearly put an end to our vegatables. I will now bring my letter to a close hopeing soon to hear from you again   I am as ever your servant

Lucy Skipwith

[Enclosed with a letter of S. N. Hardy to J. H. Cocke, July 25, 1862]

Source: #5685, Cocke Papers

Hopewell   Sept 2nd/62

mr Dear master

I Again take my seat to let you hear from me. We have not received any letter from you for some time, but I was glad to learn through mr Joe Borden that you were well.

We have had sickness here every day for two months. we have had some very sick people. we have five sick at this time, Carter, Chaptman,[1] Howell, Martha, and Betsey. they are now recovering. they have a sickly time at New Hope also. mr Powell was down here last week, and wrote to you from this place. he was very well sattisfied with things here.

I Am geting along but slow with my weaveing. I have had so many sick people to attend to that I have had but little time to weave, and unless the people are soon restored to health, I do not know when I will be able to provide winter Clothing for them. we have been haveing showers of rain for three or four days, and it is quite Cloudy to day. I think that we are going to have quite a rainny spell.

I have not seen mrs Averys Family lately, but I learn that they are well. mr Bordens Family is well also. mrs Withers has moved to greensboro to live. give my love Birthier and to my Brother William, also to master Charles if he is at home. I am as ever our servant

L. S.

Source: #2433-B Cocke deposit, Cocke Papers
1. Chapman was a field worker and a practicing Baptist. He left the Cocke lands in 1866 rather than accept Cocke's labor contract.

october 11th 1862

Dear master

I have been expecting a letter from you for nearly three months, but have received none. I do not know whither you are sick or away from home. if you have been sick I hope that you may be well by the time this reaches you, and that we may soon hear from you   The health of the people is a great deal better than it has been. we have one man sick at present but he is not dangerously sick. there are three of the Children sick at New Hope. the old people are all well. they lost a young child down there two weeks ago. mr Powell mentioned in his last letter to you the death of Jesse Dabney,[1] and Quallys[2] daughter Lucy. we received a letter from mr Powell a few days ago. he expects to be here the 21st inst   him and his family were well   we have heard from Smith Powell very lately   he was well, and wants to come and see us very bad but he cannot get off from the Army. mr Joe Borden has been very sick since he got home but he is well again. I do not know when he will return to virginia. his wife has been very sick also, but she is much better. I saw Capt Cocke yesterday   him and his family were well. mrs Averys family is well.

We have a very good Turnip patch comeing on in the Garden. I do not think that our Potatoes will be as fine as they were last year. my mother is with me at this time and desires to be remembered to you. I fear she will never get over the death of Sister mary. she will leave here the 12th inst for Columbus. I am doing all in my power to provide winter Clothes for the place. Sister martha has a very fine child three weeks old. nothing more from your ser[van]t

Lucy Skipwith

Source: Shields-Wilson deposit, Cocke Papers
1. Jesse Dabney, a field worker at New Hope.
2. Qually Johnson, one of the original settlers of Hopewell, lived at New Hope with his wife Marcia. In 1870 he reported a personal estate equal to $150 and continued to reside with his wife in the Hopewell environs.

Hopewell   Nov 17th 1862

Dear master

I have writen to you every month and hope that my letters have been received. We have not received a letter from you since June, but we have heard from you through mr Powell. I was sorry to hear of the bad state of your health. I hope that by this time your health has improved   we would be glad for you to come out and spend the winter with us if there is any way for you to get here. We are all well at present but Cain. he has a riseing in one of his Ears, but he is much better than he has been. the people at New Hope has been quite sickly this summer and fall, but they are all nearly well. We have two very nice young men Boarding here with us[1]   they are from Columbus Miss. mr Powell wrote to you about them. they walk from here to College. I am geting along very well with the peoples winter Clothes. the Children are all in good health and they are growing very fast. Etter has a very fine Child nearly two years old. I think that she will raise it as it is very healthy. We have Turnip Sallid and winter Cabbage comeing on in the garden. I have Just heard from mr Borden. they are all well but mrs Joe Borden. she is very sick. mrs Averys family. I will now bring my letter to a close hopeing soon to hear from you   I am as ever your Servant

Lucy Skipwith

Source: Shields-Wilson deposit, Cocke Papers
1. Unable to identify. After the departure of R. F. Nickles and Smith Powell for the army, Powell engaged college students, such as Sterling Hardy, to live at the plantations and provide a needed white presence. Earlier Cocke had been convicted of not keeping white persons on his plantation and fined $100. After Hardy's departure, Powell struggled to find a suitable white person for Hopewell and New Hope. His searches were generally fruitless, and only one more white person took on the overseer's duties during the war years.

Hopewell   Feb 26th 1863

my Dear master

I wrote to you nearly four weeks ago, and I have Just heard that my letter is in Greensboro at the office yet. I cannot account for it, as I sent the money with it. I will get it and send it with this.

We are all tolerable well at this time, but we have had several very bad caces of sore throat since I last wrote to you   Etta has been nearly dead with it but is nearly well. uncle Charles is laid up with it this morning. there has been some sickness at New Hope since I wrote but they are geting better. I am sorry to inform you that Washington is dead.[1] he died in Mobile workeing for the Goverment. we have three others workeing down there. Cain is going ahead plowing his land for another crop. we have commenced gardening. our Peas are up and we have some very nice Plants in the Hot Bed. we have Beded out Potatoes also. I have some Turkeys for market. I also have one for mr Powell to eat every time he comes down. The weather for the last ten days has been quite spring like. we have had several good rains during that time   The stock of all kind seem to be doing very well. the carrage mares looks very well. the old mare looks as well as ever.

mrs Averys family is well. mrs Fanny Cobb has a fine son ten

days old   I reccon that you have seen in the papers the death
of Col Isiac Croom.[2] mr Bordens family is well   give my love
to Berthier and the rest of my relations   I will now bring my
letter to a close hopeing soon to hear from you again   your
servant

Lucy Skipwith

John H Cocke

Source: Moore deposit, Cocke Papers
1. Washington was a field worker at New Hope before the Confederate government requisitioned him to build defenses in Mobile.
2. Isaac Croom was an agricultural reformer, local Whig luminary, and a planter of extensive means in Greene County.

Hopewell   march 28th 1863

my Dear master

I wrote to you four weeks ago and hope that my letter has
been received   I Have nothing new to write about   every
thing is going on as usual. We have been expecting mr Powell
every day for more than a week, but he has not arrived yet   he
had been very sick when we heard from him but was better. I
think that he will get here to day, if he can cross the river. Cain
is done planting corn and will commence planting cotton next
week. he has also planted largely of the sugar cane seed, also
the Josephs corn   I find the Josephs corn an exelent thing for
Fowles. The Garden is looking very well. our Peas are in bloom.
we have set out Cabbage and Tomatoes plants. The weather for
the last three weeks has been more or less cloudy but the sun is
shineing this morning.

The Wheat and Rye crops look very promasing   The stock of
all kind looks well. mr Hardy says that he is going to write to
you to day. I saw mr Borden yesterday   his family is well. he
got your letter. your servant

L Skipwith

[In margin] the people are all tolerable well at both places.

Source: #2433-B Cocke deposit, Cocke Papers

Hopewell   arp 30th 1863

my Dear master

We received your joint letter a few days ago, and was glad to hear from you, and to hear that your health was good. this leaves us all in our usual state of health with the exception of the Children. all of them has a very bad cough somewhat like the Whoopingcough. it makes some of them quite sick.

We have a very good garden comeing on   we have had plants in the Hot Bed in abundance. we have a plenty of cabbage and Tomatoes plants set out   Lettuce also. the cabbage is large enough to eat. I Have been to see mrs Harvy since I wrote to you last, and carried her some Butter. I found her sick confined to her bed. she was very glad to see me. she says if the War continues that she will surely die. she sends her love to you and says that she had rather see you than any one elce on earth, and that if you ever come to see again she will have some Tea for you.

mr Bordens family is well   he got your letter to him. his son William Alfred[1] got home from virginia a week ago. his daughter Marinda was married two weeks ago to a mr Clark of Eutaw Ala.[2]

mrs Averys family is well   mrs Cobb has moved to greensboro to live. I manage to clothe the people very well give my love to Berthier and all of my relations. tell Berthier to write to me.

your servant
Lucy Skipwith

John H Cocke

Source: #2433-B Cocke deposit, Cocke Papers
1. William Alfred Borden (b. 1847?) later became a small planter in Greene County.
2. Unable to identify.

Hopewell   May 31st 1863

my Dear master

We received your letter dated may 15th, and now take my seat to answer it. I was glad to hear that your health was good.

We too are injoying good health and we have had but very little sickness this spring.

The weather of late has been very hot and dry and every thing has been suffering for rain very much but now we are haveing showers of rain every day or too, and every thing is greatly revived especially the garden. we have a very good garden and it is in very good order. we have a plenty of mulberrys from the young trees as well as the old one. we have a plenty of Tomatoes comeing on. Onions and other vegatabels. I have had bad luck with my Turkeys. my Eggs hatched very badly. not more than twenty has hatched. I have had three old ones stolen from me.

I Have been to see mrs Witherspoon[1] since I received your letter, and I found that mrs Dorsey[2] had gone to Mobile, and has been there for nearly three months. mrs Witherspoon has writen to her and told her what you said about her staying here. she is in mobile with her son. mrs Witherspoon intends writeing to you soon. she and her children are well. she says she intends leting the children come and spend the day with me soon. she was very glad that I went to see her.

The behaviour of the People has been very good. I have seen but little cause for complaint about them. mr Bordens family is well. mr Joe Borden arived here a week ago. I do not know how long he will stay here.

I will now bring my letter to a close hopeing soon to hear from you again   your servant.

Lucy Skipwith

J H Cocke

Source: Shields-Wilson deposit, Cocke Papers

1. Tariffa (Cocke) Witherspoon (b. 1833), the widow of William Alfred Witherspoon, was the niece of Julia Dorsey (see below). Her children were Harrison H., Charles, Sallie, and Alfred.

2. Julia Coupland Dorsey, a distant relation to John Hartwell Cocke, moved to Mobile in 1842. She lost her home during the war and at Cocke's gracious request stayed at Hopewell from 1863 for the duration of the war. Mrs. Dorsey purchased Betsey in 1863 and kept her employed weaving and tending to household chores. After the war she returned to Mobile. In his will Cocke directed Mrs. Dorsey to receive Lucy and Maria, should they choose to remain in America.

[June 29, 1863]
my Dear master

I have writen to you regularly and I hope that my letters has been received   we have not received a letter from you for nearly two months, but we heard through mr Powell that you were well. I have nothing of importance to write about. every thing is going on as usual. We have had a very healthy summer so far   I hope that it may continue so. we have heard from mr Powell once since he went away   he was well, and will be here the 7th of July   I have seen mrs Avery and miss mary since I last wrote. they were well. I will now close. hopeing soon to hear from you.

LS

[Enclosed with a letter of S. N. Hardy to J. H. Cocke, June 29, 1863]

Source: #2433-B Cocke deposit, Cocke Papers

Hopewell   July 20th 1863
my Dear master

I received your letter dated June the 26th and was glad to hear from you. I would have writen to you sooner but as mr Powell had writen to you so lately from here, I thought best to wate untell this time.

We are all well with the exception of one of the women who is a little sick tho better than she has been.

There is one white person here at present[1] mr Hardy & the young man that was Boarding here is gone home. I do not know whither they will come back here to live or not   the young man that stayed at New Hope[2] went to see his friends and was taken sick   I have not heard how he was since he was taken sick. I am looking for him every day. I have not had it into my power to visit mrs Witherspoon since I received your letter, but will go and see her as soon as some white person comes here. she & mr Powell thinks best not for her to come here but I think that she could do very well here with her own servants to wait upon her, but mr Powell is not in favor of it. Cain is cleaning out his wheat & will finish it to day & then commence cleaning out the Rye. Cain say that he has got a splended crop of Corn & he says that the cotton looks very well   we have a plenty of vegatables to eat, Tomatoes in abundance, more than we can destroy. I never saw the like of people moveing from Mississippi   they are pasing from morning till night. I have been looking for mr Powell & master Philips people but have seen nothing of them as yet. The stock seem to be doing very well. the mare that was so sick is doing very well. mr Joe Borden has been sick but is now better. the rest of the family is well. mrs averys family is well also. I have heard of the Death of mrs Lawrence   she died in childbed with he[r] second Child since she went away from here. she had gone back to Miss. we have preaching at the Chapel twice a month. mr Brame has moved away from Greensboro & does not preach for us now. I manage to keep the people very well clothed. as I have nothing elce of importance to say I will add no more. your servant

Lucy Skipwith

J H Cocke

Source: #2433-B Cocke deposit, Cocke Papers
1. The young man's name was Shields. Nothing else is known of his history.
2. Unable to identify.

Hopewell   Aug 15th 1863

Dear master

I received your last letter & have carefully considerd its contents, & I hope to write more sattisfactory than I have done heretofore. the white people who have stayed on the plantation are always opposed to my writeing to you & always want to see my letters and that has been the reason why my letters has been short, but there is no white person here at preasent. mr Hardy is gone home to return no more. I do not know who mr Powell will get to take his place. The health of the people is not very good at preasent. we have four laid up at this time, but they are geting better. Cain has been pulling fodder for more than a week, & it will take him a week more to finish it.

The Cotton is opening very fast   it will soon be open enough to commence picking it out. The weather at preasant is quite rainy & has been for the last two or three days which maekes it bad on the fodder. There is three mulberry trees that has had fruit besides the old tree. The Scuppernong grapes have proper frames to run upon & they are full of fruit. We have two kinds of Figs the white Fig & the common Fig We have only one tree of the white Fig. there is 14/fourteen of the common Fig trees in the garden with Figs on them & 8/eight out in the fence cornors. We have 60-sixty Hogs, 32-thirty two Pigs, & 9 Sows, 53-fiftythree Sheep, 21 twentyone Lambs, 5-five Cows to the pail, 4 four young Calves, 4 four old Goats 1 one kid. the provision lots for their support is very good.

We have our morning prayers regularly. I have not kept up the sabbath school regularly. some white people in the neighborhood has said that they would punish me if they caught me at it, and I have been afraid to carry it on unless some grown white man was liveing here, but I will commence Teaching again as soon as this talk dies out.

I Have seen mrs Dorsey. I think that she is a very nice Lady. I think that Betsey will do very well with her, but she wishes you to let Betsey stay here untell she settle herself somewhere. mrs Witherspoon & the Children are well and talkes a great deal about you I sent her some butter yesterday, & I sent mrs Dorsey a Loaf of light Bread. the Children all came and spent the day with me last week. I Thank you a thousand times for what you purpose doing for Maria & myself & I hope that we may both walk sattisfactory before you while you live. I cannot tell at preasent what will be best for me to do, but I will keep the subject upon my mind & try to deside what will be best to do.[1] Maria is growing very fast and is learning to write very fast. she is a great comfort to me & to every one about her, and above all I hope that she is a true Christian.

mr Joe Borden expects to start back to the Army to day. I will now bring my leter to a close hopeing soon to hear from you again   your servant

Lucy Skipwith

Source: #2433-B Cocke deposit, Cocke Papers
1. Lucy refers to Cocke's manumission offer, which provided that she and Maria emigrate to Liberia.

Hopewell   Sept 28th 1863

my dear master

Since I last wrote to you I have been very sick & I am quite unwell at preasent but much better than I have been. We have had a great deal of sickness of late. we have five sick at preasant, Cain amoung them, but I hope that they will soon be well. The Goverment has taken eight-8-of our Men this week & sent them to Mobile to worke. it is a great bother to Cain & Armistead as they have been set back in their worke by so much sickness among the people   Armistead has not had as much sickness as we have. Cain is hawling up his fodder at preasent. he has not commenced geathering his corn. it is raining very hard this morning & all hands are at the Jin House cleaning out Rye. the Cotton patch is very white but the wormes has done great damage to the cotton   our Turnip patches has failed this year. however we have a very good one in the Garden. we have some very nice winter cabbage in the Garden also. The mares and coalts are doing very well, & the coalts are growing very fast. the old mare looks nearly as well as she ever did. our Hogs are doing much better than they were a few weeks ago   we lost a great many of them, but [that?] has stoped among them   The sheep are looking very well, the Goats also

We have not tried our Potatoes yet   I do not know how they will turn out. We have been makeing melasses   we made about 30-thirty gallons. the cane was too old & dry when we commenced makeing it. I am geting along very well with the peoples clothes and I manage to keep them from suffering

mr Smith Powell arived here a day or too ago with a wounded Leg. he was wounded in the late Battle up about Chattannooga Tenn.

Capt John Cocke went up in that neighbourhood to see his sons in the army, & has not been heard from since   he has been gone nearly six weeks. his family is very uneasy about him. mr Joe Borden is still at home sick   I do not know when he will return to the army. he lost his oldest son [illegible] three weeks ago   mrs Dorsey & mrs Witherspoon have been to see me since I last wrote to you   they think that this is a Beautiful place they & the Children are well   mr Powell went away from here two weeks ago   I have not heard from him since he went away. old mrs Winston & Dr Hardy came down with him. they were very well pleased with the place. mrs Winston was up in time in the morning & Joined us at our family prayers. your servant

Lucy Skipwith

Source: Shields-Wilson deposit, Cocke Papers

Hopewell   oct 21st 1863

my dear master

I wrote to you the last of September which letter I hope you have received. We have heard nothing from you for nearly too months. I hope that you are not sick. The health of the people is better than when I wrote last. Carter has been very sick since I wrote last. he is now better tho unable to do any worke. uncle Champion also is in very bad health. Cain is not well but he is at his busness. the health of the people at New Hope is better than it was when I last wrote. Cain is very busy geathering his corn   he will finish it this week. the Pea field is all that he has to geather. there is two cribs filled with corn & they are filling the third one.

Cain has picked a great many dry Peas, & there is a great many more to pick. he has not had much time to pick cotton, but he can pick it out before Christmas. the cotton patch is very white   there is beautiful cotton in the Lawn. it has been lately picked over. our Turnip Patches has turned out very bad but we have a very good one in the garden. our Potatoes seem to turn out very well. we have had a few dug to eat. The mares & coalts are looking very well   they have separated the coalts from the mares for the last week. The Goats are looking very well, but no more increase. mr Powell went away from here the 8th inst. he wrote to you from here & was disapointed at not receiveing a letter from you. he was very well. mr Smith Powell left here the 11th inst to Joine his company up at Chattanooga. his wound was a great deal better. he is looking very thin but says that he is willing to tuff it out untell the War ends. mr Borden has been very unwell for a week or two, but is better   mr Joe Borden is still at home in bad health. Capt John Cocke has got home after an absence of two months   I heard that the yankeys had him.

hc is looking very bad. miss Lucy & her two youngest sisters are liveing down here at her Fathers.

I Have not seen nor heard from mrs Dorsey lately, but she is still at mrs Witherspoons. I saw mrs withers not long since she was well & [inquired?] after you. she is looking well. both of her Sons are in the Army. mrs Averys family was well when I heard from them last.

I Am geting along very well Clotheing the people & manage to keep them from suffering. I make cloth for both places. we have eight 8 men still workeing in Mobile. the people all desire to be rememberd to you and says that they hope to see you again in Ala. I must now bring my letter to a close hopeing soon to hear from you   your servt

L Skipwith

Source: Shields-Wilson deposit, Cocke Papers

[November 24, 1863]

my dear master

your last letter was received, but as I had just writen to you I have defered writeing untell the present time. I Am sorry to inform you of the death of my poor Sister Etta. she died a week ago after an Illness of four days. She died with a desease of the Brain. she has left a little Boy three years old, and would have had another in about two months. she told me two weeks ago that she wanted to see you very bad, but alas, she is gone, & shortly we must follow her.

I find that I have grace to help me in this my time of need, but the Lord knows what is best & tho he slay me yet will I trust in him.

Mr Powell left here about ten days ago. he wrote to you from here. Mrs Dorsey spent two days here with him. he seemed to be very well pleased with her company. she expects to move here by the time that he comes down again. she thinks that she can live very comfortable here in your house. she has taken a room up stairs to sleep in & says that she will stay down stairs in the day time. The weather for the last week has been quite rainy but it has cleared off to day & the sun is shineing again.

We have made a very fine crop of Potatoes at both places

The desease that the Hogs had has stoped & they are doing very well   The mares and coalts are doing very well. the coalts are growing very fast   The Cows and calves are looking very well. we have six cows to the pail. they have kept us up for something to eat these hard times

The sheep looks very well   The Goats looks very well they have not had but two kids this summer. There is seven of our men are still at Mobile   one of them came three weeks ago almost dead, but he is now a great deal better. it was Matthew one of uncle Charles sons.[1]

Mr Joe Borden returned to the Army eight or ten days ago. mr B Bordens family is well & desires to be rememberd to you. your servt

L Skipwith

[Enclosed with a letter of James Hampton[2] to J. H. Cocke, November 24, 1863]

Source: #5685, Cocke Papers
1. Matthew Morse (or Moss), son of Charles and Kessiah Morse (or Moss), was a field hand who survived to 1880, working as a farm laborer near the old plantation. Matthew learned how to read and write at Lucy's school.
2. James Hampton was an overseer at Hopewell during the winter of 1863 to 1864.

Hopewell   Dec. 26th 1863

my dear Master

I wrote to you one month ago telling you of the death of Sister Etta, which letter I hope you have received. we have had sickness more or less all the fall up to the preasant time. I had Just sent for the Docter to see Marthas daughter Ann,[1] who is very sick.

Mrs Dorsey has Mooved here & seem to be very well sattisfied with her new home. she says that she intends writeing to you soon. she went up to Mrs Witherspoons Thursday to spend the Christmas. Mrs Witherspoon has paid her one visit since she has been here the widdow Randolph[2] also.

Mr Powell went away from here two weeks ago   he wrote to you from here. he told me that you was not sattisfied with my letters but I hope that they may be more sattisfactory than they have been heretofore.

We have killed 25-twenty five Hogs & have five more to kill. they killed 22-twenty two at New Hope.

our Milch Cows are not in very good order   we have six to the pail   the best one gives five quarts of milk. the rest gives from one to three quarts. we have lost two sheep from sickness of late. we have sixtythree others that seem to be doing well. the Mares & coalts are looking very well. the Coalts are growing very fast. the Goats are looking very well. they have had no kids lately   there is a very bad desease among the Poltry   I have lost a great many old Chickens, & five old Turkeys. I never saw the like of dead Hens in my life   they will be well one day & the next day they will be dead. it is Just so with capt Cockes cows. he has lost upward of twentyfive or thirty head of cattle. him & his family are well. mr Bordens family is well also. we have had two children born at New Hope lately both Boys. uncle Daniels wife & daughter had them.

The weather for the last day or two is quite rainy & to day the rain is Just poreing down. give my love to Birthier. tell him to write to me   Remember me also to master Charles. your servant

Lucy Skipwith

Source: Shields-Wilson deposit, Cocke Papers
1. Ann Morse (or Moss) was born in 1857 and lived with her parents on the Key property at least until 1870. She was Lucy's niece.
2. Ann Randolph, formerly of Virginia.

Hopewell   Mar 15th/64

dear master

I wrote to you four weeks ago & hope that my letter has been received   I have not received a letter from you this year.

The health of the people is better than it was when I last wrote but we still have some little sickness   Mr Powell was here a week ago. he was well & said that he had not received a letter from you in a long time. he wrote to you from here. Mrs Dorsey is here & sends much love to you & says that she will write to you very soon. The young man that lives here is not at home   he went to see his Father in North Alabama who is very sick

Cain commenced planting his corn nearly a week ago   he will soon finish it. Armistead is planting also   the people are all well at New Hope.

uncle Charles has the garden in hand   he has it in a very good condition. the plants in the Hot bed is large enough to set out but it is too cold at preasent. mrs Dorsey is an old gardener, & she gives him her advice. she seem to take a delight in giveing her advice about any thing on the place, & is very serviceable to us all.

Mrs Witherspoon came down with all the children & dined while mr Powell was here.

mrs Withers & nearly all the Ladies in the Neighborhood has called on mrs Dorsey. The stock of all kind are well. the young coalts are still growing. I have had bad luck with my Turkeys. I have lost all but one, & that one looks sick. it seems that there is no care for them when they get sick. I never saw the like of sick Turkeys & chickens. the chickens seem to be geting over it. I have lost nine old Turkeys. the desease is worse at Capt Cockes than it is here.

mr Powell wrote to you about the death of morris.[1] he died in Mobile. that makes three men that we have lost in Mobile. we have three men workeing there at preasent. they always take more hands from here than they do from any one about here. they have never taken but two at a time from mr Borden & four from Capt Cocke, while we send from four to eight. them that do not die in mobile come home almost dead. I am afraid that we shall never meet again on earth. if so I pray that we may meet in heaven where parting shall be no more. your servant

Lucy Skipwith

[In margin] Willy Cocke died in the Army with the small Pox

Source: #2433-B Cocke deposit, Cocke Papers
1. Morris was a field hand at Hopewell.

March 28th 1864

dear master

I wrote to you a week ago which letter I hope you have received. my busness now is this. mr Powell asked my consent to buy Maria from you, & I haveing so much respect for him hated to tell him my mind upon the subject, but later [told] him that he could perpose the thing to you & see what you say about it.

I do not wish Maria sold to him, for she is a child after my own heart & I hate to part from her. if you think propper to hire her to him I will try to make up my mind to that, but it goes hard with me to think of parting with her. I would like to see him acomadated but it seems that nothing will do for him but Maria   if he must have her I would rather be hired to him & go myself rather than be parted from her.

my other poor child came very near being ruined while liveing away from me. there is nothing like a Mothers watchful eye over a child. I hope that you will look into the matter & do what you think best   let me hear from you on the subject   your servant

Lucy Skipwith

Mr Powell went home this morning
[In margin] we are all well. mrs Dorsey wrote to you a few days ago   she sends her love.

Source: #2433-B Cocke deposit, Cocke Papers

Hopewell   May 31st 1864

my dear master
I Have been very sick since I last wrote to you, but I am well again. the rest of the people are in very good health.

The last time that I heard from you was Dr Brents letter to Mr Powell   you were very unwell at that time, but I hope by this time you are restored to your usual health again.

We got a letter from Mr Powell a few days ago. he was well, & will be here the 3rd day of June.

Cain is geting along very well with the Crop. he has Plowed the Corn over twice, & is now choping out the cotton. the Corn seem rather backward for this season of the year. it has been suffering for rain very much. we have had a few light showers but no hard rain for some time.

The wheat is ripening very fast. we cut a small Piece yesterday. it is not as good as it was last year. the Rye is ripening very fast also. The Garden is in very good order & we will soon have a plenty of vegatables. we have very nice Peas. we have a plenty of Cabbage ready for use, & various other vegatables comeing on. uncle Charles is a very good Gardener. the mulberry Trees are full of nice ripe mulberries enough for all the Plantation.

The men that we had in mobile has got home after an absence of three months and two others sent. the Goverment has taken the two best Mules that we had & valued them at twentythree (23) hundred dollars for the two. we also had one of the carrage mares stolen from the Stable the night of the 6 inst   it was the darkest mare. Lady her name was. Fancy is up at Mr Powells. we have seen nothing nor heard from the mare, but feel confident that some of the Soldiers have her as there are so many of them passing about.

The old mare has got a fine horse colt three weeks old. we have had one young kid since I wrote last but it is dead. the stock of all kind is looking well   The People are all well at New Hope   Armistead is geting along very well with his crop. The People all Joines me in love to you & hope to see you again.

L Skipwith

[In margin] give my love to Berthier & all my relations   give my love to master Charles.

Source: #2433-B Cocke deposit, Cocke Papers

Hopewell   Dec 7th 1865

my dear Master

I Received your letter a few days ago dated oct 14th it being nearly two months on the way.

I was truly glad to see that you were still alive & not yet gone the way of all the Earth & that you were able to write to me once more. I was sorry that I had to part from Armistead but I have lived a life of trouble with him, & a white man has ever had to Judge between us, & now to be turned loose from under a master, I know that I could not live with him in no peace, therefore I left him for I wish to live a life of peace & die a death of both Joy and peace & if you have any hard feelings against me on the subject, I hope that you will forgive me for Jesus sake.

I Have a great desire to come to Va to see you & my relations there & I hope that I maybe able some day to do so. I have looked over my mind in regard to going to Liberia but I cannot get my consent to go there, but I thank you for your advice. none of our people are willing to go. I am still carrying on my School on the plantation & the Children are learning very fast. I had a notion of going up to Columbus another year to be with my mother & Father, but as they have mooved down here to mr Keys,[1] I have given the notion out. I do not know what Father done in Columbus but I have not seen nor heard nothing of his drinking down here. I have been thinking of puting up a large School next year as I can do more at that than I can at any thing elce, & I can get more children than I can teach, but I do not know yet whither I will be at liberty to do so or not.

I am glad that one of your Grandsons[2] is comeing out this winter. we are looking for him every day. we have been looking for master Charles to come out, & we will be sorry not to see him.

I Have not seen mrs Dorsey for nearly three months   she is now in mobile   mrs Witherspoon & her Children are well with the exception of the Whooping cough. mr Joseph Borden is not here as Mr Powell have agreed to stay with us another year. our Turnip patch failed this year. we have a small patch in the Garden. our Crop of Potatoes were very small also. Some of every bodys black people in this Neighbourhood have left their homes but us. we are all here so far but I cannot tell how it will be another year.

I will now bring my letter to a Close hopeing soon to hear from you again   I am as ever your Servant

Lucy Skipwith

Source: Shields-Wilson deposit, Cocke Papers

1. David M. Key (b. 1815) and his mother, Rebecca Key, both originally from Georgia, operated a plantation near Hopewell during the slavery era. After the war they divided their property among sharecroppers, including several ex-slave families from Hopewell.

2. Philip B. Cabell (b. 1836), Cocke's grandson by his daughter Anne and her husband Nathaniel Francis Cabell, came to Alabama in 1866, following Cocke's death. Well educated, he later taught at a female college in Greensboro and Urbana College in Ohio. Still later, he served as a minister to the Swedenborgian church in Wilmington, Delaware. He administered the Alabama property until 1874.

Bibliographical Essay

Preface

The debate over the virtues of black-authored sources on slavery continues hot. For generations students of slavery in America discounted the reliability of slave narratives and later of the ex-slave interviews collected by the Federal Writers' Project. The most persistent critic of these sources is Kenneth Stampp: see his "Rebels and Sambos: The Search for the Negro's Personality in Slavery," *Journal of Southern History*, XXXVII (1971), 367–369 (quote); and his more vigorous attack, "Slavery—The Historian's Burden," in Harry P. Owens, ed., *Perspectives and Irony in American Slavery* (Jackson, Miss., 1976), pp. 165–170. On the other side, John W. Blassingame and Gilbert Osofsky, among others, have written persuasive defenses of the narratives: see Blassingame's, "Using the Testimony of Ex-Slaves: Approaches and Problems," *Journal of Southern History*, XLI (1975), 473–492; and Osofsky's introduction to *Puttin' on Ole Massa: The Slave Narratives of Henry Bibb, William Wells Brown, and Solomon Northup* (New York, 1969), pp. 9–44. The most convincing argument for using the Federal Writers' Project interviews is C. Vann Woodward, "History from Slave Sources: A Review Article," *American Historical Review*, 79 (1974), 470–481. On the use of nonliterary materials see Lawrence Levine, "Slave Songs and Slave Consciousness: An Exploration in Neglected Sources," in Tamara K. Hareven, ed., *Anonymous Americans: Explorations in Nineteenth-Century Social History* (Englewood Cliffs, N.J., 1971), pp. 99–130; Levine, *Black Culture and Black Consciousness* (New York, 1977); and Sterling Stuckey, "Through the Prism of Folklore: The Black Ethos in Slavery," *Massachusetts Review*, IX (1968), 417–437. New black-authored materials continue to come to light. The richest sampling is in John W. Blassingame, ed., *Slave Testimony: Two Centuries of Letters, Speeches, Interviews, and Autobiographies* (Baton Rouge, La., 1977). George P. Rawick, who edited an edition of the Federal Writers' Project interviews, has discovered many interviews which never reached the Washington office. He is publishing supplements to his *The American Slave: A Composite Autobiography* (Westport, Conn., 1972), in order to bring these materials together. The Virginia interviews have been collected in Charles L. Perdue, et al, eds., *Weevils in the Wheat: Interviews with Virginia Ex-Slaves* (Charlottesville, Va., 1976). Perdue's introduction points out the many pitfalls of the documents, largely due to the editing procedures of the Federal Writers' Project.

Introduction

The John Hartwell Cocke Papers, particularly Cocke's letters & diaries and Louisa (Maxwell) Cocke's diaries, in the Alderman Library, University of Virginia, provide a full record of Cocke's myriad interests and achievements. Cocke's correspondence with John McDonogh, in the McDonogh Papers (Tulane University), shows his growing reform interest. Several Cocke letters in the American Colonization Society Papers (Library of Congress) detail his colonization proposals and the histories of those few individuals he sent to Liberia. The best biography of Cocke is M. Boyd Coyner, "John Hartwell Cocke of Bremo: Agriculture and Slavery in the Ante-Bellum South" (doctoral dissertation, University of Virginia, 1961). A shorter, valuable study is Clement Eaton's sketch of Cocke in his *The Mind of the Old South* (revised edition, Baton Rouge, La., 1967), chapter ii. On the antecedents and context of Cocke's thought see Winthrop Jordan, *White Over Black: American Attitudes Toward the Negro, 1550–1812* (Chapel Hill, N.C., 1968), especially pp. 546–569; David Brion Davis, *The Problem of Slavery in the Age of Revolution, 1770–1823* (Ithaca, N.Y., 1975), *passim*; George M. Fredrickson, *The Black Image in the White Mind: The Debate on Afro-American Character and Destiny, 1817–1914* (New York, 1971), especially pp. 6–21; Robert McColley, *Slavery and Jeffersonian Virginia* (Urbana, Ill., 1964), *passim*; and Bertram Wyatt-Brown, *Lewis Tappan and the Evangelical War Against Slavery* (Cleveland, Ohio, 1969), which includes some revealing remarks on Cocke's relationship with "conservative" reformers such as John Tappan. Cocke's role in the shift from "liberal" to proslavery thought can be further traced in Clement Eaton, *The Freedom-of-Thought Struggle in the Old South* (revised edition, New York, 1964); and in Joseph C. Robert, *The Road from Monticello: A Study of the Virginia Slavery Debate of 1832* (Durham, N.C., 1941). The best survey of persistent antislavery in the South, and its lonely vigil, is Carl N. Degler, *The Other South: Southern Dissenters in the Nineteenth Century* (New York, 1974), especially pp. 13–96. Surprisingly, Degler does not discuss Cocke in his book. For the colonization movement per se and conservative reform in America see Philip J. Staudenraus, *The African Colonization Movement, 1816–1865* (New York, 1961).

Letters from Liberia

On the émigré experience in Liberia the following are useful: J. Gus Liebenow, *Liberia: The Evolution of Privilege* (Ithaca, N.Y., 1969), an excellent, brief survey of the emergence of a distinct Americo-Liberian community in the first two chapters; Svend E. Holsoe, "A Study of Relations between Settlers and Indigenous Peoples in Western Liberia, 1821–1847," *African Historical Studies*, IV (1971), 331–362; W. W. Schmokel, "Settlers and Tribes: The Origins of the Liberian Dilemma," in Daniel F. McCall, Norman R. Bennet, and Jeffrey Butler, eds., *Western African History*, Vol. IV of *Boston University Papers on*

Africa (New York, 1969), pp. 153–181; and James T. Sabin, "The Making of the Americo-Liberian Community: A Study of Politics and Society in Nineteenth Century Liberia" (doctoral dissertation, Columbia University, 1974). On the Liberian climate, soils, flora, and fauna see George W. Brown, *The Economic History of Liberia* (Washington, D.C., 1941), pp. 22–28; and for a full appreciation of the sponsoring society's supply, financial, and political problems in settling and maintaining the colony see Staudenraus, *The African Colonization Movement*. Useful descriptions of Liberia are found in contemporary journals, particularly the *African Repository*.

On the process of acculturation of privileged bondsmen in America and the implications for "proper" slave control, see Gerald W. Mullin, *Flight and Rebellion: Slave Resistance in Eighteenth-Century Virginia* (New York, 1972). On work incentives and labor patterns in the slave South, see Eugene Genovese, *Roll, Jordan, Roll: The World the Slaves Made* (New York, 1974), especially pp. 285–398. On the powerful family solidarity among enslaved Afro-Americans, see Genovese, *Roll, Jordan, Roll*, pp. 450–535; John W. Blassingame, *The Slave Community: Plantation Life in the Ante-Bellum South* (New York, 1972), chapter iii; Herbert Gutman, *The Black Family in Slavery and Freedom, 1750–1925* (New York, 1976); and Robert H. Abzug, "The Black Family During Reconstruction," in Nathan I. Huggins, Martin Kilson, and Daniel M. Fox, eds., *Key Issues in the Afro-American Experience* (2 vols.; New York, 1971), II, 26–41. The best discussion of the emerging Afro-American religious life in slavery is Genovese, *Roll, Jordan, Roll*, pp. 159–284. A full study of religion among the slaves is badly needed.

Letters from Alabama: The Driver

Cocke's Alabama experiment is fairly treated in Coyner, "John Hartwell Cocke," pp. 372–449. The letters of Richard D. Powell, John Cocke of Alabama, and Elam Tanner, all in the Cocke Papers, amply furnish the white side of the story. Cocke's disappointments are recorded in his various journals, all in the Cocke Papers. For an informative review of the duties and vexations of the overseer and for some provocative suggestions on driver-overseer relations, see William K. Scarborough, *The Overseer: Plantation Management in the Old South* (Baton Rouge, La., 1966). Scarborough discusses the Cocke estates at some length.

There is no full history of the slave driver, one of the most important individuals on the plantation. Several recent studies, however, have gone far toward demolishing the ogre image of the driver and have directed attention to more important questions on the driver's self-perception and his place within the plantation and slave communities. The studies are: Genovese, *Roll, Jordan, Roll*, pp. 365–388; Randall M. Miller, "The Man in the Middle: The Black Slave Driver," *American Heritage* (forthcoming); Leslie Howard Owens, *This Species of Property: Slave Life and Culture in the Old South* (New York, 1976), pp.

121–135; and Robert S. Starobin, "Privileged Bondsmen and the Process of Accommodation: The Role of Houseservants and Drivers as Seen in Their Own Letters," *Journal of Social History,* V (1971), especially 58–70.

A serviceable institutional history of slavery in Alabama, although woefully thin on black attitudes and aspirations and on the slave subculture, is James B. Sellers, *Slavery in Alabama* (University, Ala., 1950).

Letters from Alabama: The House Servant

Again, the letters of R. D. Powell and the several overseers and preachers at Hopewell offer perspectives to help understand the slave's account. For a good contemporary description of the state of religion in Greene County see also John Witherspoon to Susan McDowall, July 9, 1846, Witherspoon-McDowall Papers (Southern Historical Collection, University of North Carolina at Chapel Hill).

As is the case with the driver, the house servant has only recently come under careful review by scholars. Although he is reluctant to take affection for the planter seriously, Kenneth M. Stampp, *The Peculiar Institution: Slavery in the Ante-Bellum South* (New York, 1956), nicely describes the domestics' duties and their difficult position vis à vis slaves and masters. A more promising approach which emphasizes house servant ambivalence toward self and masters and explores strategies of accommodation rather than just overt acts of rebelliousness is that of Genovese, *Roll, Jordan, Roll,* pp. 327–365. Also useful in this regard is Owens, *Species of Property,* pp. 106–120. For additional samples of letters written by house servants, see Robert S. Starobin, ed., *Blacks in Bondage: Letters of American Slaves* (New York, 1974), pp. 63–83, which stress resistance; and Randall M. Miller, " 'Dear Master': Letters from Nashville, 1862," *Tennessee Historical Quarterly,* XXXIII (1974), 85–92; and Miller, " 'It is good to be religious': A Loyal Slave on God, Masters, and the Civil War," *North Carolina Historical Review,* LIV (1977), 66–71, which describe slave loyalty.

The postwar scene at Hopewell is covered, albeit briefly, in Coyner, "John Hartwell Cocke," pp. 557ff and 580ff, and in the letters of Philip B. Cabell and R. D. Powell in the Cocke Papers. *The Alabama Beacon* (Greensboro, Ala.) and planters' records, especially the John Parrish letters in the Henry Watson Papers (Duke University, Durham, N.C.), reveal much about economic and social conditions in Greene County after the war, but they are generally hostile to black aspirations. This is also the case with Walter L. Fleming, *Civil War and Reconstruction in Alabama* (New York, 1905). Fleming's book remains the only general survey of the period for Alabama.

The black side of the postwar history of Alabama is yet unwritten, partially for want of materials. Peter Kolchin, however, has made an excellent start with his *First Freedom: The Responses of Alabama's Blacks to Emancipation and Reconstruction* (Westport, Conn., 1972). Kolchin corrects many misconceptions about black migration, churches, and social habits. My findings support his conclusions. Although illuminating about black-white relations and social and economic conditions in the postbellum South, the records of the Freedmen's Bureau (National Archives, Washington, D.C.) and the benevolent societies working in Alabama and Virginia yielded no information about any of the Hopewell freedmen. The manuscript census schedules for Greene and Hale Counties (Greene County was split in 1867) provided the basic information for my discussion. Allen W. Trelease, *White Terror: The Ku Klux Klan Conspiracy and Southern Reconstruction* (New York, 1971), was very useful for understanding the volatile political climate in the area.

Index

An asterisk (*) following a name designates the individual as a slave. A dagger (†) designates the individual as a Liberian settler. JHC refers to John Hartwell Cocke.

"DEAR MASTER"

Designed by R. E. Rosenbaum.
Composed by The Composing Room of Michigan, Inc.
in 10 point VIP Melior, 2 points leaded,
with display lines in Melior Bold.
Printed offset by Vail-Ballou Press on
Warren's Olde Style, 60 pound basis.
Bound by Vail-Ballou Press
in Joanna book cloth
and stamped in All Purpose foil.

Library of Congress Cataloging in Publication Data
(For library cataloging purposes only)

Main entry under title:
"Dear Master."

    Bibliography. p.
    Includes index.
      1. Skipwith family. 2. Cocko, John Hartwell, 1780–1800 3. Afro-
Americans—Colonization—Liberia—Sources. 4. Slavery in the United States—
History—Sources. I. Miller, Randall M.
E444.D42   976.1'004'96073   77-90907
ISBN 0-8014-1134-3